VOICES OF THE POOR IN AFRICA

ROCHESTER STUDIES in
AFRICAN HISTORY and the DIASPORA

Toyin Falola, Senior Editor
The Frances Higginbotham Nalle Centennial Professor in History
University of Texas at Austin

(ISSN: 1092-5228)

VOICES OF THE POOR IN AFRICA

Elizabeth Isichei

UNIVERSITY OF ROCHESTER PRESS

First published 2002
by the University of Rochester Press

The University of Rochester Press
668 Mt. Hope Avenue, Rochester, NY 14620, USA
and at Boydell & Brewer, Ltd.
P.O. Box 9, Woodbridge, Suffolk 1P12 3DF, UK
www.urpress.com

ISBN 1–58046–107–7
ISSN 1092-5228

Library of Congress Cataloging-in-Publication Data
Isichei, Elizabeth Allo.
    Voices of the poor in Africa : moral economy and the popular imagination /
    Jonathan K. Gosnell.
        p. cm. — (Rochester studies in African history and the diaspora, ISSN
        1092-5228)
    Includes bibliographical references and index.
    ISBN 1-58046-107-7 (alk. paper)
      1. Ethnology—Africa.   2. Oral tradition—Africa.   3. Mythology,
African.   4. Ethnoscience—Africa.   5. Popular culture—Africa.
6. Discourse analysis, Narrative.   7. Africa—Historiography.   8. Africa—
Social life and customs.   I. Title.   II. Series.

GN645.I845 2002
305.8′0096—dc21   2002022503

British Library Cataloguing-in-Publication Data
A catalogue record for this book is available from the British Library

Designed and typeset by Straight Creek Bookmakers
Printed in the United States of America
This publication is printed on acid-free paper

CONTENTS

MAPS AND DRAWINGS

Maps

Drawings

ACKNOWLEDGMENTS

My contribution to the study of the cognitive worlds of African popular culture began with a paper presented at a conference organized by David Dorward, at ANU Canberra, in 1995. The encouragement I received there, especially from David and from John Lonsdale, changed a paper into an unrecognizably different book.

Much of the research was done on a year's sabbatical in 1997–98, divided between Nuffield College, Oxford, Clare Hall, Cambridge, Green College, UBC, Vancouver, and the University of Virginia. The writing has taken much longer. I received so much assistance and hospitality that I cannot acknowledge it adequately without writing another book. Special thanks, however, to Joe Miller, who read an early version of this study, and has been a great source of encouragement ever since.

I am immensely grateful to the University of Otago; it is the granting of sabbatical leave, and research and conference funding that made this book possible. This university is a great place to work at, as Dunedin is a great city to live in.

I am grateful to Tim Madigan, as publisher, and Toyin Falola, as series editor, for welcoming this study on to their list.

In a conversation that he has undoubtedly forgotten, on a Saturday afternoon in the 1980s, when he was still an undergraduate, my eldest son, Uche, insisted that I read Foucault. It was that conversation that, some fifteen years later, has led to this book.

The members of my family continue to provide an affection and support for which any acknowledgment is inadequate.

This book is dedicated to those of whom I write—the poor of Africa, whose voices are too seldom heard.

University of Otago, Dunedin, 2002

A Note on Terminology

In this book I usually refer to African nations by their contemporary names, for clarity's sake—Malawi, not Nyasaland, and so on. There is, of course, a certain cognitive dissonance in expressions such as "colonial Zambia," and there are several references to Tanganyika. I refer to the state which was, until recently, Zaire, as the Democratic Republic of Congo or Congo/Zaire, to distinguish it from its neighbor of the same name. The modern nation and ancient city of Benin are always distinguished.

1

INTRODUCTION: TRUTH FROM BELOW

> Four women came from Atta. . . .I asked them what their names were,
> and their answer was "Ohandum." I asked them where they came
> from, and they answered "Ohandum." I asked them what they wanted,
> and I received the same reply. I detained them, and said I was not
> going to listen to nonsense. . . .[1]
>
> A witness at the inquiry into the Women's War,
> southeastern Nigeria, 1929[1]

The Scope of the Study: Myth as True Fiction

The title of this chapter echoes that of a study of the popular press in
Africa, which inverts the words of a West African politician: "[R]umor is
not the truth. Truth comes from above; rumor comes from below.[2] This is
a book about truth from below, voices that have often been undervalued or
ignored. (They are often articulated in the poetics of memory, or of rumor—the distinction between the two is explored in a later chapter.) This
may seem paradoxical, because listening to the African voice has been central to the whole African studies enterprise since the 1960s. Unconsciously,
however, academics—myself among them—have selected their evidence
according to preconceived notions of the possible.

1

I can illustrate this from my own work. In the late 1970s, I was engaged in a major oral history project in central Nigeria. When village elders stated, for instance, that Benue valley salt producers and Jos Plateau iron workers exchanged their respective products as part of a wider network of regional trade, I accepted their evidence. When three old men separately claimed that cowries, the shell money of the slave trade, were obtained by human bait, I disregarded their testimony, because it was at variance with the known facts about cowries. I did so even when I found the same story in a 1907 document in the Kaduna archives. Years later, the same myth was independently recorded in the Republic of Benin, and it was only then that I was forced to take it seriously. I came to realize that this symbolic narrative—and many others—embodied True Fictions, encapsulating in a condensed and elliptical form, historical insights—in this instance, the fact that shell money was obtained in return for enslaved people. They corresponded to what Foucault, writing of a very different historical context, called, "subjugated knowledges."

> [B]y subjugated knowledges one should understand . . . a whole set of knowledges that have been disqualified as inadequate to their task or insufficiently elaborated: naive knowledges, located down on the hierarchy, beneath the required level of cognition or scientificity. I also believe that it is through the re-emergence of these low-ranked knowledges, these unqualified, even directly disqualified knowledges . . . that criticism performs its work.[3]

This book is an exploration of certain recurrent configurations of myth and symbol—"poetic echoes"—that have been recorded in Africa over several hundred years; they enable one to glimpse some patterns in cognitive history, albeit through a glass, darkly. It is an essay in the reconstruction of popular consciousness, past and present; in it, I seek to make unheard voices audible and to understand familiar symbols in new ways.

In a sense it is an exploration of the history of ideas in Africa, but its themes are very different from the way in which this has been defined in the past—the analysis of the speeches and writings of Africa's past and present rulers, or of the books of intellectuals such as the nineteenth-century physician and author of draft constitutions, Africanus Horton.

In conventional usage, mirrored in dictionary definitions, myth is "untrue"—a "widely held but false notion."[4] But ethnographers, in particular, have come to realize, that, to use the words Taussig applied to popular culture in Latin America,

> Magical beliefs are revelatory and fascinating not because they are ill-con-
> ceived instruments of utility but because they are poetic echoes of the ca-
> dences that guide the innermost course of the world. Magic takes language,
> symbols, and intelligibility to their uttermost limits, to explore life and thereby
> to change its destination.[5]

(Interestingly, Taussig was writing from a neo-Marxist perspective, which
has moved very far from the palaeo-Marxism that saw religion as false consciousness.)

We have learned not to marginalize a particular discourse because it is
couched in the language of myth and symbol, a language, as Fernandez and
others have argued, that is actually closer to reality than the "imageless"
discourse of abstract thought.[6]

> Thought embedded in images, symbols and actions is complex thought. . . .
> The intellectualist argument [of Robin Horton] ignores how ideas are
> squeezed out of images and how they can be again embedded in them—and
> it ignores the difficult problem of the coding of thought in images and sym-
> bolic forms.[7]

In the words of Berdyaev:

> Myth is a reality immeasurably greater than concept. It is high time that we
> stopped identifying myth with invention, with the illusions of primitive
> mentality, and with anything, in fact, which is essentially opposed to real-
> ity. . . . Myth is always concrete and expresses life better than abstract thought
> can do; its nature is bound up with that of symbol.[8]

Of course I do not mean to imply that a study of the historical meaning of myth and symbol is a substitute for history of a more conventional
kind. Like all specialized studies, this one presupposes it. Research into the
African past has advanced largely by the incorporation of new variables
into patterns of inquiry—ecology, disease, gender and "the invention of
ethnicity" among them. The study of True Fictions develops a further vari-
able.

It is not easy to integrate the world of myth and symbol with the
interpretations of the academic historian. McCaskie, a pioneer in this type
of study, provides a good example. In 1873–74, British forces defeated the
Asante. Standard histories explain this, in ways that need not detain us
here. Asante tradition, however, attributes the defeat to the fact that the
Asantehene's war charm was lost in the Pra river. These very different expla-

nations cannot be integrated into a single narrative. But if we ignore the Asante version, we are overlooking the way in which a people interprets its own past experience.[9]

The rich historiography of the Asante kingdom reflects, in microcosm, two contrasting ways of interpreting the African past. Wilks, reacting against European sources that depicted Asante as bloodthirsty and barbaric, analyzed it in the language of European political history.[10] McCaskie, in a series of penetrating essays,[11] suggested that this was not to enhance Asante but to diminish it. In nineteenth-century Kumasi, for instance, there was a building housing different European artifacts. To Wilks, this was a museum; to McCaskie it was a symbolic assertion in an ongoing symbolic struggle between nature and human culture, in which umbrellas also had a role to play.[12] Wilks's history is of enduring value, and McCaskie's work has complemented, not superseded it. There is an Igbo proverb to the effect that to appreciate a masked dancer, you must move from place to place.

There are many difficulties inherent in an attempt to penetrate a world of popular culture, past and present, where insights find expression, not in abstract statements about society, but in images. Like poetry, which, in many ways, these sources closely resemble, they have multiple layers of meaning, and their interpretation is not unlike literary criticism. Heidegger said, "Poetry proper is never merely a higher mode . . . of everyday language. It is rather the reverse: everyday language is a forgotten and therefore used-up poem."[13]

To a greater extent than with more conventional source material, each reader recreates a meaning. I have sought to decipher the coded representation and critique of social change. A Jungian analyst, for instance, would read this material in an entirely different way. The task of interpretation is facilitated by the recurrence of particular symbolic complexes in different settings. Each separate instance confirms, extends, or challenges an interpretation, and the whole is greater than its parts.

Ideally, each text should be interpreted—like any other historical source—in terms of its specific historical setting and ethno-linguistic context. In practice, in many cases, the appropriate studies do not exist; in other cases, such as that of the electric vampires of Buhaya,[14] there is a rich literature, but to explore it would be impracticable in the context of a book of this kind. (This is equally true of, for instance, national histories.) To some extent it is possible to locate the themes of this book in the context of a wider historiography—this is attempted, in necessarily brief compass, in chapters 2 and 7.

Nothing could have been further from my original intentions than to write a book about vampires, money magic, and so on. Like Bastian,

Geschiere, and others, I found that these motifs were forced on my attention because they were recurrent, even dominant, though not universal. Dylan Thomas found the reinventions of tradition in Tutuola's writings "grisly" as well as "bewitching." They cannot be disregarded because of their dark nature. To ignore the metaphors and symbols of popular culture, whether past or present, for whatever reason, is to render invisible what millions of Africans take seriously. In the words of Luise White, another pioneer in this area:

> [C]olonial vampires . . . as descriptions of things that never happened, should begin to subvert some of our ideas about what constitutes authenticity. The study of colonial vampires is authentic . . . because it involves writing about the colonial world with the images and idioms produced by the subjects themselves.[15]

Several variables seem relevant to the dark nature of many of these symbolic narratives. They are certainly not peculiar to Africa—Taussig's famous study of folk mythologies in Columbia and Peru is entitled *The Devil and Commodity Fetishism in South America.* The title of Stewart's fine account of the *exotica* (Nereids and so on) in modern Greece is not dissimilar—*Demons and the Devil, Moral Imagination in Modern Greek Culture.*[16] Marina Warner's Reith lectures dealt with themes such as Monstrous Mothers and Cannibal Tales.[17]

Vampires, witches, and shapeshifters (in the European context, werewolves rather than werelions) thread their way through western literature and contemporary film. Lycanthropy is mentioned in Webster's *The Duchess of Malfi.* Fifty werewolf films were catalogued in 1973,[18] and many more have appeared since. *The Silence of the Lambs* and *Delicatessen* are successful recent western films that deal with cannibalism. There are many novels about vampirism, among them Bram Stoker's classic, *Dracula* (1897), and Anne Rice's ongoing *Vampire Chronicles* (1976–98).

Stewart suggests, "It may be that the imagery and stories surrounding these demonic beings [in Greece] are richly detailed because evil and misfortune demand extensive commentary, while happiness is taken for granted."[19] Freud once observed that "a happy person never fantasises."[20] But in Africa at least, the simplest explanation is that these symbols reflect the real tragedies of lived experience—no imagery could be more macabre than the factual history of the Middle Passage. Are such symbols equally appropriate to the colonial or postcolonial experience? It would be easy to seek apparent confirmation in academic sources. Vansina, for instance, writing of early colonialism in Central Africa, describes "the violence of an apocalyptic conquest":

> A combination of war, destruction by fire, disease and hunger finally succeeded in breaking African resistance by 1920, at the cost of an estimated half of the total population of the area.[21]

The growing recognition of the validity and significance of "subjugated knowledges" is largely due to the fact that the continuing—though contested—crisis of independent Africa offers a radical challenge to modernist models of progress and improvement. But it is my intention to listen to the multiform and various insights of popular cultures, not to pass judgment on their validity. Were I to do so, it would imply that I understand the life situation of the African poor better than they do, which is precisely the model that Foucault critiqued (p. 2). The recent proliferation of studies of individual life histories, biographies, and autobiographies of the poor and obscure[22] reflects an increased awareness of the fact that those who experience—or endure—historical processes are the real experts.

New symbolic complexes develop in the sphere which has been called interculture, a shifting bricolage of African and Western elements. Their intuitive critique of society and its power structures has many of the same resonances as post-modernist texts. The recent proliferation of studies of Mami Wata and other spirit possession cults reflects this. As Rosenthal writes:

> In a manner of speaking, both these Vodu orders are already "postmodern" . . . in the sense of a discourse and practice that admit of a continual reworking of identity, authority and power, and a concept of changed margins and border crossings.[23]

African scholars have sometimes been sharply critical of post-modernism and of its applicability in Africa.[24] There is, as Rosenthal acknowledges, a profound irony in the idea of a post-modernity in a continent struggling with limited success towards modernity, and spirit possession cults often critique a flawed and imperfectly achieved "development."

The interface between Africa and the West has often been a source of exploitation and pain, but it has also been a place of cultural innovation—the African-Portuguese ivories of the sixteenth century, the new scripts invented by the Vai, Bamum, and others in the nineteenth, the musical form "highlife" in the twentieth. Creolized languages and pidgins comprise a different form of métissage, which both embody and express the culture of encounter. Each of the symbolic complexes studied in this book is an example of bricolage, something new created out of African and exotic elements.

Are these symbolic and mythical structures totally disparate and unconnected, or can they be interpreted in terms of an underlying model or models? Most of the complexes explored in this book are rooted to some degree in continuing reinventions of "traditional" religion, and in particular of ancient witchcraft beliefs. Each, it is important to stress, is an innovation—the cowries that feed on people, the colonial vampires, complete with Western medical apparatus. In the African context, Harms first drew attention to a particular vision of moral economy rooted in the concept of life as a zero-sum game (see below). The model fits the data well, and is adopted here, and elaborated more fully later in this chapter. Several ethnographers who began with quite different research agendas—Geschiere among the Maka of Cameroon, Bastian in the Igbo city of Onitsha—found that images linked with witchcraft were so prevalent and powerful that they became central to their inquiries.[25]

Neo-traditional religion is a source of symbols and metaphors that embody a critique of the unacceptable face of social change. Its continuing vitality has disproved two inherently reasonable assumptions.

The first is the expectation, which prevailed until relatively recently, that "traditional" religions would die out with the advance of Western education, and of Christianity and Islam. In 1969, Parrinder suggested that "In modern times these magical and witchcraft beliefs ought to disappear with the growth of education."[26] In 1982, the Nigerian novelist, Elechi Amadi, made much the same point.[27] There was a tendency to overlook the continued existence of, for instance, witchcraft accusations. Perhaps it was more comfortable to ignore aspects of African life that sat uneasily with a model of Improvement. It is now clear that modernity has not replaced tradition; instead, tradition has provided symbols with which to articulate a critique of the contemporary world.

The second expectation was that the global spread of the icons of Western consumer culture—which Barber evocatively calls McWorld[28]—would tend to obliterate local cultures. There is, of course, much evidence of the global impact of McWorld. In 1992, McDonalds and KFC attracted more customers than any other restaurants in Japan. Women cloth merchants in Togo named a particular pattern, Dallas, after the American soap opera.[29] But to see the rest of the world as the passive recipient of Western cultural imprints, is, perhaps, a contemporary equivalent of writings produced in the heyday of imperialism. Gilroy has pointed out how black music has been a major determining force in the global culture. When I was asked to give a keynote address on the global and the local, I spoke on the way in which Mami Wata crosses and recrosses the Atlantic.[30] The resurgence of local particularisms, variously rooted in language, religion, and understandings of history, is a world-wide phenomenon—it underlies regional conflicts in Africa and elsewhere, including the balkanization of the Balkans. The African reinvention of ancient religious metaphors is part of this—the paradox inherent in the title of Geschiere's *The Modernity of Witchcraft.*

Academic Contexts

Ethnographers have perhaps gone furthest in exploring the "subjugated knowledges" studied in this book—I have mentioned the work of some of them, such as Geschiere, and Rosenthal; the work of the Comaroffs and their students, in *Modernity and Its Malcontents,* has been seminal. A later chapter is deeply indebted to the ethnography of MacGaffey in Central Africa. Among historians, McCaskie's work on Asante has been profoundly influential. More recently, Austen and Luise White have made important contributions. No academic book stands in isolation, and the present work is no exception.

Similar insights are emerging among some political scientists. When African nations regained their independence in the 1960s, there was a flurry of books on their constitutions and political parties. The passage of events made most of them ephemeral, and they were followed, in due course, by studies of military regimes. There is now a tendency to focus, not on the changing political superstructure, but on civil society. Schatzberg has recently suggested that a study of African political thought "from above"—as expressed in the speeches and writings of African politicians and military rulers, and their exegesis—constitutes "a sterile, static and narrowly exegetical Afro-Saxon tradition." He advocates a study of "the dispersion of political ideas in economics, religion, social and family relationships, literature and art."[31] This is precisely what I have sought to do in this book.

There is an intuitive recognition of the truth of popular culture's True Fictions in the clear transition in much recent African creative writing from realism to a fantasy that embodies a political critique. Images from popular culture percolate into the literary canon. Azaro, the spirit child who is the central character of several of Ben Okri's novels, sees and describes the dark occult forces that underpin the Party of the Rich.

African creative literature has proved a valuable source for this study. Like any other source, it must be utilized with discrimination, for the novel is not a simple map of social relations and local symbols. The ancestry of the unicorns in Okri's *The Famished Road* lies in medieval literature and ultimately in ancient Greece, and the book as a whole is clearly indebted to that Latin American classic, Gabriel Garcia Marquez's *One Hundred Years of Solitude*.

In the 1970s, Chinweizu, Jemie, and Madubuike made a plea for a truly indigenous African literature—the depiction of a "landscape of elephants, beggars, calabashes, serpents, pumpkins, baskets, town criers, iron bells, slit drums, iron masks, hares, snakes, squirrels . . . a landscape portrayed with native eyes to which aeroplanes naturally appear as iron birds." Soyinka condemned this, and pointed out that his own imaginative world includes "precision machinery, oil rigs, hydro-electricity, my typewriter. . . ."[32] One of the most interesting themes to emerge in recent work is the incorporation of the varied icons of modernity—now computers rather than typewriters—into neo-traditional imaginative worlds.

Moral Economy and the Zero-Sum Game

This is a book about a changing symbolic universe that mirrors what has been variously called moral imagination or moral economy. In the process of analysis, it is easy to reify and essentialize its manifestations. But underlying a vast number of disparate images and myths are certain core concepts and metaphors in which a moral vision finds expression, and it is this which makes a unified analysis possible.

Stewart, writing of Greece, and Beidelman, writing of the Kaguru of Tanzania, employ the term "moral imagination."

> Imagination is an art by which individuals struggle to transform their social baggage into gear that suits urgent situational needs in terms of meanings and moral judgments.[33]

I have opted for "moral economy" because its use is currently more widespread. But a study of the literature reveals a concept almost as fluid as the bricolage of spirit possession cults. It first became part of general academic usage through the work of celebrated scholars working in non-African fields. In 1970, the English social historian, E. P. Thompson referred to moral economy in a discussion of eighteenth-century English riots about the scarcity and high price of wheat, in which he critiqued "an abbreviated view of economic man" by mapping an underlying "legitimizing notion."[34] In a widely cited study of a very different kind, dealing with village life in Southeast Asia, Scott equated moral economy with a different conceptual universe—peasant life-strategies where survival, rather than the expansion of individual income, is the paramount concern.[35]

The expression has been widely used in African contexts. Lonsdale has applied it—significantly in the plural—to the twentieth-century experience of the Kikuyu and their search for a shared moral discourse and "community of esteem."[36] Both Austen and Geschiere have used it with reference to witchcraft beliefs.[37] Watts, in studying famine in Northern Nigeria and the factors which formerly palliated its effects, suggested that during the colonial era, "the tissues of the moral economy were stripped away."[38] He was referring to horizontal and vertical social linkages that alleviated the impact of natural disasters. He took care to elaborate the many injustices of the past. "The Sokoto Caliphate was not, as I have implied, a universe of satisfied peasants, benevolent patrons. . . . The moral economy was . . . not always especially moral."[39]

Writing on moral economy focuses on the cognitive worlds of the poor and springs from a conscious attempt to move beyond simplistic notions of *homo politicus* or *homo economicus.* But for an explanatory model for the detailed and varied case studies that follow we must look elsewhere.

The Limited Good and the Zero-Sum Game

In 1965, Foster published a widely cited if somewhat controversial article based on his research in a peasant community in Mexico. He suggested that at the heart of peasant life was the belief that all things held to be of value *"exist in finite quantity* and *are always in short supply* as far as the peasant is concerned." One cannot acquire wealth by one's own efforts, so an individual who becomes rich or powerful does so at the expense of others, and peasants tend to conceal prosperity, or dissipate it in institutionalized extravagance. Sudden wealth is attributed to extraordinary events—the discovery of buried treasure, or, in modern times, a lottery win. This is, he suggests, realistic —the peasant will not become rich by working harder or longer.[40]

The model of the zero-sum game is essentially the same as that of the limited good—it is noteworthy that it has been applied by a Nigerian commentator to Nigerian politics.[41] In a study published in 1981, Harms applied it to the experience of the Bobangi, river traders of the middle Zaire basin.

> [T]he Bobangi . . . held a holistic view of human activity that made two important assumptions. First there was a fixed amount of wealth in the world. Economic activity was therefore a zero-sum game in which one person's gain was another's loss. . . . The second assumption was that material wealth, physical health and social tranquillity were interrelated.[42]

It was thought that wealth from trade could only be obtained by magical means. Riches were obtained by the astral sacrifice of one or more relatives, and if one ran out of relatives, one's own life was forfeit. The Bobangi's demographic decline was thought to reflect these choices. Discourse of this kind is profoundly egalitarian, for personal enrichment is both stolen from a limited totality of resources and obtained at an unacceptable price. Wealth in things is obtained at the cost of wealth in people.

The model of life as a zero-sum game is characteristically articulated in terms of one or both of two closely linked and overlapping symbolic complexes, which refer, respectively, to witchcraft and to gluttonous and depraved consumption. Here as elsewhere, it is profoundly unsatisfactory to generalize, and my brief account is intended as a map of territories to follow. Like all maps it is arbitrary, and intelligible only because of its exclusions.

Witchcraft, as it is imagined, is the most extreme manifestation of life as a zero-sum game, and beliefs of this kind have been interpreted as an essay in moral economy.[43] In the most ancient and widespread image of the witch, s/he is characterized by ravenous hunger. The witch defines humanity through inversion and feasts in astral banquets on the life force of the living, sometimes as a solitary individual, sometimes as a member of a coven whose members incur and pay flesh debts to each other. In this study, I call this kind of witchcraft "astral cannibalism." A recent study of Hausa neo-traditional religion refers to "soul eaters."[44] In Amos Tutuola's *My Life in the Bush of Ghosts* (1954), a "Superlady" (who escapes the fate intended for her) relates:

> My father and mother . . . were discussing within themselves with a low voice whether to kill me next week for their wizard and witch meeting which is very near, because it is our turn to prepare food for our members who will attend the meeting according to our rule, as they have no other daughter or son who is to be killed and cooked and presented to our members, because every one of them will do so whenever it is his or her turn.[45]

This is fiction, but the same pattern emerges from a vast number of ethnographies. In popular discourse past and present, exploitative social relations are condemned through the use of one or more of the associated metaphors of witch, cannibal, or vampire. Each is identified with absolute evil. All three images were applied to Mobutu's regime in Zaire, towards its end.[46]

Some of the most interesting recent research on the changing face of neotraditional religion has explored the way in which witchcraft beliefs mutate, often in response to the cash nexus. (The core imagery of indebtedness is clearly relevant here.) In some contexts, the powers of the cannibal witch were originally inherited, but now can also be purchased so that witchcraft proliferates.[47]

In parts of Cameroon and elsewhere, the concept of the cannibal witch has been supplemented or supplanted by that of the witch as the owner of zombie slaves, motivated not by hunger but by the desire for gain. Alternatively, the witch becomes a long distance trader, exporting captive souls (pp. 104).

The concept of the limited good underpins the innumerable stories of riches obtained through pacts with dangerous and capricious nature spirits or familiars—a human price is typically demanded, reminiscent of the witch's flesh debt. Harms links this astral pact with the social death inflicted by the slave trade, and cites an 1894 example.

> Bokatula . . . is said to have died as *nkila* . . . the price paid by his son for some charm. . . .Bokatula himself not so long ago went to a famous witch doctor for medicine to get rich. As *nkila,* he had to pay three lives, and shortly three of his people died.[48]

In 1985, a Kataf informant in central Nigeria told me of such a pact, made with an astral python.

> "A woman in our place wanted the most beautiful cloth money can buy. She promised she would give forty children. She wanted to pay with her grand-children, but her son threatened her with death if she did so. She became very sick. She tried to get children along the road, but she could not get any child. She died. When she died strange things happened. The mortar and pestle knocked on the wall. There were strange noises, and the woman was screaming, 'They have come to take me away.'"
> "Have your people always believed this?"
> "Always."[49]

It is a poignant commentary on village poverty that she had sought, not wealth beyond imagining, but new clothes. Pacts of this kind form a recurrent theme in this book; I call them, for convenience, Faustian, but they resemble less Marlowe's Dr. Faustus (who sacrifices his eternal salvation) than peasant stories of pacts in Latin America, where a man may grow rich through a bargain with the Devil, but will not live long if he does so.[50] They reflect a world where prosperity seems so remote that it is explicable only through the extraordinary. But although wealth is both desirable and unattainable, these narratives condemn those who sacrifice people to things, and emphasize their downfall.

An important dimension of the concept of the witch as soul-eater is that astral (or indeed literal) cannibalism commodifies the human body when it becomes food. Money or goods that become alive, and human bodies that are commodified, are a recurrent theme in counterpoint in the analysis which follows. In one symbolic complex, cowries, the shell money of the slave trade, eat people; in another, slave bodies become industrial raw material. In modern urban legends of blood or money magic, great wealth is attained by human "spare parts." Money again becomes a devouring force and people are commodified and destroyed. This is much like Marx's theory of commodity fetishism, where capital is spoken of as if it had a life of its own—galloping inflation, or bull and bear markets, and so on.[51] Taussig found this a powerful explanatory model, so much so that he incorporated it in the title of his *The Devil and Commodity Fetishism in South America*. Marx, perhaps, adds little to the argument here, but a discourse where people are sacrificed to animate money is a statement about moral economy, what Schmoll has called "a sophisticated and nuanced commentary on the problem of uncontrolled desire for power and wealth and the use of immoral means to achieve them."[52]

The witch kills and eats people, rather than animals, and s/he seeks companionship in the animal, rather than human world, inverting appropriate relations with each. S/he may have a familiar, such as a python. S/he may assume its shape, or that of a nocturnal bird. Ancient concepts of the witch as shapeshifter mutated into new forms, first documented in the late nineteenth or early twentieth centuries (depending on the locality)—images of an anonymous collectivity of male theriomorphs who assume the form not of snake or bird but of predators ("leopard men" or "lion men") and, in this form, become assassins. These movements—real or imagined—varied considerably, but were typically a response to the imposition of colonial rule, and its new power equations. This transmutation of the witch as shapeshifter forms the theme of chapter 10. Here as elsewhere, the individual human body becomes a metaphor for changes occurring in society as a whole—the body politic.

If we are to develop a view of moral economy linked with witchcraft beliefs, we must begin with certain caveats. The English word "witchcraft" is not a true equivalent to *tsav* (Tiv) or *djambe* (Maka). Its use imposes European concepts on African experience, obliterates the real distinctions between the terminology and understandings of different ethno-linguistic groups, and re-places what is often a nuanced and ambivalent category with one that implies absolute condemnation. Fisiy and Geschiere, reflecting on this critique, point out that Africans themselves use these terms,[53] but this does not solve the problem, and it seems likely that the absolute evil of, for instance, colonial vampires reflects a dualism absorbed from Western translations and categories.

Western dualisms have shaped neo-traditional religion in other ways— the theme of chapter 16. The teachings of missionary Christianity—and later, of some African Christians, especially the Born Again (to use a Nigerian expression)—have had the unintended effect of creating new polarities in neo-traditional religion. The Yoruba divinity, Eshu, is both Trickster and cosmic intermediary, but the Yoruba Bible translates the Devil as "Eshu." The Born Again acknowledge the reality of the neo-traditional world but reject it as demonic, a theme explored later in this study.

It is important to remember that there was and is much that is positive and lifeaffirming in African neo-traditional religions. There are delightful vignettes of this in Wole Soyinka's enchanting memoir of his childhood in a Christian Abeokuta household. Uncle Sanya, for instance, shares a meal with forest spirits, and with their help manages to consume fifty bean cakes![54]

Geschiere and others have documented the prevalence of witchcraft beliefs among the well educated, but nothing could be more misleading than to postulate a general credulity. There are many vigorous skeptics— including those who have never left the confines of the village. "If someone starts talking about a jini (djinn) I know he has a screw loose. I don't consult diviners. Divination is mutual self-deception."[55] In contemporary Sierra Leone, a Mende hunter told an ornithologist where he was likely to find a rare bird. An ethnographer asked him where he could find "the equally rare forest dwarves of Mende folk tradition." The hunter laughed and told him that birds and dwarves belong to different orders of reality.[56] De Rosny tells of an old man on the Cameroon coast who "took me aside one day and confided to me that, in his view, the *miengu* [water spirits] did not exist. Why? He had gone fishing, he said, since his boyhood, in the place reputed to be frequented by *miengu,* and yet had never seen a single one."[57]

Like "witchcraft," ethonyms are inherently unsatisfactory generalizations. I began my life's work as a historian of Africa with studies of "the

Igbo." I assumed that such an ethno-linguistic unit existed, because, by the time I wrote, "the Igbo" themselves took this for granted. It is now generally recognized that "the bounded tribe" is a recent invention, an artifact of the colonial experience and that ethonyms are particularly inaccurate shorthand for complex and changing realities. Like other historians of Africa, I use them because otherwise my work would be unintelligible, and to qualify them each time they are used would be impracticable. One can write of "the Igbo" or "the" Igbo, but to do so throughout this book would be an affectation. It is equally unsatisfactory, of course, to write about "the West" or "modernity." In East Africa, "the West" is Africa; in West Africa, it is the sea. There are many modernities and many different ways in which a wider world interacts with a great diversity of African societies.

The image of the witch as astral cannibal is only one of many strands in the fabric of a socio-political discourse, past and present, that is articulated in metaphors of depraved and predatory consumption, representing distorted social relations. They differ greatly in tone and intent—from the terror of rumor, to the resigned jocularity evident in terms such as "chopping bribes." "Ridicule and the crisis of the quotidian" form the theme of chapter 17.

Gender is a significant subtext in this study. The "traditional" soul-eating witch was typically an older woman; when the concept metamorphosed into new forms, there was a significant change—colonial vampires or werelions are anonymous men, acting in concert. Older concepts of the dangerous and devouring woman survive and take new forms, which are often tragic and sinister, in an age of AIDS (p. 159–60).

All slave traders, whether black or white, were men.[58] Men, women, and children were enslaved. In recent times, some women have wielded considerable clout, such as the First Lady in Banda's last years in Malawi, and some have accumulated vast fortunes in licit or illicit commerce, but independent Africa is and has been ruled by men. This is reflected in popular culture, which, significantly often equates the black ruler and the white comprador. A recurrent motif in the popular urban art of modern Congo (formerly Zaire) is *"simba bulaya,* the lions of Europe, representing the white cannibal . . . the personification of power, living off the victims brought to him by his assailants."[59] By extension, white now means powerful; in one painting of this motif, two (male) human *simba* are shown; they are dressed identically, but one is black, and one is white.[60] In 1985, in Malawi, as Kamuzu Banda's oppressive regime neared its end, a new Nyau mask appeared in a Chewa village. It took the form of a European who attacked people and demanded money. His name was Kamuzu the Warrior.[61] Popular imagination absorbs elements which were once used to invent Savage Africa and applies them to the West and to the rich and powerful close at hand.

The Global and the Local

The material that follows falls into two unequal parts. The first and shorter section delineates an alternative history of the Atlantic slave trade, expressed in symbolic terms. The second deals with perceptions of the colonial and postcolonial world. There are many parallels between them, but they are widely separated in time, and often in space as well, and I do not intend to imply that they form a continuum.

Even with this caveat, the scope of this study will inevitably be questioned. A willingness to explore ethnographic motifs beyond the local context has always been typical of continental scholarship—Lindskog's monumental study of Africa's leopard men is an example, as is, more recently, Kramer's well-received survey of spirit possession cults.[62] But African studies in Britain and North America over the last twenty-five years have tended to have a local or regional focus. My own work is no exception. I devoted three years of fieldwork and archival research to the Anaguta of central Nigeria. There are perhaps ten thousand Anaguta. Partly because of this I have, where possible, explored the motifs of this book in regional case studies. But in certain cases what is significant is the independent invention of comparable—not identical—myths over a vast area.

The emphasis on the local sprang, to a large extent, from a reaction against inventions such as "the High God in Africa" or "the Sudanic state." Writing in general terms about African cultures became profoundly unfashionable, blighted by the errors of diffusionism. And yet, curiously, it has currently become quite acceptable in the academy to generalize at the global level—we have noted *Jihad vs. McWorld* and there are many other instances.[63] This is also true of generalizations about the African experience made in such familiar contexts as that of a general history. Iliffe's well-received study, *Africans,* moves from the australopithecines to the 1990s in 284 pages of text.[64]

Like all reactions in the academy, the retreat to the particular led to new distortions, or more precisely, to misleading silences. Perhaps the single most striking aspect of African cultural and cognitive history lies in its convergences. If we ignore these, we leave some of the best documented aspects of the African past undocumented. One of the classic stories told of

the Yoruba divinity, Eshu, was also recorded in a nineteenth-century compilation of Kongo oral literature.[65] Myths about the dangers of demanding
one's pound of flesh, which center around a borrowed Spear and a swallowed Bead, were analyzed by Lienhardt as part of an ancient substratum of
Nilotic culture, but an example has been recorded far away, near the Zaire
river.[66]

Increasingly, the underlying parallels between widely separated African cultures are coming to be explicitly acknowledged. In the words of van
Binsbergen, writing of contemporary religious movements, "the same symbolic materials seem to be manipulated within narrow limits in diverse
movements."[67] Our very choice of language, —words like "witchcraft"—
presupposes the existence of continuities. One explanatory model suggests
that "the material culture is meager, so that relatively few objects and things
are available to sustain the ideological and affectual freight of the culture.
Each of these . . . sustains enormous and complex symbolic weight."[68] But
in much of Africa the material culture was a complex one and the known
and named natural world—its animals, plants, reptiles, and fungi—was
and is rich and detailed, and has now been supplemented by a whole new
symbolic universe, in which the icons of modernity—cars, telephones,
planes, computers—feature prominently. The convergences that are so striking do not reflect a lack of objects good to think with. But how does one
explain them?

As we have seen, many of the symbolic complexes found in Africa
have parallels elsewhere. A poem in Surinam Creole reflects on Copenhagen's
statue of the Little Mermaid, and recognizes how close it is to local traditions of Watra Mama.[69] Stories collected in Central Africa bear a striking
resemblance to the Garden of Eden story. Are they a local adaptation of
missionary teaching, or do they reflect "the African and Near Eastern context in which Hebrew narratives originated"?[70] These questions which, again,
I can document but not explain, lie outside the scope of this and probably
any history.

The focus here is on African, and to a lesser extent, African American
experience. The Atlantic slave trade is imaged in folk memory in Africa and
the New World. The sections dealing with the slave trade and with Mami
Wata are concerned with African American, as well as African, experience.
Indeed, one of the readers of this book suggested that I reflect this in the
title, but I felt that I had insufficiently explored African American experience, especially in the second section, for this to be accurate.

The insights explored in this book do not form a connected narrative. They are expressed in ways which are often ambiguous or inconsis-

tent, they are polysemic and pluriform, reflecting the changing interfaces between the individual, the local community and the wider society, expressed in a multitude of different utterances over a long period of time.

The image of a forest of symbols originated, not with the anthropologist, Victor Turner, but with the poet, Charles Baudelaire.[71] This chapter is, as we have seen, a map, delineating certain paths through the forest. There are other paths one might have taken, and it is possible to walk in a forest and not know a single tree by name. A proverb from Ghana suggests that truth is like the baobab tree. One person's arms cannot embrace it.

Notes

1. *Aba Commission of Inquiry, Notes of Evidence* (Dec. 1929), 256, para. 4947. The Commission was told that the words were *ohandi nyiom,* and meant "women's world." *Report of the Aba Commission of Inquiry* (Lagos, 1930), 20.

2. R. Carver, *Truth from Below* (Article 19, n.p., 1991). The words are those of President Paul Biya on Cameroon radio, in 1984, quoted in S. Ellis, "Tuning in to Pavement Radio," *African Affairs* (1989): 325.

3. M. Foucault, "Two Lectures: Lecture One: 7 Jan. 1976," in *Power/Knowledge: Selected Interviews and Other Writings* (New York, 1980), 83.

4. *The New Zealand Pocket Oxford Dictionary* (Auckland, 1986).

5. M. T. Taussig, *The Devil and Commodity Fetishism in South America* (Chapel Hill, NC, 1980), 15.

6. J. Fernandez, "African Religious Movements," *Annual Review of Anthropology* (1978): 220–29.

7. Ibid., 222.

8. Quoted in James Irwin, *An Introduction to Maori Religion* (Bedford Park, S. Australia: Australian Association for the Study of Religions, 1984), 8.

9. T. C. McCaskie, "Komfo Anokye of Asante: Meaning, History and Philosophy in an African Society," *Journal of African History* (1986): 321.

10. I. Wilks, *Asante in the Nineteenth Century: The Structure and Evolution of a Political Order,* 2nd ed. (Cambridge, 1989).

11. Now collected as T. C. McCaskie, *State and Society in Precolonial Asante* (Cambridge, 1995).

12. T. McCaskie, "Accumulation,Wealth and Belief in Asante History," I, *Africa* (1983): 28.

13. Martin Heidegger, "Language," quoted in Bruce Chatwin, *The Songlines* (London, 1987), 303.

14. B.Weiss, *The Making and Unmaking of the Haya Lived World* (Durham, NC and London, 1996), 202–19, on electric vampires. There is, in addition, a substantial historical and ethnographic literature on Buhaya.

15. L. White, "Cars Out of Place: Vampires, Technology and Labour in East and Central Africa," *Representations* (1993): 29. White's book, *Speaking with Vampires: Rumor and History in Colonial Africa* (Berkeley, 2000) appeared after this study was completed.

16. C. Stewart, *Demons and the Devil: Moral Imagination in Modern Greek Culture* (Princeton, 1991). For Taussig, see n.5 above.

17. Marina Warner, *Six Myths of Our Time* (New York, 1994).

18. W. Lee, *Reference Guide to Fantastic Films* (1973), cited in C. Otten, *A Lycanthropy Reader: Werewolves in Western Culture* (Syracuse, 1986), xiii, 1.

19. Stewart, *Moral Imagination in Modern Greek Culture*, 15

20. Quoted in D. Punter, *The Literature of Terror* (London, 1980), 409.

21. J. Vansina, *Paths in the Rainforest* (Madison, 1990), 239.

22. See for instance, M. Wright, *Strategies of Slaves and Women: Life-Stories from East/Central Africa* (London and New York, 1993), and Charles van Onselen, *The Seed is Mine: The life of Kas Maine, A South African Sharecropper 1894–1985* (New York, 1996).

23. J. Rosenthal, "Foreign Tongues and Domestic Bodies: Gendered Cultural Regions and Regionalised Sacred Flows," in M. Grosz-Ngaté and O. H. Kokole, *Gendered Encounters: Challenging Cultural Boundaries and Social Hierarchies in Africa* (New York and London, 1997), 198–99.

24. See for instance, D. Ekpo, "Towards a Post-Africanism: Contemporary Africa Thought and Postmodernism," *Textual Practice* (1995): 121–22.

25. P. Geschiere, *The Modernity of Witchcraft* (Charlottesville and London, 1997), 1; M. Bastian, "Bloodhounds Who Have No Friends: Witchcraft and Locality in the Nigerian Popular Press," in J. Comaroff and J. L. Comaroff (eds.), *Modernity and Its Malcontents* (Chicago, 1993), 129ff.

26. G. Parrinder, *Religion in Africa* (Baltimore 1969), 65.

27. Elechi Amadi, *Ethics in Nigerian Culture* (Ibadan, 1982), 20–21(writing of ritual killings).

28. B. Barber, *Jihad vs. McWorld* (New York, 1996).

29. For Japan, see Barber, *Jihad vs. McWorld*, 18; for *Dallas*, see p. 220.

30. P. Gilroy, *The Black Atlantic: Modernity and Double Consciousness* (Cambridge, Mass., 1994). My address was given at the Canada Learneds, St Johns, Newfoundland, 1997.

31. M. Schatzberg, "Power, Legitimacy and 'Democratisation' in Africa," *Africa* (1993): 445.

32. Chinweizu, "Prodigals, Come Home" (*Okike*, 4), quoted in Wole Soyinka, "Neo-Tarzanism: The Poetics of Pseudo-Tradition," *Transition* (April/June, 1975): 38. He notes, "We must add in fairness that Chinweizu rejects the use of such a landscape 'as exoticism for background effect,' nevertheless it is one which must be moved to 'the dramatic centre of poetry.'" See also Chinweizu, O. Jemie and I. Madubuike, *Towards the Decolonisation of African Literature* (Enugu, 1980).

33. T. O. Beidelman, *Moral Imagination in Kaguru Modes of Thought* (Washington, 1993), 203.

34. E. P. Thompson, "The Moral Economy of the English Crowd in the Eighteenth Century," *Past and Present* (1970): 76

35. James Scott, *The Moral Economy of the Peasant* (New Haven and London, 1976), 4.

36. J. Lonsdale, "The Moral Economy of Mau Mau: Wealth, Poverty and Civic Virtue in Kikuyu Political Thought," in B. Berman and J. Lonsdale, *Unhappy Valley* (London and Nairobi, 1992), 315ff–.

37. P. Geschiere, "Witchcraft, Kinship and the Moral Economy of Ethnicity," paper presented to the Conference on Ethnicity in Africa, Edinburgh, 1995; R. Austen, "The

Moral Economy of Witchcraft," in Comaroff and Comaroff, *Modernity and Its Malcontents,* 89ff.

38. M. Watts, *Silent Violence: Food Famine and Peasantry in Northern Nigeria* (Berkeley and Los Angeles, 1983), xxiii.

39. Ibid., 146

40. George M. Foster, "Peasant Society and the Image of Limited Good," *American Anthropologist* (1965): 293–315.

41. Shehu Othman, "Spoils of Power," *The Guardian* (London), 3 Feb. 1984.

42. R. Harms, *River of Wealth, River of Sorrow* (New Haven and London, 1981), 97.

43. Austen, "The Moral Economy of Witchcraft," 89ff.

44. P. Schmoll, "Black Stomachs, Beautiful Stones," in J. and J. Comaroff, *Modernity and Its Malcontents,* 216 n.1.

45. Amos Tutuola, *My Life in the Bush of Ghosts* (London, 1954; reprint 1978), 117

46. F. De Boeck, "Postcolonialism, Power and Identity; Local and Global Perspectives from Zaire," in R. Werbner and T. Ranger (eds.), *Postcolonial Identities in Africa* (London, 1996), 102 n.9.

47. Schmoll, "Black Stomachs," 204.

48. Harms, *River of Wealth,* 200.

49. Stephen Akut, of Samaru Kataf, 1985.

50. Taussig, *The Devil and Commodity Fetishism,* 94ff.

51. K. Marx, "Revenue and its Sources," Addenda to Part 3 of *Theories of Surplus-Value,* trans. J. Cohen and S. W. Ryazanskaya (Moscow, 1971), 461. See M. Taussig, "The Genesis of Capitalism Amongst a South American Peasantry: Devil's Labour and the Baptism of Money," *Comparative Studies in Society and History* (1977): 140.

52. Schmoll, "Black Stomachs," 205.

53. C. Fisiy and P. Geschiere, "Sorcery, Witchcraft and Accumulation: Regional Variations in South and West Cameroon," *Critique of Anthropology* (1991): 252.

54. Wole Soyinka, *Ake: The Years of Childhood* (London, 1981), 11–12.

55. Shambaa informants quoted in S. Feierman, "Therapy as a System-in-Action in Northeastern Tanzania, *Social science and Medicine* (1981): 355.

56. Paul Richards, "Natural Symbols and Natural History: Chimpanzees, Elephants and Experiments in Mende Thought," in K. Milton (ed.), *Environmentalism: The View from Anthropology* (London, 1993), 145.

57. Eric de Rosny, *Healers in the Night,* trans. R. R. Barr (Maryknoll, NY, 1985), 199.

58. A pedant would point to one (localized) exception—the signares of Senegal.

59. B. Jewsiewicki, "Painting in Zaire: From the Invention of the West to the Representation of Social Self," in S.Vogel (ed.), *Africa Explores 20th Century African Art* (New York and Munich, 1991), 148–49.

60. Tshibumba Kanda-Matulu, "Simba Bulaya" (1970s), reproduced in Vogel *Africa Explores,* 165.

61. D.Kaspin, "Chewa Visions and Revisions of Power," in J. and J. Comaroff, *Modernity andIts Malcontents,* 48–49

62. B. Lindskog, *African Leopard Men* (Uppsala, 1954); F. Kramer, *The Red Fez: Art and Spirit Possession in Africa,* trans. M. Green (London, 1993).

63. See the positive reception given to works such as E. Wolf, *Europe and the People Without History* (Berkeley, 1982), and A. Appadurai, *Modernity at Large: Cultural Dimensions of Globalization* (Minneapolis, 1996).

64. J. Iliffe, *Africans: History of a Continent* (Cambridge, 1995). This is not, of course, intended as a criticism.

65. R. E. Dennett, *Notes on the Folklore of the Fjort,* [i.e., Kongo] (1898; reprint, Nendeln, 1967), 31–32; for the Eshu story, found in many sources, and common to Yorubaland and Cuba, see U. Beier, *Yoruba Myths* (Cambridge, 1980), 55–56 and R. F. Thompson, *Black Gods and Kings* (Bloomington, 1976), chap. 4, 3–4.

66. G. Lienhardt, "Getting Your Own Back: Themes in Nilotic Myth," in J. Beattie and Lienhardt (eds), *Studies in Social Anthropology* (Oxford, 1975), 213–37; John Janzen, *Lemba 1650–193: A Drum of Affliction in Africa and the New World* (New York and London, 1982), 210–19. The story in essence tells how A threw B's spear at an elephant, which carried it away. B insisted on its return, and A recovered it after many adventures. Later, B's child swallowed A's bead, and A insisted on cutting the child open to recover it. There are many variants.

67. Quoted in Fernandez, "African Religious Movements," 226.

68. Beidelman, *Moral Imagination,* 210.

69. "Trefossa" (H. de Ziel), *Trotji* (Amsterdam, 1957), 32 and end foldout, with Dutch translation. David Dorward drew my attention to this source, and Elli Mulder helped me translate the Dutch version.

70. C. Vecsey, "Facing Death, Masking death, in Luba Myth and Art," *Journal of Religion in Africa* (1983): 31.

71. Quoted in W. Benjamin, *Charles Baudelaire, a Lyric Poet in the Era of High Capitalism,* trans. H. Zohn (London, 1973), 148.

PART I

Perceptions of the Atlantic Slave Trade

2

AN OVERVIEW

> [T]he discerning Natives account it their greatest Unhappiness, that they were ever visited by the *Europeans*. They say that we Christians introduc'd the Traffick of Slaves, and that before our Coming they liv'd in Peace.[1]

The time has come to turn from general theoretical perspectives to a specific—though vast and amorphous—phase of historical experience. The Atlantic slave trade—and domestic slavery—are vividly depicted in the alternative cognitive universe of myth and symbol. I begin, in necessarily brief compass, with an introduction to its existing historiography. The interpretation of the Atlantic slave trade has a complex history of its own, which began long before the discipline of African history began to take shape, from the 1960s on. Europeans involved in the trade sought to justify themselves by emphasizing—or inventing—the darker aspects of African life, seeking to show that captives were rescued from a Hobbesian state of nature where life was nasty, brutish and short, though scarcely solitary.[2]

Abolitionists often emphasized Africa's shadow side, to show the harm done by the slave trade. Wilberforce notoriously called Africans "fallen men."[3] They tended to depict the European as savior and civilizer, whether through missionary activity or so-called legitimate trade. The two, indeed, were often confused:

25

> "The Book says you are to grow cotton," explained Livingstone's interpreter, "and the English are to come and buy it."[4]

The ironies were not lost on Africans:

> When I told one, this morning, that the slave trade was a bad thing, and that White people worked to put an end to it altogether, he gave me an excellent answer. "Well, if White people give up buying, Black people will give up selling slaves."[5]

In a further irony, it has long been recognized that the products of nineteenth century "legitimate trade" were largely collected, produced, or processed by domestic slaves.[6] Abolitionist and allied rhetoric, paradoxically, contributed to attitudes that made colonialism possible, and clothed military invasion with a cloak of moral superiority.

By definition, the Atlantic slave trade was a global phenomenon, and many studies deal with themes which have at most an oblique relevance to the African experience. In the 1960s and 1970s, interpretations of the trade's impact on Africa tended to fall into one of two schools that I have called revisionist and radical. The first of these, which Manning calls minimalist,[7] emphasized its positive aspects. In a famous article, Fage wrote of the "close correlation, between economic development (and political development because indigenous commercial activity was largely king or state-directed) and the growth of the institution of slavery."[8] He concluded, "in West Africa [the slave trade] was part of a sustained process of economic and political development."[9] Northrup called the slave trade "an effective, though cruelly exploitative solution to the problem of economic growth in southeastern Nigeria."[10] I wrote twenty years ago:

> Radicals have sometimes felt that the revisionist view of the slave trade is . . . an attempt to whitewash Europe's crimes in the past, and, by implication, perhaps, to minimise international economic injustices . . . in the present. Revisionism . . . is, in essence a desire to break free from a historiography where the African appears as victim, dupe or comprador. It insists that the African of the past was making rational choices which benefitted the society he lived in. . . . Revisionism is generously intentioned. But it is wrong.[11]

Radicals—among whom Davidson, Rodney, and I were prominent— saw the slave trade as a source of underdevelopment and social polarization,[12] and stressed both the shoddy nature of many of the commodities sold to Africans and the fact that they often duplicated local products.

"The trade in slaves . . . was essentially an exploitative alliance between a comprador class [and] an external exploiter to prey upon the . . . population."[13]

Much research has been done since, and some elements in the original radical analysis now need revision. These include Rodney's suggestion that, in Upper Guinea at least, and perhaps elsewhere, domestic slavery did not antedate the Atlantic slave trade, and Davidson's view that the slave trade turned Benin into a City of Blood and even led to a deterioration in its art![14] But the anonymous African voices to which we listen in the pages that follow denounced the slave trade for its oppressiveness and cruelty, as Rodney did.

In research on the African past, as in other fields, a new insight is introduced, either in a seminal study or through a number of scholars moving in the same direction at much the same time; this in its turn suggests a plethora of additional research, and so on. There is usually a clear link between the state of historiography and other concerns—accounts of resistance to colonial rule in Africa flourished when political nationalism appeared triumphant, studies of Great States and long distance trade seemed to attest to African political and economic achievements in the past, and by implication, in the contemporary world. Books on women reflected a new awareness of gender issues in the West. In the 1980s, studies of ecology, epidemics, and famines were only too clearly linked to contemporary concerns of a very different kind.

In 1969, Curtin published a book which was to have a seminal impact on two decades of research. Based on printed sources, it suggested that the total number of slaves *imported to* the Americas was 9,566,100; he analyzed distribution over space and time—their diverse African origins and New World destinations and the changing role of different European slaving nations at different periods. His figures were much lower than those that had been generally accepted, which he succeeded in proving had been handed from one writer to another and had begun with a nineteenth-century American source.[15] (There has been a comparable downsizing in the statistics of those executed in the witchcraft persecutions of early modern Europe.)

Curtin's figures fitted in well with the revisionist school; Fage suggested that the export of slaves had creamed off the population increase in the eighteenth century. "For other centuries the [demographic] effect of the slave trade would have been slight."[16] Many historians—myself among them—were initially dubious about Curtin's figures; we felt that because they were based on published sources, they were likely to be too low, and that data was often collected in contexts which encouraged under-reporting. Inikori argued that the figures were too low, Henige that they are unknowable.[17] Curtin's book was followed by a great deal of specialized research in primary sources—Postma on the Dutch slave trade, Miller on the Portuguese, Daget on the French, Richardson and Eltis on the British.[18]

Some of his regional figures proved too high and others too low, but his general order of magnitude was confirmed to a remarkable degree.[19] In time, new variables entered the research, such as a study of the age and sex of captives, which in turn shed important light both on demographic change and family relationships.[20] Scholars disagree very considerably on the demographic implications, for Africa, of the Atlantic slave trade. Manning suggested that the combined demographic effects of the Atlantic, Indian Ocean, and trans-Saharan slave trades meant that the population of subSaharan Africa in 1850 was fifty rather one hundred million, and led to transformations so great that they amounted to a change in the mode of production.[21] Eltis, on the other hand, believed that "significant depopulation was unlikely" and that even when the Atlantic slave trade was at its height, Atlantic imports probably represented less than five per cent of African incomes.[22] Studies were made of the price of slaves, of imported goods, and of the currencies associated with Atlantic trade.[23] The Fishers wrote a study of slavery and enslavement in Islamic societies, relying heavily on the writings of the explorer, Nachtigal.[24] There was a proliferation of case studies of domestic slavery in Africa, some with special reference to enslaved women.[25]

There has been a marked tendency to concentrate on economic history, statistics, and the quantifiable; this research has been facilitated by the establishment of a data bank on Atlantic slave voyages at the W. E. B. Du Bois Institute at Harvard.

In 1981, however, a collection of essays appeared which drew attention to cognitive history. In *The Ideology of Slavery in Africa,* contributors wrote on three themes—the idiom of kinship in domestic slavery, varied forms of abolitionism (including slave revolt) and slavery in Muslim societies.[26]

The late 1990s saw a significant clash between exponents of western academic history and a local historian in Dakar, Senegal. Since the 1970s, the *Maison d'Ésclaves* on Gorée Island, in Dakar harbor, has become a place of pilgrimage for many African Americans largely because of the advocacy of Joseph Ndiaye, who believed that many—perhaps millions of—slaves were exported through Gorée. The academic research of Curtin and others suggested much lower figures, and it has been shown that the Maison d' Ésclaves was probably used marginally, if at all, for this purpose. The resulting controversy lies beyond the scope of this study,[27] but these debates are not immediately relevant to the present work. Ndiaye was an amateur historian, but he was expounding essentially the same kind of history as the academy. Some of the details were wrong—an experience not, of course, peculiar to Ndiaye—but the work emanated from conscious reflection on and study of the shape of past events.

The chapters that follow explore a cognitive history of an entirely different kind, expressed in myths, metaphors, and symbols. They provide us with significant, even unforgettable, reflections on the Atlantic trade. Students struggle with the statistics of the external commerce of Bristol or Nantes, but the image of vampire cowries or white slaver cannibals is compellingly apposite and vivid.

The slave trade seemed a classic illustration of life as a zero-sum game—hence the appropriateness of the associated metaphors of cannibal and witch. The most widespread of these images calls the white slave merchant a cannibal. What of the black slavers who sold these captives to foreigners? Their role is largely though not wholly elided in African American memory, but strikingly preserved by their descendants in a variety of ritual contexts ("The afflicted slaver," pp. 41–2 below).

Alternative symbolic representations suggest that the slave's exported body provided the raw material for Europe's industrial manufactures, or alternatively, that Western commodities were made under the sea for white sorcerers by zombies, enslaved African souls. Yet another complex of myths states that cowries, the shell money of the slave trade and one of its leading imports, were obtained from the ocean, using slaves as bait. Cowries, long since useless as currency, live on in popular culture, and retain symbolic links with the slave trade. African, not African American, memory is the main focus of this book. But it is impossible to ignore the latter in any cognitive history of the Atlantic slave trade. Chapter 6 explores the way in which, in the New World, the poetics of memory reinterpreted patterns of enslavement and reversed the Middle Passage.

The symbolic worlds of popular culture do not, of course, fit neatly into academic categories. Some of the material in chapter 4, for instance, concerns domestic slavery, and the study of cowries leads us into their changing ritual meanings in the twentieth century. (Similarly, many of the books cited in the footnotes to the present chapter deal, in different permutations, with domestic slavery and the slave trades of the Sahara and Indian Ocean, as well as the Atlantic slave trade.)

Implicit or explicit in all this material is a discourse on the value of wealth in people vis-à-vis wealth in things. This is often expressed in mirror images—the living slave body is commodified, and becomes food, or industrial raw material, or bait, while dead shell money takes on a predatory life of its own.

It is important to be aware of certain distinctions, which are equally applicable to the second section of this study. First, we must distinguish the poetics of rumor, dealing with contemporary events, from the poetics of memory, dealing with the past. (The distinction is easily overlooked, since the kinds of statements they make are so similar, and in some sense, thoughts about events distant in place and distant in time are comparable.) Second, some of the myths and symbols discussed in this book are found over a vast area, and have counterparts elsewhere in the world, while others are highly localized. The maps, unconventional in a history of ideas, reflect this. These symbolic complexes are undoubtedly more extensive than existing written records, or rather the selection of these of which I have knowledge. The legend that slaves were turned into statues has been recorded only among the Anaguta of the Jos Plateau, and is known to me through my fieldwork there. The legend of vampire cowries has been recorded in Benin (the modern nation, not the ancient city) and central Nigeria.

On the other hand, myths that describe white slavers as cannibals extend over a vast extent of space and time and are clearly both separate inventions and manifestations of a great international continuum that ascribes anthrophagy to the Other. Early Christian apologists, such as Tertullian and Minucius Felix, indignantly rejected claims that they practiced ritual cannibalism.[28] The (medieval) Hereford Map of the World locates *anthrophagi* in southeast Asia.[29]

Some writers in the West have accused their own culture of cannibalism, referring to its predation and cruelty. Montaigne's essay is a celebrated example—in English translation, "Of the Canniballes," it seems to have influenced *The Tempest*.[30]

More commonly, the West has stigmatized subjugated peoples by calling them—very often wrongly—cannibals. When Columbus reached Hispaniola, he thought it was an island off the coast of Asia, and called its inhabitants, Caniba, people of the Great Khan. "[I]t is the slightest of historical accidents that America is today not called Cannibalia and that its inhabitants are not known . . . as Cannibals."[31] The name of Caliban, image of the Other in Shakespeare's *Tempest*, may be an anagram of "cannibal"[32] (though Caliban himself is a nut-eating vegetarian). It is noteworthy that of the symbols discussed here, the one which appears most frequently in slave trade records is also that which has the widest international currency.

All historical writing involves an infinite number of choices or exclusions. The chapters that follow do not exhaust the possible ways of studying the slave trade in the poetics of rumor and of memory. The first version of this book included a chapter on the aquatic rainbow serpent in Whydah and elsewhere, which, in a very real sense, embodies yet another commentary on wealth and death from the sea. The mysterious gems called Popo beads or akori were thought to be its excrement; in one version, indeed, "his excrement is believed to have the power of transmuting grains of maize into cowries."[33] Maize is a New World crop, introduced during the slave trade years, as were cowries.

The rainbow serpent is well known in Casamance and Guinea, where it is sometimes adorned with diamonds and cowries, and sometimes party to a Faustian pact. The diamond serpent of Sierra Leone was documented long before the discovery of diamonds there. In Duala, a sinister aquatic serpent is the familiar of wicked sorcerers. I decided to publish my interpretation of the rainbow serpent separately, as the historical linkages are more tenuous than is the case with the rest of my material. But it is also true that to restrict these intricate mythologies to slave trade studies is both to distort and impoverish them.

The poetics of rumor and of memory are my main, but not my only, sources. Important interpretations of the slave trade are encoded in contemporary rituals (p. 44) and in language. The myth of the stealers of hearts, which flourishes and takes new forms in contemporary Madagascar, was first recorded in the nineteenth century, and was then interpreted as a memory of the slave trade. Rumors of vampirism—Chifwamba—flourished in colonial and postcolonial Malawi. The word originally referred to those who captured slaves.[34] These instances preserve, like fossil footprints, the imprints of the past.

Concealed in legend, symbol, and ritual is a history of the slave trade that focuses not on statistics but on how it was perceived and remembered. The interpretation of a particular source may be contested. But the total picture is more than the sum of its parts. In 1973, a hitherto unknown African Portuguese ivory was discovered in Italy. It was probably made by Bullom craftsmen in Sierra Leone, at some point between the mid-fifteenth and the mid-sixteenth centuries. It shows an aquiline-featured executioner in European dress. He is surrounded by severed heads, and a further victim awaits decapitation. In another ivory carving, apparently from the same hand, two naked women are savaged by crocodiles.[35] We lack the data to define these works as an indictment of the slave trade; but they are hauntingly reminiscent of stories of white cannibals.

The study of the alternative universe of myth and symbol is not, of course, a substitute for other, more conventional ways of looking at the slave trade. It simply suggests a different way of seeing the past; as we have seen, to appreciate a masked dancer, one must watch him from all possible angles. Concealed in legend, symbol, and ritual, is a history of the slave trade that focuses not on statistics but on how it was perceived and remembered.

To some African writers, the experiences of the slave-trade years continue to resound in the present. In Cheney-Coker's novel, *The Last Harmattan of Alusine Dunbar,* a modern political prisoner finds himself in a cell where slaves destined for the New World were once imprisoned.[36] Ayi Kwei Armah's *The Beautyful Ones are Not Yet Born,* set in the last days of Nkrumah's Ghana, repeatedly compares the elite of the post colony with the slave traders of an earlier day. "He could have asked if anything was supposed to have changed after all, from the days of chiefs selling their people for the trinkets of Europe."[37]

Notes

1. W. Smith, *A New Voyage to Guinea* (London, 1744), 266, citing Charles Wheeler on the Gold Coast. The bibliography on the slave trade is vast and constantly growing and lies, for the most part, beyond the scope of this study. The best source is to be found in J. Miller's bibliographies, appended each year to the journal *Slavery and Abolition,* and periodically published as separate volumes; most recently, *Slavery and Slaving in World History: A Bibliography* (Millwood, 1993). The outstanding general texts are P. Lovejoy, *Transformations in Slavery* (Cambridge, 1983), and P. Manning, *Slavery and African Life* (Cambridge, 1990).

2. See for instance W. B Cohen, *The French Encounter with Africans: White Response to Blacks, 1530–1880* (Bloomington, IN, 1980), 183. There is much further material of this kind in books written by those who visited Africa as slave traders. My discussion of the Atlantic slave trade here is necessarily extremely condensed. For a fuller and more completely documented account, see my *History of African Societies to 1870* (Cambridge, 1997), chapter 18.

3. Quoted in P. D. Curtin, *The Image of Africa* (Madison, WI, 1964), 54. There are, of course, many other strands in pro-slavery and abolitionist polemic. In addition to Curtin's and Cohen's work, see J. Walvin (ed.), *Slavery and British Society, 1776–1846* (Macmillan, 1982), D. Turley, *The Culture of English Antislavery 1780–1860* (London, 1991), S. Drescher, "The Ending of the Slave Trade and the Evolution of European Scientific Racism," in J. Inikori and S. Engerman (eds.), *The Atlantic Slave Trade* (Durham, NC, 1992), 361–96 and especially J. N. Pieterse, *White on Black* (New Haven, 1992), chapters 2–5.

4. David and Charles Livingstone, *Narrative of an Expedition to the Zambesi and Its Tributaries* (London, 1865), 77.

5. J. F. Schön and S. A. Crowther, *Journals* (London, 1842), 48 (Schön's journal, 26 Aug., 1841).

6. Lovejoy, *Transformations,* 159–83. For two pioneering studies, see R. Austen, "The Abolition of the Overseas Slave Trade: A Distorted Theme in West African History," *JHSN* (1970): 257–54, and P. Manning, "Slaves, Palm Oil and Political Power on the West African Coast," *African Historical Studies* (1969): 279–88. There is recent information on this issue in R. Law (ed.), *From Slave Trade to "Legitimate" Commerce* (Cambridge, 1995); see for instance, Law, "Introduction," 17, P. Lovejoy and D. Richardson, "The Initial 'Crisis of Adaptation . . .'", 48, and G. Austen, "Between Abolition and *Jihad,*" 100–105.

7. P. Manning (ed.), *Slave Trades, 1500–1800: Globalization of Forced Labour* (Aldershot, 1996), xxiv–xxvi.

8. J. D. Fage, "Slavery and the Slave Trade in the Context of West African history," *Journal of African History* (1969): 397. C. Wrigley wrote an equally celebrated rejoinder, "Historicism in Africa: Slavery and State Formation," *African Affairs* (1971): 113–24.

9. Fage, "Slavery and the Slave Trade," 400.

10. D. Northrup, *Trade without Rulers* (Oxford, 1978), 176.

11. Elizabeth Isichei, *A History of Nigeria* (Harlow, 1983), 108.

12. W. Rodney, *How Europe Underdeveloped Africa* (London, 1972); B. Davidson, *Black Mother: Africa the Years of Trial* (London, 1972).

13. Isichei, *A History of Nigeria,* 108.

14. B. Davidson, *Black Mother,* 205–6; W. Rodney, "African Slavery and Other Forms of Social Oppression on the Upper Guinea Coast . . . ," reprint in J. Inikori (ed.), *Forced Migrations* (London, 1982), 61–73.

15. P. D. Curtin, *The Atlantic Slave Trade: A Census* (Wisconsin, 1969).

16. Fage, "Slavery and the Slave Trade," 400.

17. D. Henige, "Measuring the Immeasurable: The Atlantic Slave Trade, West African Population and the Pyrrhonian Critic," *Journal of African History* (1986): 295–313; J. Inikori, "Measuring the Atlantic Slave Trade: An Assessment of Curtin and Anstey," *Journal of African History* (1976): 197–223.

18. J. Postma, *The Dutch in the Atlantic Slave Trade, 1600–1814* (Cambridge, 1990); J. Miller, *Way of Death: Merchant Capitalism and the Angolan Slave Trade* (Madison, WI, 1989); S. Daget, *Répertoire des expéditions négrières françaises au XVIII siècle,* 2 vols. (Paris, 1978–84); D. Eltis, *Economic Growth and the Ending of the Transatlantic Slave Trade* (Oxford, 1987); D. Richardson, "Slave Exports from West and West-central Africa, 1700–1810," *Journal of African History* (1989): 1–22.

19. See P. Lovejoy, "The Volume of the Atlantic Slave Trade: A Synthesis," *Journal of African History* (1982): 473–501.

20. D. Geggus, "Sex, Ratio, Age and Ethnicity in the Atlantic Slave Trade . . . ," *Journal of African History* (1989): 23–44; J. Thornton has written a number of papers in this field, including "The Slave Trade in Eighteenth century Angola: Effects of Demographic Structures," *Canadian Journal of African Studies* (1981): 417–27.

21. Manning, *Slavery and African Life,* 71.

22. Eltis, *Economic Growth,* 67, 72; also see 183.

23. On currencies, J. Hogendorn and M. Johnson, *The Shell Money of the Slave Trade* (Cambridge, 1986) is outstanding. R. Bean pioneered the study of slave prices in *The Brit-*

ish Trans-Atlantic Slave Trade, 1650–1775 (New York, 1975). See J. Miller, " Slave Prices in the Portuguese South Atlantic," in P. Lovejoy (ed), *Africans in Bondage* (Madison, WI, 1986), 43–77, and Eltis, *Economic Growth,* 260–64.

24. A. Fisher and H. Fisher, *Slavery and Muslim Society in Africa* (London, 1970).

25. S. Miers and I. Koytoff (eds.), *Slavery in Africa* (Madison, WI, 1977); C. Robertson and M. Klein (eds,), *Women and Slavery in Africa* (Madison, WI, 1983).

26. Paul Lovejoy (ed.), *The Ideology of Slavery in Africa* (Beverly Hills, CA, 1982).

27. There is a useful account, with bibliographic references, by R. Austen, "The Slave Trade as History and Memory: Confrontations of Slaving Voyage Documents and Communal Traditions," *William and Mary Quarterly* (2001): 229–44.

28. Minucius Felix, *Octavius,* 9; Tertullian, *Apology,* 7–8.

29. J. B. Friedman, *The Monstrous Races in Medieval Art and Thought* (Harvard, 1981), 95; see 11 for a (Caucasian) cannibal from the Sion College bestiary. Other sources locate them in Africa (102) or the New World (177).

30. A. Vaughan and V. Vaughan, *Shakespeare's Caliban: A Cultural History* (Cambridge, 1991), 47–8.

31. L. Osborne, "Does Man Eat Man? Inside the Great Cannibalism Controversy," *Lingua Franca* (April/May, 1997): 28.

32. The question is discussed in Vaughan and Vaughan, *Shakespeare's Caliban,* 26–32; as they point out, it is more likely that it is an anagram of Carib.

33. A. B. Ellis, *The Ewe Speaking Peoples of the Slave Coast of West Africa* (London, 1890), 49.

34. M. Bloch, *Placing the Dead* (London and New York, 1971), 32, on Madagascar. On Chifwamba, see p. 113.

35. V. L. Grottanelli, "Discovery of a Masterpiece: A 16th-Century Ivory Bowl from Sierra Leone," *African Arts* (1975): 14ff; E. Bassani, "Additional Notes on the Afro-Portuguese Ivories," *African Arts* (1994): 36, 39.

36. S. Cheney-Coker, *The Last Harmattan of Alusine Dunbar* (London, 1990), vii.

37. Ayi Kwei Armah, *The Beautyful Ones Are Not Yet Born* (London 1968; reprint 1971), 175.

3

THE SLAVE TRADERS

Fear rules not only those who are ruled, but
The rulers too.

Berthold Brecht, "The Anxieties of the Regime"[1]

This chapter explores two contrasting symbolic systems that represent, respectively, white and black slave traders. The first took shape in the poetics of rumor, among the enslaved and the communities from which captives were obtained. It referred specifically to Europeans, and depicted them as cannibals. Like enslavement, cannibalism is an extreme form of the zero-sum game; it annihilates its dehumanized victim in order to augment the life force of the predator. The image of the cannibal slaver is rooted not only in the cruelty and rapacity of the Atlantic slave trade, but also in a complex set of associations between whiteness, the spirit world, and the sea. It was extensively recorded during the years of the slave trade, and soon after it came to an end.

The second symbolic complex—"the afflicted slaver"—sheds significant new light on the African merchants from whom white slaving captains bought their living cargo. It is to be found in cults of affliction, which are either contemporaneous with the trade (the Lemba cult) or which are found in our own times, in communities very different from each other, whose forbears bought, sold or owned slaves.

Much of the value of studying "subjugated knowledges" lies in the way in which they challenge accepted and conventional ways of seeing. Accusations of cannibalism have often been part of an invention of Africa, a component in white racism, perpetuated by Western cartoonists into modern times (the explorer in the cooking pot, complete with sun helmet).[2]

But there have always been skeptics,[3] and Bentley, a nineteenth-century missionary in Central Africa, found that cannibalism, like the horizon, constantly receded into the distance:

> Since coming first to the Congo, the further I travelled the further cannibalism seemed to recede; everybody had it to say that their neighbours on beyond were bad, that they "eat men," till I began to grow sceptical.[4]

In a spirit possession cult in a Muslim Arabic-speaking village in the northern Sudan, cannibal sorcerers are always Zande, from far to the south. One of these spirits takes the form of a crocodile.[5] The Zande also located cannibalism at a distance, in their own remote past, where they described it with detestation. "In the past the Azande were just like animals of the bush, because they killed people and ate their fellows, just like lions, leopards and wild dogs."[6]

The present study is concerned with the history of ideas, not of diet. But one must note in passing that there is currently a major international debate as to whether cannibalism existed anywhere. Arens claims that it did not, but was a mental construct, an invention of the Other.[7] Specialists in different disciplines and regions have questioned this.[8]

Many—probably most—texts that Westerners believed described cannibalism in Africa actually referred to the astral cannibalism ascribed to witches, the "traditional"—and constantly reinvented —idiom through which an absolute evil is imagined. (The same confusion is evident in the title of a book by a modern academic, Kalous's *Cannibals and Tongo Players of Sierra Leone* ("Cannibal" was nineteenth-century Krio usage for wereleopards).

White Cannibals in West Africa c.1500–c.1780

The belief that whites bought captives in order to eat them is by far the most extensively documented symbolic representation of the slave trade. To some extent, this reflects the fact that it was of practical importance to

European slavers, as the despair it produced often led to suicide, attempts to escape, or revolt. (The cannibal's victim is seemingly passive, but the myth often led to action.)

Literal cannibalism and the astral cannibalism of the witch merge into each other, as symbols of absolute evil. In many parts of Africa—including the Igbo culture area—suicide was an abomination. (An Igbo suicide was denied burial, and the body was discarded in what was called the evil forest.) The fact that it was seen as preferable to falling victim to cannibalism shows the horror with which anthrophagy was regarded.

The idea that European slave traders were cannibals was first recorded in the first decade of the sixteenth century, with reference to an earlier Portuguese expedition up the Gambia. When the Portuguese said that they had come, not to make war, but to trade,

> They replied that they knew well how trade had been carried on on the *Canaga,* and that the Christians ate human flesh and that all the slaves they bought they carried away to eat.[9]

There is abundant later evidence of these fears. Jean Barbot made several slaving voyages to West Africa, and in a book written in 1688, he explained how the dread of European cannibals often led to suicide.[10]

Bosman, who traded in West Africa, mainly on the Gold Coast, from 1688 to 1702, took the stereotype of the white cannibal as evidence that black ones existed,[11] and noted that at Whydah, the great slave port in what is now the Republic of Benin,

> We are sometimes sufficiently plagued with a parcel of Slaves, who come from a far In-land Country, who very innocently perswade one another, that we buy them only to fatten and afterwards eat them as a Delicacy.[12]

Snelgrave's first slaving voyage, in 1704, was to Calabar, in southeastern Nigeria. In the late 1720s, he captained slave ships to Whydah, and visited the king of Dahomey. Like earlier writers, he documented the terror felt by the enslaved at the prospect of being devoured by white cannibals, and the way in which this led to shipboard revolts.[13] Atkins, writing of a slaving voyage in 1722, observed

> as many of them think themselves bought to eat, and more, that Death will send them into their own Country, there has not been wanting Examples of slaves rising and killing Ship's Company, distant from Land, tho' not so often as on the Coast. . . .[14]

The idea that death returned the enslaved to their homes is well documented in African American traditions (p. 81–2).

Newton bought slaves in the Sherbro (Sierra Leone) in the early 1750s. Thirty odd years later, he recalled how slaves "often bring with them an apprehension they are bought to be eaten. . . . It is always taken for granted, that they will attempt to gain their liberty if possible."[15]

Matthews, writing of late eighteenth-century Sierra Leone, described the terror of the captive who "imagines the white man buys him either to offer him as a sacrifice to his God, or to devour him as food."[16]

As Bosman pointed out, the image of the white cannibal slaver was found not only on the coast but also far inland. Mungo Park described it among slaves travelling from Segu to the Gambia.[17] Although they were sold on the coast, captives were obtained in inland communities, which lacked first-hand knowledge of Europeans, or the sea. The poetics of rumor flourished accordingly.

So widespread were these concepts, that when the occasional victim of the Atlantic slave trade returned home, he was greeted with surprise. Ayuba Suleiman of Bondu returned to Africa in 1734. "What he said took away a great deal of the Horror of the Pholeys [Fulbe] for the State of Slavery amongst the English; for they before generally imagined, that all who were sold for slaves, were generally either eaten or murdered, since none ever returned."[18]

When written by slaving captains, stories of white cannibals often include an element of propaganda, the idea being to contrast these imaginary horrors with a less catastrophic reality in the New World. They are accounts—not always independent—from without, though they are mutually reinforcing. But the rare autobiographies of the enslaved confirm them.

First-Hand Accounts c.1750–c.1827

Olaudah Equiano, born in Igboland in c.1745, enslaved as a child, and emancipated in 1766, wrote vividly of his terror at the prospect of white cannibalism.[19] Ali Eisami was born in Borno in the 1780s; he was captured, lived as a slave for a time in Old Oyo, and sold at Porto Novo in 1818. The slave ship was intercepted, and he was released in Freetown. Many years later, he remembered his initial meeting with a missionary in the village of Bathurst, and the words of his companions, "The white man has taken Ali, and put him into the house, in order to slaughter him."[20]

The man whom history knows as Bishop Samuel Ajayi Crowther was born in the Yoruba town of Osogun in c.1806; he was enslaved, and placed on a ship bound for Brazil. He too was freed on the high seas, and liberated in Freetown in 1822. When he first boarded the naval vessel and saw roasting pigs and cannon balls, he and his companions at first assumed that they saw human flesh and heads.[21] Joseph Wright was another Yoruba, an Egba, who was sold in Lagos in c.1827, and liberated at sea. Later, he remembered his initial fears,which would soon be confirmed by the cynical manipulation of the slave ship's crew.

> [F]or we had heard that the Portuguese were going to eat us when we got to their country. This put [us] more to despair. . . .Next day we saw an English man-of-war coming. When the Portuguese saw this, it put them to disquietness and confusion. They then told us that these were the people which will eat us, if we suffered them to prize us.[22]

The myth outlived the slave trade—it was documented on the lower Niger during the 1841 expedition[23] and in Dahomey in 1863.[24]

The fear of white cannibal slavers was not confined to West Africa. In about 1870, a young trader visited a port south of the Zaire river, where the slave trade had ended twenty years earlier, and described how the dread of cannibalism had driven captives to attempt escape, and their owners to draconian reprisals.[25]

A True Fiction?

Accounts of the white cannibal slaver, documented over a vast area over a time span of nearly three hundred years, undoubtedly represent multiple independent responses to the same situation. They are, as we have seen, by far the most common symbolic description of the Atlantic slave trade and collectively constitute a powerful essay in moral economy. They encapsulate the way in which the trade killed many of its victims, destroyed the social identity of the survivors, and condemned them to an often cruel servitude in an alien land. More than one authority has acknowledged the essential truth of these accounts. Pierson wrote in words that are, perhaps, truer of the Atlantic slave trade than of colonialism:

> The great Molochs of American slavery and European colonialism consumed generations of African men, women and children.[26]

White cannibalism is a core symbol in *Sacred Hunger,* Barry Unsworth's historical novel about the Atlantic slave trade. In one episode, at a London banquet, English sugar merchants dismember and consume a chocolate model of an African woman.[27] The book is based in part on an atrocity which occurred in 1783, when the master of the *Zong* threw 122 ailing slaves overboard, because insurance would not cover the loss if they died a natural death. In 1840, the English artist, Turner, painted a famous picture of this tragedy. Marina Warner sees it as an image of white cannibals: "Turner's whiskered, jowly, and even pink sea monsters moving in to feed on flesh stand for the well-fed but still hungry, pink, whiskery merchants who trade in Africans."[28]

The symbols in these alternative histories have multiple layers of meaning. It is this, as much as anything, that brings them close to the ambiguities and complexities of lived experience. At one level, the white cannibal is a metaphor for the cruelty, destructiveness, and exploitation of the slave trade. Cannibal stories were sometimes told in a spirit of conscious manipulation. Some nineteenth-century slaving captains encouraged their victims to believe that the naval vessels that pursued them were crewed by cannibals—the passage from Wright, cited above, is an example.[29] Africans, as well as Europeans, made use of these fears. Burton described how, in Somalia, fathers kept their sons in check by threatening them "with the jaws of that ogre, the white stranger."[30] African merchants often told Europeans that their own local rivals or enemies were cannibals, to exclude the latter from foreign trade and direct contact with a powerful potential ally.[31] African coastal brokers sometimes consciously disseminated frightening images of the whites in an attempt to preserve their own middleman role. "They [Akwamu] painted us Europeans as horrid; that we were sea monsters."[32] In late nineteenth-century Gabon, these stereotypes were used to dissuade the Okande from leading a French party to the Gabon interior— "the Poutou [Europeans] only buy slaves to fatten them up and eat them."[33]

It is evident that Europeans—but not their black trading partners— were seen as cannibals, not only because of the cruelty of the slave trade, but also because they were unfamiliar and strange. In many widely separated African cultures, spirits were thought of as white, and the water is often seen as the abode of supernatural beings (pp. 56–8). Equiano, enslaved in c.1756, recalled, "I was now persuaded that I had gotten into a world of bad spirits, and that they were going to kill me."[34] On the opposite side of Africa, more than a century later, Livingstone recorded a conversation with a local inhabitant by the Ruvuma river:

> On inquiry if he had ever heard of cannibals, or people with tails, he replied, "Yes, but we have always understood that these and other monstrosities are met with only among you sea-going people."[35]

The young Crowther was terrified by his first sight of Lagos lagoon. "Nothing now frightened me more than the river, and the thought of going into another world."[36]

The image of the white slaver as cannibal merges with that of the European witch, and with that of a supernatural world located under the sea, which as we shall see still flourishes in the popular imagination (p. 224, 227–8). The cannibal is a metaphor both for predatory relations and for the Other. "In metaphor we see the use of the essentials of one experience to grasp another. And it is interactive and integrative in the sense that both experiences have something in common."[37]

The body has been called "the symbolic stage upon which the drama of socialization is enacted."[38] One of the most striking continuities in African socio-political discourse is a tendency for the individual body to become a metaphor for society as a whole. Threats to the body politic are expressed as threats to the individual. Patricia Turner, writing of the African American experience, reflects on why social relations are often personalized in this way. "One way to make sense of large-scale uninvited domination is to reduce it to a more personal plane. . . .[M]etaphors are generated that collapse the threat to the group into a threat to an individual."[39]

In the poetics of rumor, and of memory, the impact of the Atlantic slave trade is described in terms of the microcosm of the grossly abused and commodified body. The slave becomes food, bait, or industrial raw material.

The Afflicted Slaver

After the initial contact period, slaves were invariably obtained by purchase, from African middlemen on or near the coast. "The trade of slaves is in a more peculiar manner the business of kings, rich men, and prime merchants, exclusive of the inferior sort of Blacks."[40] Despite their power and prosperity, in West Central Africa members of the elite developed a characteristic affliction known as Lemba sickness. Not all, of course, were directly involved in the slave trade.

Lemba was a cult of affliction, first recorded in the mid seventeenth century, which died out in the 1920s. When first described, by Dapper, it was a royal cult in Loango, but later, it covered a much larger area, becoming a secret society, which also regulated trade routes. Those who joined it, often because they suffered from Lemba sickness, were rulers, merchants, and *nganga* (ritual specialists) whose success "made them vulnerable to the envy of their kinsmen, and thus in a sense marginal in the society and "sick" with the Lemba affliction."[41] In a sense, Janzen's superb study, the source for this account, was "a book about a seventeenth century 'cure for capitalism, created by insightful Congo coast people who perceived that the great trade was destroying their society.'"[42] But their affliction seems to have been rooted, not in guilt about the slave trade, but in the fear that because of their prosperity they would be regarded as witches. Since there was a finite amount of wealth in the world, their enrichment meant the impoverishment of others—life as a zero-sum game.

Lemba initiation was expensive; in the 1880s, it cost between 1000 and 2000 currency units of imported wire. At the time, the average price of a slave was 500 to 600 units.[43] Lemba died out in the 1920s, partly because the old caravan routes had been superseded, and partly because of the attacks of Christian prophets, such as Kimbangu.

But paradoxically, although Lemba members were drawn from the elite, the enslaved carried the cult to the New World. Lemba still survives in Haiti, and has undergone a striking transformation.

> We are but poor folk
> who beg your mercy.
> O Earth, our mother and patron! . . .
> you know that we are not of this land.[44]

It was the only Haitian ritual which was celebrated in secret.[45]

Ritual Memories of the Slave Trade: Dahomey and Whydah

The "Fon" or "Aja" founded a powerful kingdom, which expanded towards the coast from its inland nucleus at Abomey in the late seventeenth and early eighteenth centuries, conquering the great slave port of Whydah in 1727.

The ocean acquired greater ritual importance in Whydah, as foreign trade expanded. In the mid nineteenth century, it was said that

> The youngest brother of the triad [of gods] is Hu, the ocean or sea. Formerly it was subject to chastisement, if idle or useless. The Hu-no, or ocean priest, is now considered the highest of all, a fetish king, at Whydah. . . .[46]

The importance of foreign commerce was symbolically acknowledged in other ways. The Dahomey king "Agaja [reg.c. 1716–40] . . . took a

Portuguese ship as his emblem. . . . The *vodun* took responsibilities for new trade and new diseases (Sakpata became the god of smallpox.)"[47] By the mid nineteenth century, the serpent shrine at Whydah, had "a . . . fresco of a ship under full sail."[48]

The last slave ship sailed from the port of Whydah in 1865. Shortly before this, Burton described a ritual where the ocean was placated by the sacrifice of a man dressed as a courtier.

> At times the King sends as an ocean sacrifice from Agbome a man carried in a hammock, with the dress, the stool, and the umbrella of a caboceer; a canoe takes him out to sea where he is thrown to the sharks.[49]

The elite who enriched themselves through the slave trade appeased the sea by the offering of a man dressed in their own image. But paradoxically, some of their members were among the victims of the Atlantic trade.

The mother of a future king of Dahomey, Gezo, was enslaved, together with her adherents, as a result of royal rivalries. She spent twenty-four years in America, and was finally restored to Dahomey, through her son's efforts, in c.1840. From her, the court learned what happened to the victims of the trans-Atlantic slave trade. (It is striking that slave traders seem to have known as little about captives' ultimate destinations as their victims.)

In about 1930, Melville and Frances Herskovits observed a court ritual, where a bullock and a goat were slaughtered "for the unknown dead, among whom are the descendants of those sold into slavery." The words of the invocation were recorded as:

> Oh, ancestors, do all in your power that princes and nobles who today rule never be sent away from here as slaves to Ame'ica. . . . We pray you to do all in your power to punish the people who bought our kinsmen. . . .And it is not enough. The English must bring guns. The Portuguese must bring powder. The Spaniards must bring the small stones which give fire to our firesticks. The Americans must bring the cloths and the rum made by our kinsmen who are there. . . .[50]

The Herskovits' driver was a man called Felix, who came from Popo, now Aného and called himself "a Mina." The sack of Accra in 1677 and the conquest of Akwamu in 1730 had led to the creation of new refugee polities east of the Volta, one of which was Popo.[51] Felix remembered the history of his family as a flight to the east, away from slave raiders. His grandfather had told him that Portuguese slave traders took captives to Freetown, to father children, who were subsequently sold,[52] another example of the poetics of rumor. When Felix was told of New World slavery, he wept.

The court ritual described here reflects a sense of guilt about an export of slaves that had ended over sixty years earlier, less because of the suffering it inflicted than because its victims had included aristocrats and kin. The appetite for foreign goods—rum, cloth and firearms—is undiminished.

Ritual Memories of Slavery and Enslavement in Small-Scale States

Small scale states were often a source of captives—sometimes because of the predation of more powerful neighbors, but often because individuals and rival villages preyed on each other. Equiano, in a pattern very typical of Igboland as a whole, fell victim not to war but to kidnapping (on the forms of enslavement, see p. 77–8). The Diola of southwest Senegal also lived in small-scale states. Many Diola were among the victims of the slave trade and their public traditions reflect this, but a different kind of memory was fossilized in secret family rituals.

Wooden fetters were preserved on the family altar, and women used iron ones as musical instruments during festivals. In the community Baum studied, family shrines, which were originally the focus of cults of affliction, changed in the late eighteenth century, so that to become a priest one had to capture a slave and sacrifice large quantities of livestock. A new shrine was introduced, which was hidden in the family rice granary, which offered protection from the supernatural consequences of kidnapping and/or selling local children, a practice seen as akin to witchcraft (the consumption of life force). These rituals are still performed in secret.[53] As among the Igbo, some individuals captured slaves while others fell victim to enslavement.

The Ewe

"Ewe" communities live near the sea, in southeastern Ghana and southern Togo, and speak the same language as the "Aja" or "Fon" of the old Dahomey kingdom, now of the modern Republic of Benin. It is a good example of the artificiality of ethno-linguistic labels. The "Ewe," however, lived not in a centralized state but in a hundred separate villages, scattered amid the coastal lagoons. Here, slavery is remembered in rituals of atonement; the referent is not the Atlantic slave trade, but the import and ownership of domestic slaves from the north.

The Ewe honor the spirits of former slaves by placing cowries, the shell money of the slave trade, on family shrines (p. 71). They preserve ritual memories of domestic slavery, and in particular, of slaves from the north, who have become the focus of spirit possession cults, significantly named Gorovodu (kola nut spirits) and Mama Tchamba (a town in central Togo). These spirits are linked with wealth, both because it is recognized that their labor contributed to the community's resources, and because they are believed to have brought valuables with them. In the words of a Gorovodu woman priest:

> The *Voduwo* are slave spirits. Hundreds of years ago peoples of the north—Hausa, Mossi, Tchamba and Kabye—passed through Eweland. Some of them suffered hardships and had to sell their children to our ancestors. These children . . . worked their whole lives and made their masters rich. When they grew old and died, the objects we had taken from them upon their arrival—cloths, bracelets, fetishes, sandals—these things became the Vodu, and the slave spirits came and settled in them and became our gods, If we do not serve them . . . we become ill and die.[54]

In a striking reversal, the living descendants of the freeborn serve the spirits of slaves. Their devotees wear a red fez and the sandals of Asante royals. Mama Tchamba receives offerings of trade beads, called "grandmother jewels" that are, like the fez, bought from northern traders for ritual purposes. Ewe children are sometimes called by northern names, or *Donko*, slave, as a ritual protection. But there is a profound ambiguity, for threatened children are often given a name which means "worthless"—so that a dangerous spirit will not bother with them. "Woven metal bracelets" (fetters?) are sometimes found, and when this happens it is thought that the finder is called to the service of slave spirits.

As Rosenthal points out in the absorbing ethnography on which my account is based, these cults have much in common with that of the mermaid, Mami Wata, and the links are locally recognized. Cults which honor the spirits of dead slaves negate the guilt of remembered injustices by re-writing the past in an idealized way. The honor paid them in contemporary ritual contrasts with the fact that in the late nineteenth century, the victims of an illegal slave trade among the Anlo Ewe were concealed in the cult houses of a secret society.[55]

Mama Tchamba and Gorovodu are part of a wider geography of supernatural and class relations. The Asante equated slave, *odonko,* with the peoples of the northern savannahs, who were distinguished by their facial scars. Now, the Asante and other Akan peoples consider that witchfinding cults such as Tigari come from the north. "Many of the spirits which inhabit these [cult] objects are, like their patriarch spirits, from Northern Ghana, and they commonly speak the Mosi language."[56]

What is most striking, perhaps, in the various accounts of the afflicted slaver and his descendants is their complexity and ambiguity. Lemba sickness afflicted slave traders, but not, it seems, because they dealt in slaves, but because they were rich. The Dahomey court offered sacrifices for the transgressions of the past, because those enslaved had included kin and aristocrats. Ewe rituals acknowledge the wealth created by the toil of now dead domestic slaves. All these accounts are generic; for a legend about the eternal isolation of a single black slaver one must turn to African American memory (p. 79–80).

Notes

1. Berthold Brecht, "The Anxieties of the Regime," in J. Willett and R. Manheim (eds.), *German Satires (Poems)* (London, 1976), 297.

2. See J. N. Pieterse, *White on Black: Image of Africans and Blacks in Western Popular Culture* (New Haven, 1992), 113–22.

3. See for instance, J. Atkins, *A Voyage to Guinea, Brazil and the West Indies* (1735; reprint, London, 1970), 123; T. Winterbottom, *An Account of the Native Africans in the Neighbourhood of Sierra Leone,* 2 vols. (1803; 2nd ed. London, 1969), I: 166.

4. W. Holman Bentley, *Pioneering on the Congo* (1900; reprint, London, 1970), vol. 2: 94–95. In the end he believed he met real cannibals on the upper Zaire. R. Harms, *River of Wealth, River of Sorrow* (New Haven and London, 1981), 240 n.15, discusses the question of cannibalism in West Central Africa and concludes that it did indeed exist.

5. J. Boddy, *Wombs and Alien Spirits: Women, Men and the Zar Cult in Northern Sudan* (Madison, WI, 1989), 299–301.

6. E. Evans-Pritchard, "Cannibalism: a Zande text," *Africa* (1956): 73–4.

7. W. Arens, *The Man-Eating Myth: Anthropology and Anthropophaghy* (New York, 1979). His conclusions have been extensively criticized. Cf. Reeves Sanday, *Divine Hunger, Cannibalism as a Cultural System* (Cambridge, 1986), 9 and *passim.*

8. L. Osborne, "Does Man eat Man? Inside the great cannibalism controversy," *Lingua Franca* (April/May, 1997): 28–38, is a useful recent survey.

9. V. Fernandes, *Description de la Côte Occidentale d'Afrique. [1506–10],* ed. and trans. T. Monod, A. Texeira da Mota, and R. Mauny (Bissau, 1951), 34–5.

10. J. Barbot, *A Description of the Coasts of North and South Guinea* (1746), 272; (MS written 1688). Much has been written on the borrowings in the printed version, which has led to a new edition. For present purposes—the documenting of widespread and long enduring stereotypes—the eighteenth-century edition is acceptable.

11. W. Bosman, *A New and Accurate Description o f the Coast of Guinea* (1705, 2nd ed. London, 1967), 489 (first published in Dutch in 1704). His book was written in the form of letters, the first dated 1700.

12. Bosman, *A New and Accurate Description,* 365.

13. W. Snelgrave, *A New Account of Some Parts of Guinea, and the Slave Trade* (London, 1734), 163.

14. Atkins, *A Voyage to Guinea,* 175.

15. John Newton, *Thoughts upon the African Slave Trade* (London, 1788), in B. Martin and M. Spurrell (eds.), *The Journal of a Slave Trader* (London, 1962).

16. J. Matthews, *A Voyage to the River Sierra-Leone* (London, 1788), 152.

17. Mungo Park, *The Life and Travels of Mungo Park* (Edinburgh, 1896), 262.

18. Francis Moore, *Travels into the Inland Parts of Africa . . .* (London, 1739), extract in E. Donnan, *Documents Illustrative of the History of the Slave Trade to America* (Washington, 1931), vol. 2: 417.

19. *The Life of Olaudah Equiano,* ed. P. Edwards (Harlow, 1988), 22, 26–7 and 31.

20. P.Curtin (ed.), *Africa Remembered* (Madison, WI, 1967), 215. An editorial footnote links this passage with the fear of cannibalism.

21. Curtin, *Africa Remembered,* 313.

22. Ibid., 331.

23. J. F. Schön and S. Crowther, *Journals,* 2nd ed. (London, 1970), 42; Schön's journal, 22 Aug. 1841.

24. R. Burton, *A Mission to Gelele King of Dahome* (1864; 2nd ed. C. Newbury, London, 1966), 305.

25. C. Jeannest, *Quatre Annees au Congo [1869–73]* (Paris 1883), 127.

26. W. D.Pierson, *Black Legacy: America's Hidden Heritage* (Amherst, MA, 1993), 12.

27. Barry Unsworth, *Sacred Hunger* (New York, 1992), 417, 618.

28. Marina Warner, *Six Myths of Our Time* (London, 1994), 86.

29. See also F. H. Rankin, *The White Man's Grave: A Visit to Sierra Leone in 1834*(London 1836), vol 2: 104; also W.Winwood Reade, *Savage Africa* (London, 1863), 18; C. Snouck Hurgronje, *Mekka in the Latter Part of the 19th Century,* trans. J. H. Monahan (Leyden and London, 1931), 20 n.1.

30. R. Burton, *First Footsteps in East Africa* (1886; London, 1966), 108.

31. Harms, *River of Wealth,* 240 n.15.

32. L. Roemer, quoted in R. Atkinson, "Old Akyem and the Origins of Akyems Abuakwa and Kotoku," in R. B. Swartz and R. Dumett (eds.), *West African Culture Dynamics* (The Hague, 1982), 355.

33. V. de Compiègne, *L'Afrique Équatoriale Okanda Bangouens-Osyéba* (Paris, 1885), 129.

34. *The Life of Olaudah Equiano,* 22.

35. H. Waller (ed.), *The Last Journals of David Livingstone* (London, 1874), I: 60, journal entry for 25 June 1866.

36. Curtin, *Africa Remembered,* 309.

37. J. Fernandez, "Fang representations under acculturation," in P. Curtin(ed.), *Africa and the West* (Madison, WI, 1972), 14.

38. T. Turner, quoted in H. Hendrickson, "Introduction," to Hendrickson (ed.), *Clothing and Difference* (Durham, NC, and London, 1996), 3.

39. Patricia A. Turner, *I Heard It Through the Grapevine: Rumor in African-American Culture* (Berkely, 1993), 32.

40. Barbot, *A Description of the Coasts of North and South Guinea,* 270.

41. John Janzen, *Lemba 1650–1930: A Drum of Affliction in Africa and the New World* (New York and London, 1982), 4.

42. Ibid., xiii, summarizing the perceptions of "friends and colleagues."

43. Ibid., 36.

44. This rite was described by Jean Price–Mars in the 1930s; he stumbled on it while hunting.. Quoted in Janzen, *Lemba,* 288.

45. Ibid., 279.

46. R. Burton, *A Mission to Gelele King of Dahome* (1864; 2nd ed., London, 1966), 295.

47. P. Manning, "Coastal Society in the Republic of Bénin: Reproduction of a Regional System," *Cahiers d'Études africaines* (1989): 250.

48. Burton, *A Mission to Gelele,* 73.

49. Ibid., 295.

50. Herskovits, "A Footnote to the History of Negro Slaving," in F. Herskovits (ed.), *The New World Negro* (Bloomington, 1966), 86–7; also 88–9 for Gezo's mother.

51. Mina is an Ewe ethnym for people who call themselves Ge and are often called a variant of this, such as Guan. The Mina and Ewe languages are closely related.

52. Herskovits, "A Footnote to the History of Negro Slaving," 84.

53. Robert Baum, "The Slave Trade in Diola (Senegal) Oral Tradition," paper presented to a conference on the Slave Trade in African and African American Memory, University of Chicago, June 1997.

54. Quoted in J. Rosenthal, "Foreign Tongues and Domestic Bodies: Gendered Cultural Regions and Regionalised Sacred Flows," in M. Grosz-Ngaté and O. H. Kokole, *Gendered Encounters: Challenging Cultural Boundaries and Social Hierarchies in Africa* (New York and London, 1997), 183. This outstanding analysis is the basis for my account here.

55. Sandra Greene, *Ethnicity and Social Change on the Upper Slave Coast* (Portsmouth, 1996), 98 (on the Anlo Ewe).

56. Gabriel Bannerman-Richter, *The Practice of Witchcraft in Ghana* (Winona, MN, 1982), 55.

4

THE IMPORTED COMMODITIES

> . . . It is as if
> Men turning into things, as comedy,
> Stood, dressed in antic symbols, to display
> The truth about themselves, having lost, as things,
> That power to conceal they had as men.
> Wallace Stevens, "An Ordinary Evening in New Haven"[1]

Introduction: The Imports

The commodities imported to Africa during the centuries of the external slave trade varied with place and time, and have been the subject of much detailed research. In West and West Central Africa as a whole, textiles came to be the most important import, and a slave was often called a piece (that is, of cloth) a grim symbol of human commodification. In West Central Africa the next most important imports were spirits (such as Brazilian sugar brandy) and tobacco. On the "Slave Coast" (west of Lagos), currency, in the form of cowries, was the leading import. (The shell money of the slave trade, and its multiple dimensions of symbolic meaning, form the theme of the following chapter.) The next most important import consisted of metals, first iron, and later, copper. Iron, like cloth, was already produced locally on a large scale. It was used for tools and weaponry, and sometimes made into currency. Copper and its alloys likewise had been smelted and worked locally long before the European advent; it was valued as currency—manillas, copper bars, and copper wires—but was also used for jewelry and sculpture. Firearms and ammunition were also of great importance—in the late eighteenth century, West Africa imported between 283 and 394 thousand guns per annum, and the Congo-Loango area, some 50 thousand.[2]

In this chapter, I explore two contrasting symbolic complexes that offer explanations of the sources of imported western goods. In one, which is very similar to the myth of the slave as food (and often juxtaposed with it), commodities are manufactured out of the slave's body. In the second, enslaved African souls—zombies—toil for white sorcerers under the sea, manufacturing western goods. The first was recorded during the Atlantic slave trade, or soon after its close, in what is clearly a set of independent responses, in regions at vast distances from each other. The second was elaborated in the late nineteenth and early twentieth centuries, in a single mythical complex, in West Central Africa. Both sets of symbolic statements constitute powerful essays in moral economy, denouncing the extraction of profit from the destruction of the powerless.

The Slave as Raw Material

These myths described, in a condensed and elliptical way, how the slave was sold to buy alcohol, currency, cloth, arms, and gunpowder. In these symbolic statements, the slave's body became the raw material from which these commodities were made. The following examples are drawn from the lower Niger, in what is now Nigeria, from West Central Africa, and from Madagascar.

The earliest example known to me was recorded by a doctor at Luanda, on the Angolan coast, in 1770—he wrote of themes in the poetics of rumor, which are strikingly reminiscent of the horrors of white cannibals—the brains pressed into cheese, the human fat processed as cooking oil, the bones turned into gunpowder.[3] A German visitor to the Congo in 1857 was told that the olive oil sold there was made from slaves exported to America and sold to cannibals.[4] It is worth noting that Leopold of the Belgians, creator of the most inappropriately named Congo Free State, described his ambitions in the region in these terms, in 1877: "We cannot lose the chance acquiring a piece of this magnificent African cake."[5]

In the early 1830s, Oldfield, in the course of an expedition up the Niger, spoke with two different Nupe people who told him that "It is well known . . . that in their own country they [Europeans] eat black men, and dye red cloth with their blood."[6] Similar views were recorded further down the Niger, closer to the sea. Simon Jonas, an Igbo interpreter on a later Niger expedition, was a liberated slave from Sierra Leone. When he reached the Lower Niger, in 1841, he found that "The Ibo man could hardly credit it. He had hitherto believed that slaves were purchased by the White people to be killed and eaten, and that their blood was used to make red cloth."[7] In most of these texts, the concepts of the slave as food and the slave as raw material are closely linked. They might have been echoed, some sixty years later, when it was said of the Igbo on the Lower Niger that "if a man sees red cloth in a dream, it means that one, either of his own immediate household, or near connection will shortly die."[8]

In early nineteenth-century Madagascar, the same interwoven ideas of the slave as food and as raw material were recorded. The enslaved "imagined that the whites wish to eat them, that they make red wine from their blood and cannon powder from their bones."[9] The belief that the blood of slaves became a dye forms a theme in counterpoint with the African American tradition that slaves were lured aboard slave ships with red cloth (p. 78–9).

As with rumors of white-slaver cannibals, a whole historical epoch is condensed in the microcosm of the individual body. These accounts are True Fictions, which describe, briefly, but with piercing insight, the nature of a trade that exchanged living people for imported goods.

The Slave As Statue

The idea of living slaves coated with clay and turned into statues is a comparable image of human commodification. This symbolic complex mirrors the slave's weakness and lack of choices, rather than the patterns of trade. It refers, not to the Atlantic trade, but to slaves sent as tribute in the nineteenth century from the small-scale communities of the Jos Plateau to their northern neighbor, the emirate of Bauchi. It was recorded in the early 1980s, in the course of fieldwork among the Anaguta, a small people who live near the modern city of Jos, more than a hundred years after the events to which it refers. It is thus part of the poetics of memory. Like the traditions of vampire cowries in Sokoto (see chapter 5) the narrative looks to the north, not the south.

In the small-scale societies of the Jos Plateau, the fiction of the slave as an adopted child or prospective wife came very close to social realities, at

least in the modern memories of the host community—"a slave was expected to behave as a perfect son."[10] But when their own members were
sent as tribute to an emirate or became its captives,[11] the experience was
perceived as profoundly dehumanizing. This is symbolically stated in oral
testimonies claiming that tribute of a boy and a girl was sent annually to
the emirate of Bauchi, and that when they discovered the children were
covered with clay and turned into statues, they sent no more.

The legend is narrated to explain an (historic) incursion by a Bauchi
raiding party, in c.1873, that local people succeeded in driving back.[12] They
cherish the memory of a successful act of opposition to a dehumanizing
infliction; the conflict is periodically re-enacted in ritual.

People forcibly separated from their community lost their social identity.
The first generation slave lacked neither kin nor history, which were absent
only in terms of the cognitive world of the captor society. It is at the point of
sale that the slave was most clearly a commodity. As time went on the slave in
Africa began to reacquire a social identity, and the rights that go with it, a
process accelerated in the second generation slave. A "slave" could be a great
courtier, or a king's wife. Commoditization, as Kopytoff has pointed out, is
not a condition but a process, and "the commodity-slave becomes in effect
reindividualized. . . . But the slave usually remains a potential commodity."[13]
The process of enslavement cut the victims off forever from their neighbors
and kin, to whom their later destiny remained unknown. And if a funeral sacrifice
was needed, the African slave could abruptly become a commodity again.

The Zombie

A complex of traditions extensively recorded in West Central Africa, from
the late nineteenth century on, describes Europeans not as cannibals but as
sorcerers who compel the enslaved souls of dead Africans to produce manufactured goods under the sea. In this symbolic narrative, the slave's role is
eternally perpetuated in the world of the dead. The zombie myth is also
documented in colonial and/or postcolonial Cameroon and East Africa,
where it seems to have developed in the course of the twentieth century,
and where its resonances are of forced or ill-paid labor. These twentieth-
century developments of the zombie motif explain, not international economic relations, but local differences between the (relatively) prosperous
and the poor, and form the theme of a later chapter.

The zombie beliefs of Haiti are much better known than those recorded in Africa. The Haitian word zombie apparently comes from kiKongo,

nzambi, meaning, generically, human as opposed to animal.[14] If this derivation is accurate, its meaning has changed mysteriously. (Ardener suggested an alternative but less likely possibility—the Bakweri *a mo sombi o nyongo,* has pledged him in *nyongo*[sorcery].[15]) A further semantic transformation took place in New Orleans, where the serpent, Danbala, the most important spirit in the houdoun pantheon, was called *li grand Zombie.*[16]

Haiti specialists disagree as to whether actual zombification was achieved by drugs and hypnosis or whether it is part of the Invention of the Other.[17] Haiti was the first nation in the New World to abolish slavery, and it is a tragic irony that it endured in the mind, in the form of zombie fears. It is unclear whether Haiti's zombie beliefs came from Africa or were independently invented.

The Enslaved Soul in West Central Africa

In West Central Africa, the idea that the enslaved African dead work for sorcerers under the sea was first recorded in a compilation by a Dutch geographer, in 1668. Writing of seventeenth-century Loango, he describes the belief that sorcerers enslave the dead and that salt undoes the spell. (The reference to salt is arresting, for this is a well-known element in zombie lore in Haiti.[18])

> [T]he belief [is] that no one dies except through the malice and enchantment of his enemy, who, by the same spells, revives him, transports him to deserted places, and makes him work there to enrich him.[19]

Kikokoo was an *nkissi* (ritual object) in human form found, significantly, on the coast, near a cemetery.

> It is said that Kikokoo is there to protect the dead, and to prevent sorcerers from making them leave their graves to force them to work and to fish with those of the night. This *Nkissi* also presides over the sea, prevents storms and tempests, and brings ships to safe harbour.[20]

In these accounts, the sorcerers are not Europeans, but local fishermen. The trans-Atlantic export of slaves from West Central Africa shrank in the 1830s and 1840s and effectively ended in 1850, when illegal exports to Brazil came to a close. The idea of the enslaved soul, however, survived and took new forms. By the late nineteenth century, the slave-owning sorcerers were Europeans, who were thought to buy the souls of the dead and make them work under the sea, producing the textiles and other manufactures sold in Africa. The myth provided an explanation of the manufacturing capacity of industrial Europe. As in Haiti, slavery endured in the popular imagination long after the slave trade—though not domestic slavery—had ended.

Bentley was a Baptist missionary who worked in the Congo in the late nineteenth century, and his writings provide much data on the myth of the enslaved soul. "Many believed that if the mysterious strangers settled there the local witches would have every facility, and would be able to sell everybody to the white men—not as slaves, but that they would sell their spirits."[21] On a supernatural plane, the witch fills the role of the African slave trader—the comprador role largely, though not entirely, elided in New World memory (p. 79–80).

Significantly, the sources often refer specifically to cloth manufacture. In 1879, at San Salvador (the ancient Kongo capital, in northern Angola), "They considered that when a white man wanted cloth, he opened a bale and got it. . . . Everyone said that the cloth was made by dead men under the sea."[22]

The otherwise inexplicable material resources of the West are attributed to the labor of zombie slaves. It is, again, a True Fiction, for innumerable living slaves worked and died in the American South in the service of King Cotton, and textiles were, as we have seen, among the leading imports of the African slave trade.

Another missionary in West Central Africa, Claridge, also documented the concept that Europeans purchased African souls as slaves. Again, there is an emphasis on cloth manufacture and the role of the African witch or sorcerer as a supernatural slave trader. Containers of foreign provenance imprisoned captive souls, until they could be sent abroad, as did the barracoons where living slaves were penned.

> The sole work of the witch is to cause sickness and death, which is done by drawing off the soul of the victim. That soul or spirit is then sold to white men who hide them in their travelling trunks, water-tanks, salmon tins, etc, until they are able to despatch them to Europe, or to the bottom of the sea, or to some equally secure place far away where they spin cotton and weave cloth for their new taskmasters.[23]

We have seen how when the export of slaves to the Americas ended, domestic slavery often expanded (p. 26). The so-called "legitimate trade" of the later nineteenth century consisted largely of the export of commodities produced, collected, and/or transported by domestic slaves. Ivory hunting was as dangerous to the hunter as to the elephant, and it was not for nothing that Western philanthropists writing of the Belgian Congo used the expression Red Rubber.

The symbolic equation of commerce, foreigners and witchcraft was also applied to the ivory trade, and tusks, rather than salmon tins, become the prison for captive souls.

> The natives who did not travel always accused of witchcraft those who went to the coast. They believed that when a man went to sell ivory at the coast, he took with him, in the ivory, the spirits of some of his relatives and friends. In this way natives who traded were constantly annoyed with accusations of witchcraft. . . .[24]

The ivory trade was blamed for a high mortality rate, not because of its undoubted dangers, but because of the link with sorcery. A Makuta ruler told the Baptists, "If we let white men into the country, they will soon make an end of us. It is bad enough to have them on the coast. The ivory traders take down too many spirits in the tusks and sell them; we had better stop the trade in ivory altogether; we are dying too fast."[25]

In a late nineteenth-century source, the white sorcerers whose slaves toil under the sea are described in conjunction with dangerous water spirits who have much in common with later accounts of Mami Wata.

> Zimini has towns under the sand in the sea; and at times he comes up and seizes a man or a woman, and takes him or her down to his place. There are stories in which the white man is said to have his town under the sea, and to take thither all the slaves he captures and buys to help him to make his cloth.[26]

The Continuing Concept of the Enslaved Soul

The myths of the white sorcerer and of the enslaved soul were to have a long history. In 1960, the year of Congo/Zaire's independence, a kiKongo newspaper editorial demanded

> the immediate return of the entire Kongo generation exploited in 1350 [sic]. . . .all those powers that have exploited the Kongo people, transforming them into merchandise, should return this human body which was conveyed in a chemical product.[27]

Here, arrestingly, two symbolic complexes coalesce—the slave body as industrial raw material, and the idea that commodities imprisoned Africans destined for zombie servitude.

MacGaffey wrote of that year: "For some it was a dangerous time, when *mundele wa mwinda,* the white man with a lantern, went about to steal souls."[28] (The symbols of cannibal and zombie sorcerer merge; in another 1960 account, the man with a lamp was a European cannibal.[29])

In 1968, MacGaffey noted, "Even now there are those who "have heard" that the slave-trade still goes on. The sea-passage of slaves is not fully distinguished from the passage of souls, the slave-trader from the witch, the geographical America from the land of the dead."[30] A 1969 document written by members of a local independent church described how Catholics keep dead Africans in chains under the earth.[31]

In a tradition collected in 1970, in Matadi, it is the Belgians, the former colonial authority, who masterminded the sale of souls.

> In that commerce, from the time of our ancestors it was our custom to sell people, but they did not die entirely. They were sold to the Portuguese who afterwards stuffed them into ships for transportation to Belgium. . . .When a man dies he has no means of knowing that he is going to Belgium. All those people who are sold end up in Europe.[32]

In these traditions, a powerful and enduring symbolic history is encoded in the poetics of rumor and of memory. It is concerned not only with the Atlantic slave trade and the ivory trade, which to some extent replaced it, but also with the origins of Western manufactures and the technological superiority that produced them, suggesting an answer to a question to which we return in a later chapter, "Why are blacks poor and whites rich?"

The World Beneath the Sea

The image of Europeans who buy African souls from sorcerers so that they can profit from their toil is, like other symbolic depictions of the Atlantic slave trade, a dark one. But wealth from the sea was also compellingly attractive, and had this not been the case, the slave trade could not have existed. "The sea," wrote Livingstone, "is the Taprobane of the African."[33] Taprobane is Sri Lanka, mentioned in a number of Greek and Roman texts as a source of fabulous treasures.

Exotic manufactures were valued both for their real or presumed utility and as status symbols, which bolstered the public reputation of Big Men and enabled them to reward their supporters. These alternative histories give us an insight into the lure of exotic goods, which is invisible in statistical surveys of imports. The sources studied in this chapter reflect a core ambiguity in popular sensibility—the horror of the sufferings imposed on slaves on one hand, and the magnetic attraction of a world of things on the other. The improper consumption of witch or cannibal is a core symbol in symbolic statements of African moral economy; in a different version of same terminology we speak of "consumer goods". The resonances are thought-provoking.

The attractiveness and mystery of exotic imports is reflected in different but related narratives that describe the Europeans as rich magicians who live beneath the sea. In 1853, on the upper Zambezi, Livingstone wrote eloquently of the allure of imported textiles and beads, and their association with the sea.

> The Mambari told the Makololo, when questioned as to the origin of the [Manchester] prints so curiously written upon, that they came out of the sea. Beads are believed to be collected on its shore.[34]

A song recorded in Equatorial Africa in the mid nineteenth century anticipates many twentieth-century accounts of Mami Wata. The European lives in the sea, surrounded with riches. His house is made of money, in the form of brass rods, and his garden is strewn with pearls. It has gone through a process of double translation, and may well have been romanticized by its European transcriber.

> In the blue palace of the deep sea
> Dwells a strange creature:
> His skin as white as salt,
> His hair long and tangled as the seaweed.
> He is more great than the princes of the earth.
> He is clothed with the skins of fishes,
> Fishes more beautiful than birds.
> His house is built of brass rods;
> His garden is a forest of tobacco.
> On his soil white beads are scattered
> Like sand-grains in the sea-shore.[35]

In inland Gabon, according to an 1863 account, people "suppose that we live under the sea; that our clothes are the skins of those strange

monsters which dwell in deep waters; and that Manchester cloth is pre-
pared from a marine vegetable."[36] In many versions, the white sorcerers
beneath the sea were resurrected African ancestors. On the upper Zaire
river, nine hundred miles from the sea, it was said "that white people were
the returned spirits of the dead, who lived at the bottom of the ocean."[37] In
an 1872 account of Gabon, the European is a resurrected Fang ancestor
with "direct contact with Nzama (the creator) who gives him cloth, guns,
powder, etc."[38]

These images are rooted in ancient cosmologies. Their details vary, as
one might expect, but there are recurrent linkages between water, whiteness, and the spirits of the dead. In a well-documented Kongo instance, the
dead are white, and water is the point of contact between their world and
that of the living.[39] By identifying the white sorcerers with the African
dead, one restores a dimension of local autonomy to history—a pattern
evident in other contexts (see p. 169–70).

At least since the nineteenth century there has been a tendency to
identify the world of the dead with Mputu (Europe) or "America." Mputu
is generally thought to be short for Mputulukeezo, a form of "Portuguese,"
but in the nineteenth century it referred to the great cataracts of the lower
Zaire, or the surf of the Atlantic coast.[40] An alternative derivation is *vutuka,* to
return—the meaning being the place from which one does not return,[41] which
was equally applicable to the dead and to most victims of the slave trade.

The association of the world beneath the sea with the manufacture of
Western goods has been documented in the West Africa of the 1990s, but
it is attributed now not to European sorcerers but, as we will see later, to
Satanic agency.

Notes

1. Wallace Stevens, "An Ordinary Evening in New Haven," *Collected Poems* (London, 1984), 471.

2. For a more detailed discussion, with references, see E. Isichei, *A History of African
Societies, to 1870* (Cambridge, 1997), 335–37.

3. F. D. Cosme, "Tractado das queixas endemicas (1770)," cited in J. Miller, *Way of
Death: Merchant Capitalism and the Angolan Slave Trade 1730–1830* (London, 1988), 389.
See also p. 5.

4. Adolf Bastian, quoted in S. Axelson, *Culture Confrontation in the Lower Congo*
(Uppsala, 1970), 188.

5. Leopold II to Solvyns, 17 Nov. 1877, quoted in J. Stengers, "Leopold II and the
Association Internationale du Congo," in S. Forster, W. Mommsen, and R. Robinson, *Bis-
marck: Europe and Africa* (Oxford, 1988), 237 n.43.

6. Oldfield's journal, in MacGregor Laird and R. A. K. Oldfield, *Narrative of an Expedition into the Interior of Africa* (1837; reprint London, 1971), vol. 2, 77, 106..

7. J. F. Schön and S. Crowther, *Journals,* 2nd ed. (London, 1970), 42; Schön's journal, 22 Aug. 1841.

8. A. G. Leonard, *The Lower Niger and Its Tribes* (London, 1906), 146.

9. J. H. Bernardin de Saint-Pierre, *Voyage à l'Île de France* (Paris, 1818), 154, quoted in W. D. Pierson, *Black Legacy: America's Hidden Heritage* (Amherst, MA, 1993), 9.

10. T. M. Baker, "The Social Organisation of the Birom" (Ph.D. diss., University of London, 1954), 119. I recorded similar memories of the slave as adopted son among the Anaguta.

11. Some, but not all, Plateau peoples paid tribute to the emirates of Bauchi or Zaria. For details, see E. Isichei, "On Being Invisible: An Historical Perspective of the Anaguta and Their Neighbours," *International Journal of African Historical Studies* (1991): 537–38.

12. The accounts of the human statues were obtained from Pozo Kauda of Andrigiza, in Babale, and Pozo Usuman Barde, also of Andrigiza, in Kunga, both in Nov., 1983. A Bauchi participant, who was still alive in 1915, told the story of the raid to a colonial official. (National Archives, Kaduna, Josprof, 2/257, 1934, Abdu Wazirin Wunti of Lemme, testimony in P. Lonsdale, D. O. Bauchi Division to Resident, Naraguta Division, 4 Jan. 1915. encl. in S. E. M. Stobart, "Assessment Report on Anaguta and Jarawa tribes.")

13. I. Kopytoff, "The Cultural Biography of Things: Commoditization as Process," in A. Appadurai, *The Social Life of Things: Commodities in Cultural Perspective* (Cambridge, 1986), 65.

14. W. MacGaffey, personal communiction, 20 Aug. 1996; see also his *Religion and Society in Central Africa: The BaKongo of Lower Zaire* (Chicago and London, 1986), 6, 75. Nzambi Mpungi, the Highest Nzambi, is the supreme God.

15. E. Ardener, "Witchcraft, Economics and the Continuity of Belief," in M. Douglas, *Witchcraft Confessions and Accusations* (London, 1970), 149, and 158 n.9. There are two problems here. The first is that *nyongo* sorcery is a modern phenomenon and reached the Bakweri early this century. The second is that, unlike the Kongo, the Bakweri are a tiny group—hence unlikely to have had a formative impact in a New World society.

16. N. N. Puckett, *Folk Beliefs of the Southern Negro* (1926; reprint, New York, 1975), 179.

17. Wade Davis, *The Serpent and the Rainbow* (London, 1986) is an account of an ethno-botanist's research into the question. Karen MacCarthy Brown, *Mama Lola: A Vodou Priestess in Brooklyn* (Berkeley, 1991) writes "It is impossible to know how much of so-called black magic is actually practised in Haiti, but it is much discussed" (189). She describes popular belief in the (usually male) sorcerer, *boko,* who may entrap a wandering soul in a rock or bottle to do his bidding.

18. A. Métraux, *Haiti Black Peasants and their Religion,* trans. P. Lengyel (London, 1960), 96; Davis, *The Serpent,* 80.

19. O. Dapper, *Description d l'Afrique* (Amsterdam, 1686), 334. I read this in the French version, from which these extracts are translated. The original Dutch version of 1668 is fuller, but I did not have access to it, nor indeed do I read Dutch. Dapper (1636–1689) was an Amsterdam doctor who never visited Africa; he compiled information obtained from others, particularly an unpublished account by a merchant who did visit Africa, Samuel Blommaart. Ryder, writing of Benin, states that the material does not extend beyond 1644. A. F. C. Ryder, *Benin and the Europeans* (London and Harlow, 1969), 87–8.

20. Dapper, *Description,* 337.

21. W. H. Bentley, *Pioneering on the Congo* (London, 1900), I: 82.

22. Ibid., 160

23. G. C. Claridge, *Wild Bush Tribes of Tropical Africa* (London, 1922), 147. Claridge lived in West Central Africa for twelve years.

24. Bentley, *Pioneering on the Congo,* I: 278.

25. Ibid., 81.

26. R. E. Dennett, *Notes on the Folklore of the Fjort [Kongo] (French Congo)* (1898; reprint Nendeln, 1967), 8–9.

27. *Kongo dia Ngunga (Kinshasa)* 1 Oct. 1960, quoted in W. MacGaffey, *Modern Kongo Prophets* (Bloomington, 1983), 134.

28. W. MacGaffey, "Kongo and the King of the Americans," *The Journal of Modern African Studies* (1968), 175.

29. [Marcel] d'Hertefelt, in the published discussion of W. Friedland, "Some Urban Myths of East Africa," in A. Dubb (ed.), *Myth in Modern Africa* (Rhodes Livingstone Institute, Lusaka, 1960), 146, for Leopoldville (Kinshasa).

30. MacGaffey, "Kongo and the King of the Americans," 177.

31. The followers of Simon Mpadi, founder of *L'Église des Noirs,* 15 Mar. 1969, quoted in MacGaffey, *Modern Kongo Prophets,* 135.

32. Quoted in MacGaffey, *Modern Kongo Prophets,* 137.

33. David Livingstone, *Livingstone's African Journal 1853–6,* ed. I. Schapera (London, 1963), 32 (entry 31 Dec. 1863).

34. Ibid.

35. Sung by Ananga and translated by Mafuk, in W. Winwood Reade, *Savage Africa* (London, 1863), 228.

36. Winwood Reade, *Savage Africa,* 186.

37. R. Harms, *River of Wealth, River of Sorrow* (New Haven and London, 1981), 2.

38. Quoted in C. Chamberlin, "The Migration of the Fang into Central During the Nineteenth Century: a New Interpretation," *International Journal of African Historical Studies* (1978): 452. Fang is another unsatisfactory ethnym; the Fang of Gabon are linguistically and culturally the same as the Cameroon people once called Pahouin; scholars now tend to refer to the Fang/Bulu/Beti cluster (though other groups are also included, such as the Ewondo). Vansina calls them "the Sanaga-Ntem group." J. Vansina, *Paths in the Rainforest* (Madison, WI, 1990), 337 n.8.

39. A. Jacobson-Widding, *Red-White-Black as a Mode of Thought* (Uppsala, 1979), 334–35. An important source for this (and MacGaffey's) account of the world of the dead is Fu-Kiau Bunseki-Lumanisa, *Le Mukongo et le monde qui l'entourit* (Kinshasa, 1969). See also Jacobson-Widding, *Red-White-Black,* 332.

40. MacGaffey, *Religion and Society,* 62; his source is H. M. Stanley, who first visited the lower Zaire in 1877.

41. Ibid., 62.

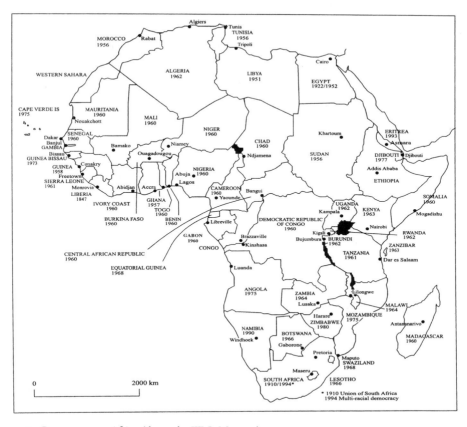

1. Contemporary Africa (drawn by W. J. Mooney)

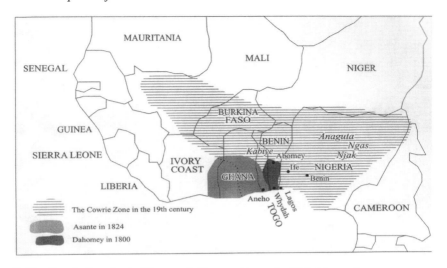

2. The Cowrie Zone in the Nineteenth Century (drawn by W. J. Mooney)

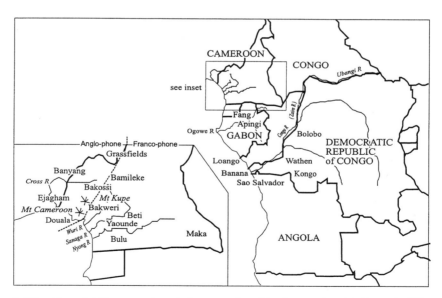

3. West Central Africa—people and places mentioned in chapters 4 and 8 (drawn by W. J. Mooney)

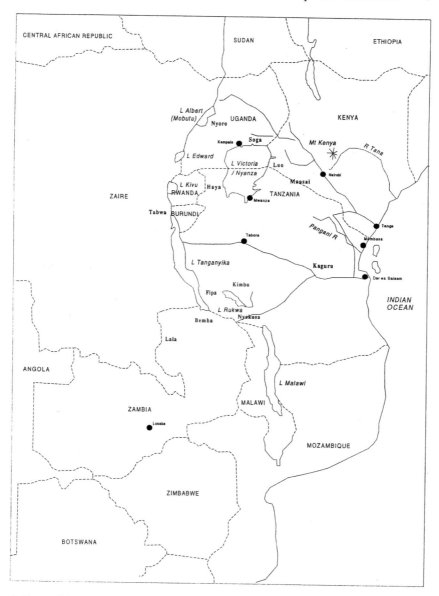

4. East and East Central Africa—people and places mentioned in chapter 9 (drawn by W. J. Mooney)

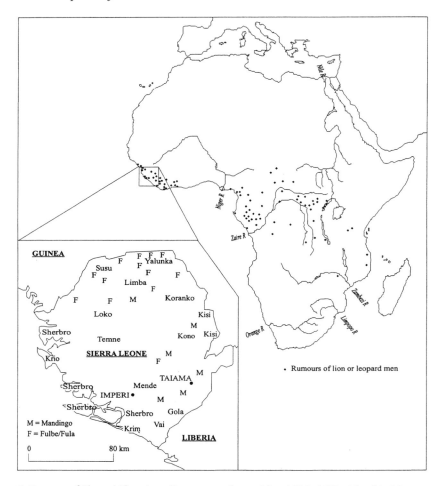

5. Rumors of Shapeshifters (werelions or wereleopards) c. 1880–1920. After Lindskog (drawn by W. J. Mooney)

5

COWRIES

> It is very singular that . . . the contemptible shells of the Maldives
> prove the price of Mankind.
>
> Fragment in the Sri Lanka National Archives[1]

In recent years, scholars have become increasingly aware that money is far
more than a simple medium of exchange. Cultural values shape the way it
is perceived, and it acquires dimensions of symbolic meaning that were
often invisible in older models of *homo economicus* and that encapsulate
particular views of moral economy.[2] In the words of a major recent study,
"Money is an anthropology. Its meanings are multiple. They deeply affect
and are deeply affected by culture."[3]

This chapter explores the symbolic meaning of the shell money of the
slave trade, and begins with the widely distributed myth that living cowries
were obtained in water, with slaves used as bait. Shell money that feeds on
people constitutes a theme in counterpoint with the images of the
commodified slave body explored in the two preceding chapters.

Perhaps few would question whether a myth of cowries that feed on
slaves is an explicit denunciation of the Atlantic slave trade. But cowries
also figure in other symbolic narratives, where they form part of a much
wider discourse on wealth in people and wealth in things. Cowries are

embedded in a complex symbolic discourse about gambling, debt, and enslavement, and myths of living cowries which multiply—but only for those already prosperous—help to explain the gap between rich and poor. Long since obsolete as currency, cowries live on in symbolic discourse. In many contexts, the shell money of the slave trade has proved enduringly good to think with.

Cowries in West and West Central Africa

Very early European accounts of West Africa and of the Kongo kingdom refer to shell currencies. Pereira's oddly entitled *Esmeraldo de Situ Orbis,* a mariner's guide written in c.1505–8, states:

> The negroes of these islands pick up small shells . . . which they call "zinbos." These are used as money in the country of Maniconguo [Mani Kongo]. . . . In the country of Beny [Benin] . . . they use as money shells which they call "iguou" . . . they use them to buy everything and he who has most of them is the richest.[4]

The ritual use of cowries reflects their monetarization, but they have much wider magical meanings that extend far beyond black Africa, and cannot be explored here.[5] A late fifteenth-century Castilian account of early European trade with the Gold Coast states that shells from the Canaries were in great demand, because they were thought to provide protection against lightning. Its author never visited Africa, and cowries did not come from the Canaries, but this is probably the earliest account of the magical power of shells (shell money?) in West Africa.[6]

Cowries were the monetary form that came closest to a modern currency, abstract symbols of value that could not readily be put to other uses apart from bodily adornment. On the "Slave Coast" (between the Volta and Lagos) they became the most important import. Burton, who visited Dahomey in 1863, called "cloth, cowries and rum—the notes, silver and copper of the country."[7] By the nineteenth century, their use had spread far inland.

In oral traditions—first recorded in 1907, far from the sea—the cowrie, the exo-skeleton of a dead sea creature, becomes the consumer of human flesh and blood. The legend is a True Fiction, a symbolic account of wealth obtained in exchange for slaves at an immense cost in human deaths, suffering, and trauma. The slave ships were called *tombeiros,* floating tombs. As in accounts of white cannibal slavers, depraved and distorted consumption symbolizes exploitative social relations. Cowries, like vampires, feast on human blood; they are dead shells, but feed and multiply. Money feeds on people, and people, separated from their community, and losing control over their labor and lives, turn into things.

The myth of the vampire cowries has been independently recorded in central Nigeria, the Republic of Benin, and Togo. Its remote historical roots may lie in the practice, common in coastal merchant states, of offering human sacrifices "as votive offerings to the sea, to direct vessels to bend their course to this horrid climate."[8] But the numbers of human sacrifices offered in such rituals was miniscule compared with those exacted by the Atlantic slave trade, and the vampire cowrie legend is primarily an indictment of the latter.

The myth that cowries were obtained with human bait was first recorded in 1907, hundreds of miles from the sea, in central Nigeria:

> [N]one of the Hill Angass have ever seen a cowrie, yet they have a word of their own for it, "jermadu"; & further they have a story in connection with it to the effect that in the days of their fathers, a man used to go to a certain water and dip himself in it; the cowries, which were alive, fastened themselves on his body, & when he came out they were taken off him & put in the sun to dry.[9]

In this version, the bait is a volunteer, and survives. In 1978, a more sinister version was recorded elsewhere in Central Nigeria—from three separate informants among the Njak, a small Goemai-related people in the Benue valley. This account links the myth of human bait for cowries with enslavement and the Hausa trading networks.

> Later people started to use cowries which were introduced by the Hausa traders. The cowries, we were told, were obtained in the ocean. These cowries were obtained by throwing human beings into the ocean. These cowries would then come and stick to the bodies of these human beings and killed the human beings by sucking all their blood. After sucking the human blood they did not fall off but remained stuck to the dead human flesh. . . . Some of our enslaved brothers and sisters were used as victims to obtain these cowries. I do not know where this ocean was but the Hausa traders who brought the cowries knew where they were obtained and they did not tell anybody.[10]

Another elder explained

> There was a special water place for these cowries. They were obtained only in this place. A person was caught and thrown into this special water and the

cowries would stick to his body, killing him. He was drawn up and the cowries were then plucked off from his body. Some of the people who were sent from here were used for this purpose. The special water was probably there around Sokoto. People saw the cowrie shells without knowing exactly where they originated from.[11]

Each of these versions was recorded long after the Atlantic slave trade came to an end—they belong, in other words, to the poetics of memory. They are particularly striking because they were found so far from the sea. One source, significantly, locates the vampire cowries in the *north*, at Sokoto. They may be contextualized in terms of very widespread traditions that cowries were found in local rivers. "Yoruba men still tell of finding cowries in streams."[12]

The legend of the vampire cowries has been independently recorded by Iroko, in the coastal lagoons of the Republic of Benin,[13] that is, in a marine environment, though not one where cowries were found. Further inland, in Kabiyè, the northern massif of Togo, it is said that the slave trade and cowries arrived at the same time; a slave cost from twelve thousand to twenty thousand cowries, and children were often sold in time of famine. Here, Verdier recorded the same myth with an accretion of macabre detail. "Slaves were taken to the coast and killed at Anèho. Their lower limbs were torn off and their thighs thrown into a large pool where cowries attached themselves."[14]

The kings of Dahomey are said to have buried vast quantities of cowries in the bush and then killed the slaves who had done the work. It is also said that human blood was poured on to cowries, to make them grow,[15] a story clearly akin to that of vampire cowries.

In Chatwin's historical novel, *The Viceroy of Ouidah*, the legend (which he presumably heard in Whydah) is located in the New World, retaining the association with a slave victim.

> Mama Benz asked what a cowrie really was.
> "Cowrie is a snail," he said. It lives in a river called Mississippi. In the old days, the Americans would throw a slave in the river, the cowries would feed on the body, and then they'd haul it up and that's how they got money to buy more slaves.[16]

Were stories of vampire cowries independently invented, or were they carried along the inland trade routes? Any answer would be sheer surmise. There are, however, hints of an underlying and enormously widespread mytheme. The novelist Tansi relates a tradition from the distant Zaire river which differs in detail, but may offer us a glimpse of an underlying cognitive world.

> This last idea put him in mind of an old custom where he came from: when a man was good and dead they used him to catch fish . . . they caught the fish using the body as bait. The custom had died out, but it left traces in people's memories.[17]

Contemporary urban legends, collected in Zambia and Zimbabwe, are strikingly similar—they suggest that diamonds can be obtained from stomachs of sea creatures, by using kidnapped children as bait (p. 143).

In each of these sources, money (or wealth in a different form) becomes a devouring force which consumes the living. A slave poet in Cuba made much the same point:

> With twenty hours of unremitting toil
> Twelve in the field and eight to boil
> Or grind the cane—believe me few grow old
> But life is cheap, and sugar, Sir—is gold.[18]

Gambling, Debt and Enslavement

A different but associated symbolic complex traces the intricate linkages between money, debt, enslavement, gambling, and witchcraft. The growth of a commercial economy, and the inequalities it engendered, encouraged the spread both of gambling and of indebtedness.[19] Bosman, referring to Whydah in the 1690s, traced the links between gambling, debt, and enslavement.

> They are very great Gamesters, and willingly stake all they are masters of in the World at play; and when Money and Goods are wanting . . . they stake first Wife and Children, and then Land and Body.[20]

Often, gambling took the form of tossing cowrie shells. "The drama of enrichment or impoverishment by the vagaries of the market was . . . parodied by popular games of chance."[21] In 1863 Burton wrote perceptively of Whydah that "Slave exporting is like gambling, a form of intense excitement which becomes a passion."[22] Gambling was also popular among the Bobangi river traders on the Zaire. "Players relied on magical charms to bring them luck. Lobesi [a game of chance] represented a concrete manifestation of the way money changed hands in the world. The person with the most powerful magic got the most money."[23]

Individuals were often enslaved because they were thought to be witches. The imagery of indebtedness—the flesh debt—is central to witchcraft beliefs in many cultures. Among the Gonja

> an *egbe* is held to be able to fly, to consume people's souls while they sleep, to belong to a coven, to incur flesh debts. . . . A part of the initiation is the bringing by the novice of one of his or her own kin to serve as the first meal of human flesh and the admission price to the coven.[24]

In the slave trade era, food or goods were sometimes left on the ground; anyone who picked them up, and could not pay the "debt," was enslaved for it.[25] In modern urban legends, in Nigeria and elsewhere, witches are thought to entrap victims by leaving money in the street. Whoever picks it up, falls into the witch's power. Witchcraft, debt, and enslavement are intricately entwined in the forest of symbols.

The Living Money of the Rich

Some accounts omit the murdered slaves, but interpret cowries as living beings that grow and multiply. Because of their shape, cowries are often perceived as symbols of female sexuality—an image found far beyond West Africa.[26]

A legend current among the Samo of Burkina Faso—far from the sea—tells of "a giant living cowrie who lives buried deep, somewhere in the bush, and gives birth to cowries, as the termite queen does to termites." People dreamed of finding her, but never did so, though sometimes newborn cowries were found, emerging from the ground. An otherwise unattainable wealth can be realized only by magic, but it always eludes the poor. At the time of the French conquest, the Samo were short of food but rich in cowries, which were used largely for prestige purposes, such as in the manufacture of expensive—and very heavy—dance costumes.[27]

Currency shells were also used on the Zaire river, where they were called *nsi* or *nji*. The Nunu of the middle Zaire believed that they sometimes contained a living creature that might multiply if kept in water. Everyone kept their shells in water, but most were disappointed.

> If you put *nsi* money in a pot of water, the shell would give birth. But that didn't happen to everybody, only to rich people. The *nsi* of the rich gave birth; those of the poor did not.[28]

Magic explains the otherwise inexplicable gulf between rich and poor.

A Grave for Cowries

Centuries of imports undermined the value of cowries, until they were suited only for very small transactions. In the colonial era they became worthless, as did other precolonial currencies. In Dahomey, "the French government expropriated and destroyed cowries where possible, replacing them with francs."[29] As the cowries for which such a high price had been paid became valueless, their owners abandoned their treasure. Ofonagoro writes eloquently of their fate in Nigeria, where

> the bitter decision [was made] to abandon them as junk. Stocks of . . . cowries hoarded by being buried in the ground, a testimony to centuries of accumulation, have since been abandoned in their permanent graves.[30]

Thus cowries, so often described as living, were consigned to the grave.

But paradoxically, they lived on in popular culture, and in some cases continued to embody a memory of the slave trade. Among the Ewe of coastal Togo and Ghana, in colonial times and later, cowries came to symbolize an age of domestic slavery. Families that had once owned slaves, fearing that their spirits would exact revenge, honored them with strings of cowries attached to a family shrine. "Today, when someone finds a [buried] pot of cowries, it is usually taken as a sign that the finder has a link with a slave spirit or with Ablo, the spirit of wealth, less frequently, with Mami Wata."[31]

The word for cowrie has come to mean money in Ewe and related languages.[32] This is also true of the Edo culture area, where cowrie, *igo,* now means money in general.[33] Halfway between Benin and the port of Ughoton lies a village called Igo; its ruler is the priest of the sea divinity, Olokun.[34] And *Olowo,* owner of cowries, is one of three modern Yoruba words for a rich man. Perhaps oddly, it has acquired this meaning only in modern times.[35]

In 1983, a Nigerian woman church leader published a pamphlet on Mami Wata and other water spirits, which she viewed as demonic, and referred to as "marines." She believed that they hid objects in the bodies of their victims. "To some marine gives cowries. The cowries show that your heart is in the control of mammy water."[36]

Eshu, Cowries, and the Market

The continuing ritual and symbolic life of cowries can also be linked to the divinity known as Eshu to the Yoruba, as Legba to the Fon, and often called a Trickster in academic studies.[37] His cult was taken by the enslaved to the New World, where he is Legba in Haiti, Elegba in Cuba, and Eshu in Brazil.

Both in the nineteenth and twentieth centuries, Eshu has been closely linked with cowries. Farrow, who lived in Yorubaland from 1889 to 1894, wrote, "he may just as reliably be called the 'god of wealth,' because his wooden images are always adorned with strings of cowries and cowries . . . are a constant offering to him."[38] The association with cowries was documented in the 1950s. "Elegba [Eshu] hides behind cowries."[39] In words sung at that time during his annual festival in Oyo, "Eshu brought cowries to men."[40]

He remains closely associated with the market. In (modern) Oyo, it is controlled by two officials, a man and a woman. Each is a priest of Eshu, and every market has his shrine.[41]

Eshu is a profoundly paradoxical figure. He has no home, and is linked with the crossroads and the threshold, loci of ambiguity. He is both very old and very young.[42] Carvings of him disconcerted nineteenth-century Europeans by their overt sexuality. Violence, unpredictability, and paradox are at the heart of Eshu's personality. Modern Eshu statuary is black—the color of witchcraft—and covered with cowries and coins.[43] His shrines now incorporate a mirror and a comb, both of which are central in modern Mami Wata iconography.[44] He is symbolized by a broken calabash, unlike the Orisha Funfun ("cool" gods such as Obatala), who are symbolized by a complete calabash.[45] In Whydah by 1863, this symbol of division and disruption was still emerging.[46]

The devotee of another divinity suggested that his link with money and the market comes at the cost of wealth in people:

> Eshu has no wives and no children; he is too wicked. No one will live with him and that is why he is homeless and must live in the crossroad and the market.[47]

But Eshu also has a cosmic role, as intermediary between the gods and humanity. In some interpretations, he embarked on his Trickster activities to save the gods from hunger, at the same time introducing divination. Those who suffer from his afflictions seek the advice of a diviner and are urged to make the offerings that nourish the gods.[48] The link between Eshu, cowries, and divination is mirrored in a Cuban source:

[T]he Lucumi [Yoruba] told the future. This they did with *diloggunes* which are round, white shells from Africa with mystery inside. The god Eleggua [Elegba]'s eyes are made from this shell.[49]

In a Fon version, Legba is a linguist, the only bridge of communication between Mawu and the lesser divinities who are her children.[50] In Haitian voudoun, he controls the gate between the human and the spirit worlds, "the spirit of communication between all spheres."[51]

> Papa Legba ouvri bayè-a pou mwen
> Pou mwen pase.
> (Papa Legba, open the gate for me,
> So that I can go through.)[52]

Twentieth century sources stressed the links between Eshu and colonial Europeans. "Esu brought the British to Nigeria."[53] In Lagos, in 1931, a man from Warri related a version of the Genesis story in which God excluded Eshu from the knowledge of how to create mankind, lest he share the knowledge with the whites, who would have manufactured a black labor force.[54] In the mid 1950s, an Oyo market official explained that "Eshu is the father of all Europeans because he taught them more about work than all other people; that is why whites have more power than blacks."[55] In a different development examined later in this study, Eshu became identified with Satan (p. 230). Clearly, there is a view of moral economy embedded in the linkages between Eshu, cowries, Europeans, and the market. A Yoruba proverb (which has an Igbo equivalent) suggests the market is a microcosm of society as a whole. "The world is a market, the market is the world."[56]

In the poetics of memory, cowries, which are the monetarized exoskeletons of a dead sea creature, became vampires that feed on the bodies of slaves. But their symbolic meanings are rich and complex, and have survived into our own times. Cowries, long since worthless as currency, live on in popular culture. In 1982 Lekan Oyegoke published a novel about a young Yoruba man in Ibadan who attempts to buy a human skull to practice money magic and kills himself to escape detection. It is called *Cowrie Tears.*[57]

Notes

1. Epigraph to J. Hogendorn and M. Johnson, *The Shell Money of the Slave Trade* (Cambridge, 1986). This is the standard history of cowrie currencies.

2. See, for instance, J. Parry and M. Bloch (eds.), *Money and the Morality of Exchange* (Cambridge, 1989).

3. A. Leyshon and N. Thrift, *Money/Space: Geographies of Monetary Transformation* (London and New York, 1997), 1.

4. Duarte Pacheco Pereira, *Esmeraldo de Situ Orbis,* trans. and ed. G. H. T. Kimble (Hakluyt, 2nd series, vol. 79, 1937), 145.

5. E. G. Gobert, "Le pudendum magique, le problème des cauris," *Revue Africaine* (1951): 5–62.

6. Hernando del Pulgar (d. 1492), *Crónica de los senores reyes católicos* . . . extract in J. W. Blake (ed.), *Europeans in West Africa, 1450–1560* (Hakluyt, 2nd ser. vol. 86, 1941), 206–207.

7. R. Burton, *A Mission to Gelele, King of Dahome* (1894; 2nd ed., London, 1966), 190; on the Cowrie House in the Dahomey king's palace, see 326.

8. John Adams, *Sketches, taken during ten voyages to Africa between the years 1786 and 1800* (London, n.d.), 32.

9. H. D. Foulkes, "Some Preliminary Notes on the Angass [Ngas]," 1907 (Nigeria National Archives, Kaduna, SNP K 3328.) He adds that they also had a word for a boat, but no first-hand knowledge of one, nor of any lake or river suitable for boating.

10. Naankwor Bawul of Namu, aged 70, Aug., 1978.

11. Usman Shindai of Shindai, Aug., 1978; also Dagum Fogotnaan of Shindai, aged c.70, Aug., 1978.

12. B. Belasco, *The Entrepreneur as Culture Hero: Preadaptations in Nigerian Economic Development* (New York, 1980), 43

13. A. F. Iroko, "Cauris et esclaves en Afrique occidentale entre le xvie et le xixe siècles," in S. Daget (ed.), *Colloque international sur la traite des Noirs I* (Nantes, 1985), 199–200.

14. Namdà of Lamabow, quoted in R. Verdier, *Le Pays Kabiyè* (Paris, 1982), 104,

15. Iroko, "Cauris et esclaves," 200–201.

16. B. Chatwin, *The Viceroy of Ouidah* (London, 1980), 26. For a critical account of Chatwin's historical credentials, see R. Law, "The White Slaves and the African Prince: European and American Depictions of Pre-Colonial Dahomey," in Martin Gray and Robin Law (eds.), *Images of Africa: The Depiction of Precolonial Africa in Creative Literature* (Stirling, 1990), 31–34.

17. Sony Labou Tansi, *The Antipeople,* trans. J. A. Underwood (London and New York, 1988), 130.

18. Juan Francisco Manzano, quoted in an 1830s' translation in Joseph M. Murphy, *Santería* (1988; reprint, Boston, 1993), 24.

19. R. Law, *The Slave Coast of West Africa, 1550–1750* (Oxford, 1991), 69. See 199–200 for the importance of cowries.

20. W. Bosman, *A New and Accurate Description of the Coast of Guinea* (1705; reprint, London, 1967), 354.

21. Law, *The Slave Coast,* 69.

22. Burton, *A Mission to Gelele,* 84.

23. R. Harms, *River of Wealth, River of Sorrow* (New Haven and London, 1981), 199.

24. Esther Goody, "Legitimate and Illegitimate Aggression in a West African State," in M. Douglas, *Witchcraft Confessions and Accusations* (London, 1970), 209.

25. For an arresting Chokwe (Central Africa) instance, see A. von Oppen, *Terms of Trade and Terms of Trust* (Münster n.d., *Studien zur Afrikanischen Geschichte,* 6), 391; for an instance of artificial debt creation in this way, in the Kasai in 1854, see David Livingstone, *Livingstone's African Journal 1853–1856,* ed. I. Schapera (London, 1963), 96–7.

26. Gobert, "Le pudendum magique," 5–62.

27. F. Héritier, "Des cauris et des hommes:production d'esclaves et accumulation de cauris chez les Samo (Haute-Volta)," in C. Meillassoux (ed.), *L'esclavage en Afrique précoloniale* (Paris, 1975), 492.

28. Oral testimony, quoted in R. Harms, *Games Against Nature: An Eco Cultural History of the Nunu of Equatorial Africa* (Cambridge, 1987), 127.

29. P. Manning, "Coastal Society in the Republic of Bénin: Reproduction of a Regional System," *Cahiers d'Études africaines* (1989): 251.

30. W. Ofonagoro, quoted in J. Hogendorn and M. Johnson, *The Shell Money of the Slave Trade* (Cambridge, 1986), 154.

31. Tobias Wendl, *Mami Wata oder ein Kult zwischen den Kulturen,* Kulturanthropologische Studien (Münster, 1991), 279 n.25.

32. Manning, "Coastal Society in the Republic of Bénin," 245, citing F. Iroko.

33. A. F. C. Ryder, *Benin and the Europeans,*(London, 1969), 60.

34. Ibid., 207.

35. W. Bascom, "Social Status Wealth and Individual Differences Among the Yoruba," *American Anthropologist* (1951): 491; cf. Belasco, *The Entrepreneur,* 42.

36. Victoria Eto, *Exposition on Water Spirits* (privately printed, Warri, Nigeria. 1983, 1989), 40.

37. J. Pemberton, "Eshu-Elegba: The Yoruba Trickster God," *African Arts* (1975), 20–27; R. Pelton, "Legba: Master of the Fon Dialectic," and "Legba and Eshu: Writers of Destiny," in R.D. Pelton, *The Trickster in West Africa: A Study of Mythic Irony and Sacred Delight* (Berkeley, 1980), 113–63.

38. S. Farrow, *Faith, Fancies and Fetich or Yoruba Paganism* (1926; reprint, New York, 1969), 86; the previous passage deals with the phallic aspect of Eshu.

39. J.Wescott, "The Sculpture and Myths of Eshu-Elegba, the Yoruba Trickster," *Africa* (1962): 345; this study is based on fieldwork in 1955–57.The account that follows is indebted to Belasco, *The Entrepreneur.*

40. Wescott, "The Sculpture and Myths of Eshu-Elegba," 346.

41. P. Morton-Williams, "An Outline of the Cosomology and Cult Organization of the Oyo Yoruba," *Africa* (1964): 258–59.

42. Wescott, "The Sculpture and Myths of Eshu-Elegba," 337–40.

43. See the illustrations in Pemberton, "Eshu-Elegba," 21, 24.

44. Wescott, "The Sculpture and Myths of Eshu-Elegba," 346; Eshu iconography also often includes a phallus, a smoking pipe, and a spoon (for the offerings he controls) as well as a distinctive projecting hair style.

45. Ibid., 34.

46. Burton, *A Mission to Gelele,* 67.

47. Wescott, "The Sculpture and Myths of Eshu-Elegba," 339; cf. Farrow, *Faith, Fancies and Fetich,* 84: "He is not taken into dwelling-houses; but has his shrine in the street." Farrow lived in Yorubaland from 1889 to 1894.

48. L. Frobenius, *The Voice of Africa,* I(1913; reprint, New York, 1968), 229–32; his source, he says, is an informant from the "Kukuruku" [Afenmai] borderland.

49. Esteban Montejo, *The Autobiography of a Runaway Slave,* trans. J. Innes (New York, 1968), 35.

50. Pelton, "Legba: Master of the Fon Dialectic," in Pelton, *The Trickster in West Africa,* 73.

51. Wade Davis, *The Serpent and the Rainbow* (London, 1986), 172.

52. Quoted in L. Hurbon, Voodoo, *Search for the Spirit,* trans. L. Frankel (New York and London, 1995), 72.

53. Cited in Belasco, *The Entrepreneur,* ix.

54. M. J. Herskovits and F. S. Herskovits, "Tales in Pidgin English from Nigeria," *Journal of American Folk-Lore* (1931): 455.

55. Wescott, "The Sculpture and Myths of Eshu-Elegba," 346; this study is based on fieldwork in 1955–57.

56. Belasco, *The Entrepreneur,* 21

57. Lekan Oyegoke, *Cowrie Tears* (Harlow, 1982).

6

TRANSFORMATIONS:

ENSLAVEMENT AND THE MIDDLE PASSAGE IN AFRICAN AMERICAN MEMORY

> *Jammè Jammè*
> *M'pa blieye Ginen ray-o.*
> (Never, never,
> I'll not forget the ranks of Africa.)
>
> Haitian voudoun song, recorded in the 1980s[1]

It is impossible to do justice to the way in which the Atlantic slave trade is represented in the poetics of memory if we ignore the re-configuration of enslavement and the Middle Passage in African American tradition. I deal with this material in brief compass, as my main focus—and area of expertise—is the African experience.

The Mode of Enslavement

Much is known about the actual mechanics of enslavement in Africa. A visitor to the Senegambia said in 1594, in words which have a much wider applicability, "The slaves which they own and sell they enslave by war or by judicial decisions, or are kidnapped."[2] In the mid nineteenth century, a missionary collected language data from informants in Sierra Leone, 179 of whom were former slaves liberated by the British naval squadron on the high seas, and resettled in Freetown. Of those who provided information on the way in which they had been enslaved, 34% were war captives, 30% had been kidnapped, 7% had been sold by rulers or relations, and 11% had been enslaved for real or supposed crimes.[3] (The last two categories are not necessarily mutually exclusive.) In the Bight of Benin, war was the most important source of captives, in the Bight of Biafra, kidnapping. The prospect of selling slaves at a profit led to a distortion of judicial processes, and in particular, to an expansion of witchcraft accusations.[4]

Captives were often obtained far inland, passing from hand to hand until they reached the coast. After the earliest phase, Europeans always acquired slaves by purchase from African coastal middlemen.

African American narratives of enslavement, which have a striking mutual consistency, tend to elide the role of the black comprador.[5] They tell of white slavers who kidnapped people—often children—on the shore or lured them on board slave ships by offering them red cloth.

The image of the kidnapped child symbolizes the captive's powerlessness, and, perhaps, innocence. Interestingly, those relating their own life histories also often stated that they were kidnapped by white sailors as children.[6]

Esteban Montejo was born into slavery in Cuba in 1860, the son of an Oyo Yoruba, and lived to tell his life story in 1963. His striking narrative includes a mention of "magical insects" that protected Africa from white settlement, perhaps a reference to mosquitoes and tropical diseases, which in many regions did just this..

> The strongest gods are African. . . .I don't know how they permitted slavery. . . .To my mind it all started with the scarlet handkerchiefs, the day they crossed the wall. There was an old wall in Africa, right round the coast, made of palm-bark and magic insects which stung like the devil. For years they frightened away all the whites who tried to set foot in Africa. It was the scarlet which did for the Africans; both the kings and the rest surrendered without a struggle. When the kings saw that the whites—I think the Portuguese were the first—were taking out these scarlet handkerchiefs as if they were waving, they told the blacks, "Go on then, go and get a scarlet handkerchief," and the blacks were so excited by the scarlet that they ran down to the ships like sheep and there they were captured.[7]

Another account, recorded from a former first-generation slave in South Carolina and published in 1928, tells of men, women, and children lured onto a slave ship with gifts of calico, beads, and red flannel.[8]

There are many versions of this story. Its omission of the role of the black slave merchant stresses an essential truth, for the Atlantic slave trade was created by white demand. Narratives of people who lost their freedom out of folly or cupidity, outwitted by the wily European, bear a strong resemblance to Trickster stories, and ancient legends of choices of dimly understood but momentous consequences (p. 175–80). These New World narratives were recorded by whites, and may well have been shaped to please the interlocutor.

> Got one mind for white folks to see,
> 'Nother for what I know is me,
> He don't know, he don't know my mind.[9]

Red cloth was distinctively foreign—the characteristic local dye was indigo—and red is the color of blood. These traditions form a theme in counterpoint with the poetics of rumor in Africa, where, as we have seen, the blood of slaves sometimes became a dye.

Red has magical and ritual associations which have been very extensively documented in different African cultures, though the specifics of this color symbolism vary.[10] When a Kongo royal died, he was wrapped in a red shroud.[11] Modern ancestral spirit mediums in Dande, in Zimbabwe, believe that they will die if they see something red.[12] Among the Yoruba of western Nigeria, "the original three cloths of Egungun [an ancestral mask] were of the colour red. They terrorized the witches. They terrorized the forces of pestilence."[13]

(These very different examples are quoted for illustrative purposes only, and each is embedded in a different ritual and ethno-linguistic context.)

The ritual importance of red cloth has been widely documented in black communities in the New World. Thus among houdoun worshippers in late nineteenth century New Orleans,

> the members . . . girding their loins with red handkerchiefs, of which the king wears a greater number . . . his head draped with some crimson stuff . . . The queen is dressed . . . with red garments and a red sash.[14]

An African Slave Trader

The role of the African merchant who sold slaves is not always elided. A collection of narratives recorded among African Americans in South Carolina, and published in 1928, includes a story about King Buzzard, an African ruler who had tricked his people into boarding slave ships. In the end, he was betrayed by his white trading partners, and was in his turn enslaved. After his death, he became a homeless and solitary ghost, feeding on carrion.[15] The dead African slave merchant is condemned to solitude and must feed on the dead. Bereft of community, he retains forever the empty title of king, spending eternity not in Africa but in perpetual exile. This eloquent True Fiction affirms the importance of the community, from which the slaver king is eternally separated.

By separating his victims from their loved ones, the slaver inflicted spiritual as well as physical death. Gullah Joe was a captive who survived, and later described, the horrors of the Middle Passage. He outlived slavery and created a new life for himself in South Carolina. But he did not forget his original home in Africa.

> I'm an old man now, but I have a longing to walk in the feenda [bush]. I have a wife and children here, but when I think of my tribe, and my friends, and my father and my mother, and the great feenda, a feeling rises up in my throat and my eyes well with tears.[16]

Matthews, in the late eighteenth century, was one of many involved in the slave trade who claimed that those torn apart from their families felt little or no distress.[17] By contrast, during his last journey, Livingstone wrote, "The strangest disease I have seen in this country seems really to be broken-heartedness, and it attacks free men who have been captured and made slaves. . . .They ascribed their only pain to the heart."[18]

Enslavement and Class

The Atlantic slave trade tended to lead to social polarization—slave traders became richer and more powerful, and domestic slavery expanded. In the New World, in a situation where African identity became identified with slave status, many cherished a belief, which was sometimes but not always literally true, that their forebears were of princely status.[19] Those who made these claims were often treated with much greater respect by their white masters. The True Fiction embedded in these narratives is, to borrow the title of Henderson's fine study of the Onitsha Igbo, that of *The King in Every Man.* It is very much alive today.

> My forefather was a king;
> He wore fat gold chains. . . .ruby rings.

Nobody believes this to be true—
Maybe it's because my eyes ain't blue.[20]

In a society where African identity was equated with slave identity or descent, supernatural powers, as well as royal ancestry, redressed the balance. In the late 1930s, in coastal Georgia, an old man pointed out that Moses turned his rod into a snake. "That happened in Africa, the Bible says. And that shows that Africa was a land of magic power, since the beginning of history."[21]

The Middle Passage Reversed: Flying Back to Africa

In eighteenth-century West Africa, recently embarked slaves were said to believe "that Death will send them into their own Country."[22] Mysterious traditions recorded in coastal Georgia tell of first generation slaves who flew back to Africa, often to escape cruel corporal punishment.[23] Sometimes this pattern—an escape from brutality by flight—is described as a transformation into birds. In one version, those concerned are specifically identified as newly arrived Igbo, flogged because of their failure to understand orders in English, who fly back to Africa in the form of buzzards.[24] There is an arresting contrast with King Buzzard, the African slave trader doomed to an eternity of solitude as in the New World.

The idea of a return to Africa through death persists in Haitian voudoun—the mermaid, Lasyrenn, calls people back to Africa.

> When people catch a glimpse of Lasyrenn beneath the water, they feel her beckoning them to come with her back to Ginen, to Africa, the ancestral home and the dwelling place of the *lwa* [divinities]. . . .[25]

Those who seek to come closer to her may drown. Again, death restores one to Africa. The Haitian great grandfather of a contemporary voudoun medium was a noted healer; he was called *franginen,* from Africa (though his father was French). When he grew old, he disappeared; he told his wife in a dream that he had returned to Africa.[26]

What is the meaning of the persistent traditions of flight to Africa? At one level it is an example of the attribution of supernatural powers to Africans, which are, in a sense, a counterpoise to their slave status. It has often been suggested that they represent suicides, particularly Igbo suicides, and frequently by drowning.[27] Enslaved Igbo in the New World were notoriously prone to suicide, although in their homeland, it was a "bad death" that excluded one from appropriate burial rites and hence from the community of the living and the ancestors. In Igboland, suicide excises the individual from the community. In the inhuman world of the newly arrived slave, a kind of mirror image developed, and suicide seemed to provide the only possible road home. In the late eighteenth century, Jamaican slaves sang:

> If me want to go in a Ebo,
> Me can't go there!
> Since dem tief me from a Guinea,
> Me can't go there![28]

Esteban Montejo rejected the stories of slave suicides:

> [O]ne [story] I am convinced is a fabrication because I never saw such a thing, and that is that some Negroes committed suicide. . . . the Negroes did not do that, they escaped by flying. They flew through the sky and returned to their own lands. . . .[29]

The Gods in Exile

In West Africa, the divinities are sometimes slave owners—in a famous Yoruba myth, Orisanla acquires a named slave at a specified market.[30] In Haiti, it is thought that African gods took part in the involuntary migration of the enslaved:

> The faithful believe that the *lwa* come from Africa, more specifically a section of Africa confined to Guinea, irretrievably lost and considered purely mythical. . . the *lwa* in their turn made the voyage out of Africa to the Caribbean.[31]
> The spirits live beneath the great water, sharing their time between Haiti and the mythical homeland of Guinée.[32]

In Haitian folk art, the leafless tree with its branches lopped symbolizes the way in which the enslaved were cut off from their past. The ancient serpent, Danbala, represents the forbears of whom memory is lost.[33]

In Haitian voudoun rituals, recorded in Brooklyn in the 1980s, devotees reflected on their enduring relationship with Ginen.

> Mezanmi, tout sa m'ape fè-a
> Nan Ginen tande.
> (My friends, everything I am doing
> is heard in Africa.)[34]

Se Kreyòl nou ye
Pa genyen Ginen ankò.
(We are Creoles,
Who have Africa no longer.)[35]

Conclusion

In chapter 3, I mentioned Turner's famous painting, "The Slave Ship." The drowning slaves are almost invisible; a manacled leg and despairing hands break the water, and because their heads are submerged, they are voiceless. A modern poet from Guyana has written a cycle of poems to speak for them. But he can only create "an imagined landscape, where most of the names of birds, animals and fruit are made up."[36] Just as the enslaved were ignorant of their destination, he cannot know the precise origins of the Zong's victims.

In one of these poems, a diviner tears his string of beads apart, and tells the watching children

> That in the future time each must learn to live
> Beadless in a foreign land; or perish.
> Or each must learn to make new jouti,
> Arrange them by instinct, imagination, study. . . .
> . . . .Each
> Will be barren of ancestral memory. . . .[37]

It is a wonderfully rich evocation of the continuing life of Ginen in the New World. But it is impossible to recapture those silenced voices. Modern Haitian voudoun rites specifically mention "All those I do not know and do not remember."[38]

The True Fictions of African American memory force us to understand the history of the Atlantic slave trade in new ways, whether they elide the role of the black comprador, or stress the isolation of the story of King Buzzard, who is himself a victim. Looking back on a life of suffering and solitude, the former slave, Esteban Montejan, reflected, "But this is not sad, because it is true."[39]

Notes

1. Quoted in Karen MacCarthy Brown, *Mama Lola: A Vodou Priestess in Brooklyn* (Berkeley, 1991), 283.

2. Quoted in J. D. Fage, "Slaves and Society in Western Africa, c. 1445–c.1700," *Journal of African History* (1980): 306.

3. P. E. H. Hair, "The Enslavement of Koelle's Informants," *Journal of African History* (1965): 196–203.

4. T. Clarkson, *The Substance of the Evidence* (London, 1789), 120, for Baggs's evidence; W. Rodney, *A History of the Upper Guinea Coast* (Oxford, 1970), 106–8 and 114–15.

5. But for an exception, see p. 79–80.

6. "The African Servant," in Alexander Mott and M. S. Wood (compilers), *Narratives of Coloured Americans* (1877; reprint, Freeport, NY, 1971), 90. Curiously, this reprint gives Lindley Murray as the author—it was originally published through a bequest he left. Many slave autobiographies, of course, record various forms of African agency in their capture.

7. Esteban Montejo, *The Autobiography of a Runaway Slave,* trans. J. Innes (New York, 1968), 16.

8. Gullah Joe, in E. C. L. Adams, *Nigger to Nigger* (New York and London, 1928), 227. Versions of the story were recorded in Georgia and published in Georgia Writers' Project, *Drums and Shadows: Survival Studies* (Athens, GA, 1940). See also W. D. Pierson, *Black Legacy: America's Hidden Heritage* (Amherst, MA, 1993), 34–49.

9. W. Levine, *Black Culture and Black Consciousness* (New York, 1977), xiii.

10. A. Jacobson-Widding, *Red-White-Black as a Mode of Thought* (Uppsala, 1979), 155 and 301; V. Turner, "Colour Classification in Ndembu Ritual:A Problem in Primitive Classification," in M. Banton (ed.), *Anthropological Approaches to the Study of Religion* (London, 1966), 53.

11. Jacobson-Widding, *Red-White-Black,* 168; there are further instances of red shrouds on p. 213.

12. D. Lan, "Resistance to the Present by the Past: Mediums and Money in Zimbabwe," in J. Parry and M. Bloch, *Money and the Morality of Exchange* (Cambridge, 1989), 195. The ancestors are eternal, and blood is a reminder of mortality.

13. Robert F. Thompson, *African Art in Motion* (Los Angeles, 1979), 219.

14. N. N. Puckett, *Folk Beliefs of the Southern Negro* (1926; reprint, New York, 1975), 181, citing H. C. Castellanos, *New Orleans as it Was* (New Orleans, 1895). For Haiti, see L. E. Moreau de Saint-Méry, *Description Topographique, Physique, Civile, Politique and Historique de la Partie Française de l'Ile de Saint-Dominique, 1797,* extract in L. Hurbon, *Voodoo: Search for the Spirit,* trans. L. Frankel (New York and London, 1995), 132.

15. Thaddeus Goodson, "The King Buzzard," in Adams, *Nigger to Nigger,* 12–15.

16. Gullah Joe in Adams, *Nigger to Nigger,* 229. I have rewritten the original (which purports to mirror Gullah Joe's dialect) into standard English.

17. J. Matthews, *A Voyage to the River Sierra-Leone* (London, 1788), 153.

18. Quoted in T. Jeal, *Livingstone* (London, 1993), 327.

19. For a recent well-documented survey, which stresses the truth of such claims, see Pierson, *Black Legacy,* 74ff. Also see Wylie Sypher, *Guinea's Captive Kings,*(New York, 1969).

20. Jungle Brothers, "Acknowledge Your Own History," rap lyric quoted in Pierson, *Black Legacy,* 214 n.53.

21. Thomas Smith, quoted in Georgia Writers' Project, *Drums and Shadows,* 28. I have changed the original to standard English.

22. J. Atkins, *A Voyage to Guinea, Brazil and the West Indies* (1735; London, 1970), 175.

23. Shad Hall, quoted in Georgia Writers' Project, *Drums and Shadows,* 169.

24. Wallace Quartermain, 1844–1938, in *Drums and Shadows,* 150–51; a number of other sources in this volume speak of flight to Africa. In Cuba, Montejo, *Autobiography,* 44, identified the fliers as "Musundi Congolese."

25. Brown, *Mama Lola,* 223.

26. Ibid., 29, 33.

27. Michael A. Gomez, *Exchanging Our Country Marks* (Chapel Hill, NC, and London, 1998), 117ff.

28. J. B. Moreton, *West India Customs and Manners* (London, 1793), 153, quoted in Pierson, *Black Legacy,* 45.

29. Montejo, *Autobiography,* 43–4.

30. E. B. Idowu, *Oludumare: God in Yoruba Belief* (New York, 1963), 39; there is a different version in Ulli Beier, *Yoruba Myths* (Cambridge, 1980), 6–7.

31. Hurbon, *Voodoo,* 69.

32. Wade Davis, *The Serpent and the Rainbow* (London, 1986), 172.

33. Brown, *Mama Lola,* 273.

34. Ibid., 272–73.

35. Ibid., 280–81.

36. David Dabydeen, *Turner: New and Selected Poems* (London, 1994), ix.

37. Dabydeen, "Turner," in *Turner, New and Selected Poems,* 33. "Jouti" is an example of an invented word.

38. Brown, *Mama Lola,* 279.

39. Montejo, *Autobiography,* 18.

PART II

Interpreting the Colonial and Postcolonial Experience

7

AN OVERVIEW

Like the baby chick which was captured by a kite, "My cry is for the world to know that I am finished, not that I should be released from captivity."

Letter to a Nigerian newspaper in 1973[1]

In the second and longer section of this book we turn to a very different aspect of historical experience—the colony and post-colony. Some of the sources studied in the first section were written in the twentieth century—they included, for instance, interviews conducted in the field in 1983. But their subject was the Atlantic slave trade or slavery, as viewed in the poetics of memory.

There are striking continuities in content and symbolic representation between both sections, which is why I have chosen to discuss them in a single book, rather than, as some readers suggested, in two.

In the 1930s, a mask performance in a northern Igbo village

was opened by a hooded character called "Government." He had no face and was crowned with a Homberg hat; . . . he read in ghostly gibberish from an important looking document. He [was] succeeded by a parade of ghostly policemen and court messengers. . . .[2]

The image of a faceless Government speaking unintelligibly (after more than twenty-five years of colonial rule) gives us a piercing insight into the sensibilities of colonial subjects. It is hauntingly reminiscent of the dialogue that forms the epigraph to chapter 1, where the words of village women are dismissed as nonsense. The following chapters explore various True Fictions created during the colonial period and after. These images are often deeply disquieting, a fact in itself of historiographic significance.

Interpretations of the Colony and Post-Colony

In Africa, historical studies have often embodied a conscious or unconscious condemnation of the preceding era. The writings of colonial rulers and their advocates tended to accentuate the negative when writing of the precolonial past, in order to justify their own role as a "civilizing mission." Later, Africanist, interpretations of the colonial experience were first formulated in a reaction to this; the response was multifaceted, stressing the glories of precolonial African civilizations, the violence with which colonial jurisdictions were imposed and maintained or the way in which colonial economic structures were subordinated to the needs of the metropolitan power. The achievements of African Improvers such as entrepreneurial peasants or pioneer teachers were celebrated, as were the apparent victories of political nationalism. The brevity of the colonial experience was emphasised—in 1969, a distinguished Nigerian historian called it "an episode."[3] Now, in a significant semantic shift, African scholars such as Mbembe write of the "post-colony."[4]

For a time, the shortcomings of Africa's newly independent nations were attributed to the deforming impact of colonialism, such as its arbitrary boundaries. Imperceptibly, the location of the Promised Land shifted, first to the former Portuguese colonies, and later to states as small as Eritrea and the Cape Verde islands.[5] When South Africa adopted majority rule, there were the same high expectations; later, as the expectations of the poor remained largely (though inevitably) disappointed, the initial hopes began to dim.

It is possible that a conspiracy of optimism has been replaced by a conspiracy of pessimism in African studies. Is "the crisis of Africa" at least partly an invention, like the dark images of Savage Africa in the writings of so many missionaries and colonial invaders? Is it appropriate or premature to acclaim an African Renaissance? These issues question the very foundations of an older historiography. In 1993, Chinua Achebe summed up the hopes and disappointments of a generation of Nigerians.

Any Nigerian who is old enough to remember October 1, 1960, cannot forget the high and heady feeling of hope and optimism that marked our dawn of freedom from foreign rule. I . . . can recall particularly how good one felt to be a Nigerian abroad and carry the new and exciting green passport. Today, Nigeria is a hopeless mess, its economy is in a shambles, crime is rampant, our judiciary is a standing joke. A once vibrant and proud people have been reduced in a few years to destitution and shame.[6]

The growing awareness of the significance of "subjugated knowledges" reflects the search for a symbolic universe closer to lived experience than a dream of progress and modernization, which for most has not been realized. However, it is important to remember that not all colonial and postcolonial subjects perceived their life situation in terms of crisis and threat. For many, the twentieth century opened up not only new opportunities, but also a novel freedom from imagined terrors. "Nothing in Tiv," wrote Akiga Sai in the 1930s, "is so illusory as *tsav*[astral cannibalism]."[7]

To the historian, Africa's twentieth-century history divides almost automatically into contrasting phases, colonial and postcolonial. It is striking that no such distinction appears in the parallel universe of popular symbolism, and this draws our attention to important continuities. Sometimes popular culture specifically equates oppression in the colony and postcolony. For instance, "La Colonie Belge" was one of the three main themes in the popular urban art of independent Zaire; its images of soldiers, floggings, or executions and a dominant flag constituted an unmistakable indictment of Mobutu's regime.[8]

Rumor has often been perceived as subversive by both colonial and postcolonial authorities. The French ethnographer, Bourdieu, began his career with research in Algeria, during and after its war of independence. Over the years he has elaborated his insights into "symbolic domination." In 1972, he wrote, profoundly, "Every established order tends to produce . . . the naturalization of its own arbitrariness."[9] All governments rely heavily on the tendency to regard political arrangements as part of the natural order.

Political subversion presupposes cognitive subversion, a conversion of the vision of the world . . . .Heretical subversion exploits the possibility of changing the social world by changing the representation of this world which contributes to its reality . . . by counterposing a *paradoxical pre-vision* . . . to the ordinary vision which apprehends the social world as a natural world.[10]

Historians of twentieth-century Africa, in recent years, have been moving towards a much more subtle and nuanced understanding of the way in which both colonial and postcolonial governments were sustained, not only by violence and the capacity for violence, and by the support of their diverse beneficiaries, but also by complex cognitive worlds. These were constructed in an intricate process of bricolage, as were the symbolic statements in which colonialism or the post-colony was critiqued or rejected. An alternative vision of the world is a necessary prelude to changing it.

In postcolonial Africa, the powerful have often explicitly acknowledged the subversive power of the poetics of rumor. The words of President Biya of Cameroon, quoted at the beginning of chapter 1, are a good example. In 1965, the death penalty for treason became mandatory in Malawi. President Banda explained what he meant by treason. "He doesn't have to march at all; if he thinks about it, talks to others about it . . . no-one should be left in doubt of what treason is."[11]

The cognitive worlds of popular culture continue to shape behavior in a great variety of ways—to anticipate a case study explored later in this book, the Bakweri of Mount Cameroon long shunned the rewards of cash crop cultivation because they feared being thought zombie-owning witches. "Development" projects fail with notorious frequency; there are many reasons for this, among them a failure to understand the life strategies of those involved, which are rooted in a particular cognitive universe. One of the major obstacles to Nyerere's policy of concentrating rural populations into ujamaa villages was a fear of living close to those suspected of witchcraft—a fear which drove some into exile.[12] In 1996, an article appeared in *World Development* on "Magic and Witchcraft: Implications for Democratization and Poverty-Alleviating Aid in Africa."[13]

There is a significant reflection on historiography in Ben Okri's *Infinite Riches,* the sequel to *The Famished Road.* As a prelude to independence, the Governor General rewrites the nation's history; in doing so, he "forgot the slave trade."

> [T]he Governor General made our history begin with the arrival of his people on our shores. . . . [He] deprived us of language, of poetry, of stories . . . he deprived us of history.[14]

But it was preserved by an old woman in a forest, who collected fragments, and "pressed on with the weavings of our true secret history."

> And with this language of signs and symbols, of angles and colours and forms, she recorded legends and fragments of history lost to her people. . . .She recorded oral poems of famous bards whose words had entered com-

munal memory, whose names had been forgotten because of their great fame, but whose true names lay coded in their songs..

Again, one remembers the words of the women from Atta (p. 1) that colonial officials dismissed as nonsense. The old woman preserved

a history that was frightening and wondrous, bloody and comic, labyrinthine, circular, always turning, always surprising, with events becoming signs and signs becoming reality.[15]

The first section of this book focused on the poetics of rumor and of memory, and these themes are further explored in the chapters which follow. The approach I have adopted is that of a detailed investigation of one or more case studies, to which is added a short account of comparable material from elsewhere. Ancient witchcraft beliefs have metamorphosed into new collective terrors, in the shape of anonymous male predators—zombie owners, vampires, shapeshifters (such as leopard men), and those who practice money magic.

Zombie beliefs, explored in Cameroon, are the counterpart of—but significantly different from—the earlier accounts of the enslaved soul recorded in the Congo and described in chapter 4. What seems to be a single complex of vampire rumors was widely disseminated in East and East Central Africa, in the last three decades of colonialism; the vampires were often identified with the employees of the colonial state. Rumors of shapeshifters—lion- or leopard-men—seem to have developed between 1880 and 1920. The case study here is Sierra Leone. Rumors of money magic—explored here in Ghana and Nigeria—became widespread after colonialism came to an end. All of these mythic complexes describe predators who were believed to prey on the helpless and poor. Each exemplifies the concept of life as a zero-sum game, and employs the metaphor of depraved consumption to represent social exploitation. The image of anonymous male predators, acting collectively, contrasts with the continuing concept of the Dangerous Woman, documented in chapter 12, and a discourse on AIDs which is often associated with it.

Chapter 13 introduces the village intellectual, who reflects on the shape of contemporary history and attempts to make it morally intelligible. Chapter 14 explores some of the many complexities of the mermaid, Mami Wata, while chapter 15 studies an associated theme, the way in which the varied commodities of contemporary material culture are used to construct new symbolic worlds. Chapter 16 examines the strange convergences between neo-traditional thought and those who condemn it as demonic. Finally, in chapter 17, I turn to a different but very important mode of conscious social criticism, which relies on humor and word play—but still, in many cases, uses the metaphor of improper consumption.

Gender

I began this book with the words of village women, and it is an old woman who, in Okri's novel, preserves the true history of her people. One of the most thought-provoking aspects of the mythemes of twentieth-century popular culture lies in the light they shed on concepts of gender. The "traditional" witch, as we have seen, was often thought to be an older woman, and the association still persists, images of the dangerous devouring woman acquiring a new significance in an age of AIDS. But vampires, shapeshifters, and zombie owners—twentieth-century adaptations of witchcraft idioms— were male. The mermaid, Mami Wata, as depicted by male artists in Congo, is a classic sex object. Her cult, in West Africa, is dominated by women, but the suffix *-isi* in *Mamisi* (Mami Wata devotee) means "wife of." In Igboland, an Oguta priestess of Mami Wata claims the male title, *eze*; she holds the male symbols of chieftaincy—the horn, the eagle's feather, the horse hair whisk,[16] and Mami Wata is often called *Eze Mmili,* Water King. In a striking way, Mami Wata devotees blur conventional gender boundaries.

Spirit Possession

The most subtle and nuanced popular representation of social change is to be found in the mimesis of masking and spirit-possession cults. Mimesis is multidimensional and concrete, like life itself; it comes closer to experience than abstract analysis. Two very different examples shed light on how, in the complicated and polysemic language of ritual, a changing world is both mirrored and critiqued.

A sophisticated study by Boddy shows how village women act out a mirror image of a wider world, and critique it in the process of depiction. The cult of zar spirits can be found over a vast expanse of (Islamic) northeast Africa, in the Sudan, Somalia, and elsewhere. In a village near Khartoum, it dates from the 1920s, and is dominated by women, who are drawn to it by particular kinds of sickness. The possessed enact roles, including that of an American physician called Dona Bey who hunts miniature antelope with an elephant gun—a telling commentary on the inefficiency and de-structiveness of much Western technology in the Third World.[17]

Hauka is a male spirit-possession cult which appeared in Niger in 1920. It had spread to Ghana by the 1930s; in 1953, it became the subject of a celebrated ethnographic film by Jean Rouch, *Les maîtres fous* (the mad masters). Initiates played the roles of different colonial authorities—such as the governor, or the Wicked Major (who had persecuted Hauka in its early days in Niger). They wore white sun helmets, and carried whips and wooden rifles, marched on parade, and held a Round Table conference. The colonial government, sensitive to the subversive power of mimesis, banned the film in the then Gold Coast.

Hauka was not an exercise in amateur theatricals; initiates frothed at the mouth, smeared themselves with the blood from animal sacrifices and plunged their arms into boiling water. Stoller, who has made an extensive study of Hauka rituals in Niger, calls the film "a kind of voyeuristic colonial cannibalism . . . the cinematic equivalent of Artaud's Theatre of Cruelty."[18]

Hauka died out in Ghana after Independence, but survived in Niger, perhaps in a response to the powerful continuing French presence there. It was a classic form of interculture, derived both from ancient Songhay traditions of spirit possession and the experience of colonial rule. Those possessed spoke both Songhay and pidgin. It was part of the satire that those who played the role of colonial officials spoke in an interlanguage which the latter despised.

> Possession ceremonies are theaters of Songhay experience-in-the-world. . . .Once people in Songhay were masters of their own destinies. Co-lonialism transformed the social order, creating a new dimension of power-lessness. . . .Colonialism created a deep social void. . . .Through their terrify-ing burlesque the Hauka attempted to make sense of European influences. . . . [T]he powerless ridicule the powerful.[19]

Hauka embodies an alternative history, which oscillates between satire and terror.

Spirit possession is only one of the ways in which aspects of the West are enacted. embodied, or critiqued. The dance societies of late nineteenth- and early twentieth-century Mombasa mirrored both the hierarchies and the divisions of the colonizing power, and their members dressed as Scotchi or members of the House of Lords.[20] Long ago, the great historian, ibn Khaldun, said wisely, "The vanquished always seek to imitate their victors in their dress, insignia, belief and other customs and usages."[21]

While some spirit possession cults mimic manifestations of the West-ern world and modernity, others adamantly reject them. Books are among the exotic objects on Mami Wata shrines in Togo, but in Cameroon, water spirits abhor them, and their devotees, while possessed, shun Western artifacts.

The mediums of the Shona of Zimbabwe have been extensively studied; they are called *mhondoro,* lion spirits, and are possessed by the spirits of dead kings. Most mhondoro mediums are men. It is a full-time occupation that imposes many restrictions, among them a ban on Western clothes. Contemporary mediums in the Zambezi valley consider it dangerous to see or by seen by Europeans, though their nineteenth-century predecessors mixed with them freely.[22] As Lan points out, what the ancestors objected to were acts of white injustice.

In the chapters that follow, I have attempted to construct a mosaic from fragments less of the politics than of the poetics[23] of life on the periphery of world capitalism. Such a poetics expresses a multiple indictment of a world its authors have not made, and will not change. Globally speaking, these myths and symbols are constructed by the captives of power, and in a sense, it is here that the power of captives is to be found.[24] In his classic study of a Malaysian village, Scott suggests that the power of the poor lies primarily in their thoughts: "it is at the level of beliefs and interpretations . . . that subordinate classes are least trammeled."[25] But often, the poor do not hope to change anything, and seek only to be heard.

In 1934, in Northern Rhodesia, an advocate of an African newspaper told a meeting, "We understand what Europeans are doing but they do not know what we are doing and what we feel. . . . We are not content without a paper because we do not say what we see, hear or think."[26]

An African novelist, writing, significantly, under a pseudonym stated in 1972:

> The difficulty of writing this novel was not to construct my story. . . . [T]he problem was [how] to be one of the hundreds of millions of anonymous men of the Third World, whose faces no one knows, and who suddenly whispers, as if embarrassed at disturbing people: "You know nothing about me, nothing at all; please listen to my story.[27]

Notes

1. Quoted in E. Isichei, *A History of the Igbo People* (Basingstoke, 1976), 256.
2. G. I. Jones, *The Art of Eastern Nigeria* (Cambridge, 1984), 59.
3. J. F. A. Ajayi, "Colonialism: An Episode in African History," in L. H. Gann and P. Duignan, *Colonialism in Africa 1870–1960* (Cambridge, 1969), I: 497–509.

4. A. Mbembe, "Provisional Notes on the Postcolony," *Africa* (1992): 3–37.

5. This is clearly reflected in successive books by Basil Davidson.

6. Chinua Achebe, "Anniversary of Regrets," *The African News Weekly* (1993), quoted in extenso in Ebenezer Babatope, *The Abacha Regime and the June 12 Crisis: A Struggle for Democracy* (Lagos, 1995), 38.

7. R. East, trans. and ed., *Akiga's Story* (Oxford, 1939), 240.

8. B. Jewsiewicki, "Painting in Zaire, From the Invention of the West to the Representation of Social Self," in S. Vogel (ed.), *Africa Explores 20th Century African Art* (New York and Munich, 1991), 136–37.

9. Pierre Bourdieu, *Outline of a Theory of Practice,* trans. R. Nice (Cambridge, 1977), 164.

10. Pierre Bourdieu, *Language and Symbolic Power* (Cambridge, 1991), 127–28.

11. Quoted in T. D. Williams, *Malawi the Politics of Despair* (Ithaca and London, 1978), 229.

12. R. Brain, "Witchcraft and development," *African Affairs* (1982): 378.

13. D. Kohnert, "Magic and Witchcraft: Implications for Democratization and Poverty-Alleviating Aid in Africa," *World Development* (1996): 1347ff.

14. Ben Okri, *Infinite Riches* (London, 1998), 110–14.

15. Ibid., 112.

16. Depicted in a video by Sabine Jell-Bahlsen, "Mammy Water: In Search of the Water Spirits in Nigeria," (Cailfornia, 1989).

17. J. Boddy, *Wombs and Alien Spirits: Women, Men and the Zar Cult in Northern Sudan* (Madison, WI, 1989). For Dona Bey, 289–91.

18. P. Stoller, "Embodying Colonial Memories," *American Anthropologist* (1994): 636.

19. P. Stoller, *Fusion of the Worlds: An Ethnography of Possession Among the Songhay of Niger* (Chicago, 1989), 162–63. My account of Hauka is based on this study, on the same author's "Embodying Colonial Memories," and on Rouch's film.

20. T. O. Ranger, *Dance and Society* (London, 1975).

21. Charles Issawi, ed., *An Arab Philosophy of History* (London, 1950), 53.

22. D. Lan, "Resistance to the Present by the Past: Mediums and Money in Zimbabwe," in J. Parry and M. Bloch, *Money and the Morality of Exchange* (Cambridge, 1989), 200.

23. Cf. J. Clifford and G. Marcus, *Writing Culture: The Poetics and Politics of Ethnography* (Berkeley and Los Angeles, 1986); the title of this very important collection resounds through other works, as do the ideas it expresses.

24. See Marc-Henri Piault, "Captifs du pouvoir et pouvoir des captifs," in C. Meillassoux (ed.), *L'esclavage precoloniale* (Paris, 1970).

25. James Scott, *Weapons of the Weak: Everyday Forms of Peasant Resistance* (New Haven and London, 1985), 322; he is explicitly critiquing Gramsci.

26. Quoted in H. Meebelo, *Reaction to Colonialism: A Prelude to the Politics of Independence in Northern Zambia 1893–1939* (Manchester, 1971), 250.

27. "Alioum Fantouré," in an epigraph to *Tropical Circle* [*Le Cercle des Tropiques*], trans. D. Blair (Harlow, 1981).

8

THE ENTREPRENEUR AND THE ZOMBIE

> All this is to do with the spirit world, and we should face it without
> fear. The living are more dangerous.
> Esteban Montejo, *The Autobiography of a Runaway Slave*[1]

In late nineteenth-century Central Africa, Europeans, as we have seen, were
often thought to be sorcerers, manufacturing Western goods under the sea,
with a labor force of enslaved African souls, who were sold to them by an
African witch comprador, the astral equivalent of the indigenous slave trader
who supplied living captives to the Atlantic slave trade. These myths provided an explanation of Europe's industrial pre-eminence and of the unequal global distribution of resources. In twentieth-century Cameroon,
Tanzania, and South Africa, those who believe in zombie sorcery are more
concerned with the relative—and often very limited—prosperity of African neighbors.

In village society, even very modest prosperity sometimes seems so
unattainable that it must be explained by supernatural means, and in particular, by the theft of others' life force or resources. It is a vision of moral
economy rooted in the concept of the limited good or zero-sum game.

This chapter begins with an exploration of the zombie motif in
Cameroon, where the documentation is relatively full and reflects the spread

of a particular concept of witchcraft inland from the coast. This is followed by an account of the mysterious supernatural geographies of north-south trade, and of the sparser data available for Tanzania and South Africa.

These beliefs, recorded at different times and in different places, do not constitute a continuum; they are independent responses to particular social and political circumstances, and clearly draw on ancient memories of slavery.

The Zombie in Twentieth-Century Cameroon

In Cameroon, as elsewhere, the concept of the witch as an astral cannibal was much older than that of the witch as slave owner.[2] By 1960, among the Duala, "lemba and ewusu [cannibal sorcery] had fallen into relative desuetude, while ekong had redoubled its vigor."[3] *Ekong* is the Duala word for zombie sorcery, which the Beti call *kong*, and the Bakweri, *nyongo*. The ekoneur—to use a Duala neologism—is a male sorcerer who enslaves the dead and puts them to work on plantations on Mount Kupe, the magic mountain which is also a real landmark, sixty miles north of Douala. Its supernatural reputation extends to Yaoundé, and to northeast Cameroon.[4]

Through the labors of zombie slaves, the sorcerer becomes rich. Like witches in general, he is most likely to sacrifice members of his own family. "Self-betterment resulted from the killing of fellow Bakweri (particularly one's own children) and using the dead bodies to work as zombies."[5]

In a sense, ekong is a folk memory of the Atlantic slave trade.

> Cameroonians who dream they are being carried off, with hands bound, toward a river or the ocean as a slave, without being able to recognise the face of their abductors, are most anxious to find an *nganga* [ritual specialist] as soon as possible. Further, the peoples who dwell in the interior say that the *ekong* sorcery that rages among them comes from the coast.[6]

But the Atlantic slave trade in Cameroon came to an end in the 1830s and the immediate model seems to be the forced labor of the colonial era, and work on plantations owned first by Europeans, and later by black entrepreneurs.

A 1962 account describes how the Duala sorcerer makes a Faustian pact.

> People think that ekong is a power acquired in an ultra-secret society. The preliminary condition for admission is to agree to the death of a person, if possible a very close relative, one's mother or one's son. The candidate goes

to an ekoneur . . . who induces a hypnotic sleep. In his dreams, the person sees a land where money flows in streams and where many servants are at his service. A big estate owner offers him his plantation in return for the life of, for instance, his mother. . . .When he wake up, the ekoneur says, "Now you have seen what you have to do."[7]

Ekong seems to have originated among the Duala, the original and now outnumbered inhabitants of the coastal city that bears their name; according to de Rosny, ekong has changed considerably over the last hundred years. Eric de Rosny is a French Jesuit who entered deeply into the life of the city's ritual specialists. He believes that ekong was originally an association of chiefs and merchants, very different from *lemba* (cannibal) sorcerers, who enriched themselves with the help of a snake familiar, *nyungu*. "But nowadays *ekong* . . . is available to all. . . .It has taken its place in the hierarchy of horrors."[8]

An aged Douala informant said

Selling persons? Yes, that still goes on today. They're sold for prices that are different from ours. They're sold for *ndimsi* money. Someone can be sold for anywhere from two to twenty-five francs.[9]

In 1971, de Rosny attended a ritual to release a zombie. He was told that

Din himself [the *nganga*] is in reality far away now, to the west, on Mount Kupe . . . where the person to be saved tonight is being held prisoner. It seems that some sorcerers are making her work for them on their infamous plantations. . . . She is called Engome, the woman lying along the wall. . . .In appearance she is there but her essential person dwells on Kupe. . . .[10]

Ekong traveled inland rapidly, perhaps because of the status the Duala had enjoyed as brokers in coastal trade. At the same time, leopard societies expanded in the opposite direction, towards the sea.[11]

The earliest references to Mount Kupe, significantly, associate it with sorcery and wealth, but not with the labor of zombies. In a study of the Bakossi, who live near Kupe, Balz quotes older missionary sources concerning "going to Koupe" (also called *ekom*) in order to obtain all sorts of wealth and blessings from the invisible meetings of wizards and other spirits there."[12]

In a book published in 1900, a missionary said that Mount Kupe was the source of Bakossi wealth and power. "The people were therefore much afraid that I could discover the secret and carry it away.[13] He was told that the secret was linked with the stealing of souls. A different missionary account of the Bakossi, published in 1913, stated that "The best medicine of all, according to the pagans, is *ekom*. Whoever owns this medicine can go wherever he wants, even into the white man's shops, and carry away whatever he wants, without anybody getting aware of it."[14] In a report written in 1929, Mount Kupe is described as a market where spirits meet to trade.

> [Stone] says that there is a powerful spirit "at the bottom of the lake near the summit of Mount Kupe in Kumba Division. In the latter lake there is a great spirit market and spirits from all over the world are thought to meet there and barter their goods. *The new Nigerian coinage and paper money* were said first to have been introduced in this spirit market."[15]

The quotation is from an unpublished report of 1929 which "leans heavily on the work of the late Mr Steane, a Bakweri teacher of Victoria." (The hidden subtext of often literate African informants flashes into a brief visibility at third hand—the ethnographer quotes Stone who is summarizing Steane.)

A missionary study of beliefs about Kupe, published in 1930, describes how *ekong* sorcerers climb the mountain in search of wealth. If one of them fails to offer a human sacrifice, he falls to his death. These sacrifices were termed " *ein unsichtbarer Kinderhandel,*" an invisible trade in children—an echo of the slave trade—but there was no suggestion of forced labor on astral plantations.[16] On the mountain, they fight for packages whose contents are unknown, which may contain either wealth or diseases and other afflictions. Some die in these struggles, and others unwittingly bring harmful diseases to their home villages.

A book published in 1929 describes ekong sorcery among the Bakoko and does refer to the zombie, but not to the creation of wealth, or to Mount Kupe.

> Popular belief imagines that the bat'ekong have the power to bewitch and kill people at a distance. They have at their service the disembodied soul of a corpse which they have stolen from the grave, and they take the body at night and during a violent storm. Their "medicine" is made of the bones of the corpse, in which the appropriate rituals have forced the soul to remain. The mot'ekong clearly has, as well as his power to bewitch at a distance, the arts of a skilled poisoner.[17]

It seems clear that the belief in ekong sorcery as astral slave ownership took its present form well into the twentieth century. A Bakossi author wrote in 1971:

The invisible town on Kupe is something like a labor camp. . . . the great men have invisible estates there and they need people to cultivate them. The source of this labor supply is widespread.[18]

The Bakweri Experience

The Bakweri live on the slopes of Mount Cameroon, within (distant) sight of the sea. Like the Duala they are a small people, numbering perhaps sixteeen thousand, and like them, were often described in colonial times as declining. The belief in the enslaved dead reached them from the Duala at the time of the First World War.[19] While familiar with the word *ekong* (mirrored in *yekongi*), they tend to call this form of witchcraft *nyongo,* a word related to *nyungu,* the dangerous rainbow serpent which assists Duala sorcerers. Zombies, *yekongi,* work on Mount Kupe, where their toil benefits African entrepreneurs, whose prosperity is reflected in houses with corrugated iron roofs. Until the mid 1950s, the owners of such houses were afraid to live in them, lest they be accused of zombie sorcery. Ardener preserves "a record masquerading as a real instant . . . .A crowd howl at an old man hiding under a bed. Dismantled sheets of rusty corrugated iron lie in the vicinity."[20] As so often, the wealth of the supposed sorcerer was pathetically limited.

These stereotypes clearly discouraged people from acquiring property, which was what made the *ekoneu*r visible. When the Bakweri prospered during a banana boom, they spent large sums on importing a crocodile mask called Obasinjom, from Mamfe, in 1955. The mask's role was to eradicate witchcraft, and, for a time, these fears were assuaged.

In 1963, during a recession, a new rumor developed that money was being left on the ground to entrap those who picked it up. "Frenchmen" would employ these victims as zombies in port construction, or sacrifice them to appease the water people.[21] By the 1970s, Obasinjom seemed "something of the past." In 1988, perhaps because of the effects of government austerity measures, belief in *nyongo* revived and Obasinjom reappeared.[22] The people of Mamfe themselves, the Banyang, had obtained Obasinjom from the Ejagham during the colonial period. Its name, which means the mask society of God (Obassi), its titles, and most of its songs are in the latter's language. Its form and function are the same as those of a mask introduced in Oban in 1909, from Okuri in Cameroon.[23]

The belief in ekong, like mask cults, could be abandoned as well as adopted. Balz writes of a Bakossi community:

[N]obody is believed to go to Kupe any longer. Before dying the last *ekom* men . . . left a message . . . to the Nyasoso people that there is nothing—or at least nothing good—to be found on Koupe any longer, and that people who want to get wealthy should better take their cutlasses and open large farms in the bush. This message, it is true, has not yet reached the whole of Bakossi, and in some other areas people still believe in "going to Koupe."[24]

"Bamileke" is an ethonym invented in the colonial era for a mountain people in French-speaking Cameroon, who formerly lived in independent chieftaincies, under rulers called Fon. "The Bamileke" have become a monolithic entity, as have "the Beti"—another ethnym which has come to include many other ethnic identities.[25] The Bamileke are often successful entrepreneurs, said to have gained their riches through the same type of sorcery—called, significantly, *famla, nyongo,* or *kupe.* In the anglophone area of the Grassfields, it is thought that zombies are taken to Mount Kupe, or to a section of the town of Bafoussam called Famla.

Fisiy and Geschiere write of "frequent hints by *Radio Trottoir*" and in the newspapers about the *famla* to which the Bamileke entrepreneurs would owe their riches but add that the young say that they migrate from their homeland to *escape* it. "In the Grassfields these ideas still seem to be quite new."[26] Some individuals driven away as famla sorcerers have been welcomed back when they grew rich and contributed to community projects.

In the Yaoundé area, the Beti call this type of sorcery "kong." It is

a new form of witchcraft which is supposed to have spread in this area especially after independence. . . .[T]he fear of this new form of witchcraft has created a general panic.[27]

A Cameroonian Catholic priest, Mani, was excommunicated for his attacks on *kong* sorcery, and went on to found a new witch-detecting movement. The Maka, farther east, know of ekong sorcery elsewhere, but do not think it is practiced in their own villages.[28]

Bureau wrote of Douala, in 1960, that belief in ekong had never been so strong or so widespread. "Everyone shares it—the old and perhaps still more the young, town and country people, the educated as much as the rest, both Catholic and Protestant Christians, together with the few pagans who are left."[29] *Ekong* is a symbolic expression of the pain of poverty which voices both resentment at the good fortune of others and bewilderment as to how it is attained. Among the Bakossi, *ekon* means envy.[30]

"North" and "South": Supernatural Geographies of Class Relations

Earlier in this study we examined several examples of the transformation of class and regional relations into mysterious geographies of the supernatural—modern Ewe cults of dead northern slaves, Asante associations of "the north" with former slaves and witchcraft eradication.

In coastal Cameroon, concepts of ekong sorcery are sometimes integrated with accounts of long distance trade between North and South. "The Hausa transform people into cattle which they pasture among their herds; they sell their victims to the ekoneurs."[31] Southerners see northerners as sorcerers who turn their victims not into zombies, but cattle.

A study of the Mamprusi of northern Ghana reflects comparable interpretations of long-distance trade from a northern perspective. In the 1960s, witchcraft was little spoken of; the form it took was astral cannibalism. By the 1990s, witchcraft fears were more extensive, and a new concept had developed:

> Haven't you seen those herds of sheep and goats going south to the Techiman market? Those are the people witches have caught and turned into animals. And the smoked bush-meat for sale in the Accra market? Have you not seen it? That too is people caught by witches.[32]

Here, it is southerners who export and sell transformed northern victims. Drucker suggests that this encapsulates both a memory of the southward export of Mamprusi as slaves and a commentary on the contemporary political and economic dominance of the south.[33]

Like zombie beliefs, these legends of commerce in human livestock represent the addition of concepts of trade and profit to ancient witchcraft beliefs. Witchcraft has come to satisfy a hunger for money, rather than meat.

Sometimes it is the helplessness of the victim that is stressed in myths of transformation and long-distance transport, rather than edibility. In late nineteenth-century Congo, it was thought that souls were carried to the coast in elephant tusks (p. 55). In late twentieth-century Mamprusi

> I was told of a witch who changed her victims into the seeds inside a gourd, the better to transport them to a southern market. . . .Most often victims are described as changed into small helpless creatures, usually insects.[34]

The shrinking of victims symbolizes their powerlessness; it facilitates transport and capital accumulation, both of which are of central importance to the entrepreneur.

Again, there are echoes in the postcolonial novel. Ouologuem's novel, *Le Devoir de Violence,* first published in 1968, provides a different northern perspective—that of a Dogon from Mali—on the symbolism of zombies and long-distance trade. In this version, the zombie owning sorcerers include both Africans and Europeans.

> [H]e explained to Vandame . . . that he had been buried alive, then removed from his grave, drugged, and sent to the East to work for a Flencessi [French-man] . . . who dosed him with women and drugs, passed him off as dead, and finally sent him to the South, to Tal Idriss, a friend of Saif, to whom in exchange Tal was to send *his* living corpses. All those people who had died in the last six months, Sankolo revealed, were zombies like himself: living corpses enslaved, used as unpaid labor by Blacks and Whites, and ultimately shipped to Arabia as slaves at times when the normal supply was low.[35]

The narrator managed to return home, only to be killed again by the agents of an African tyrant.

The Zombie in Tanzania

Zombie myths have been widely recorded in Tanzania. In most cases they are mentioned in passing, and the neglect of the theme in academic litera-ture contrasts with the proliferation of studies of vampire rumors. There is little evidence about their history, but it seems likely that, like their Cameroon counterparts, zombie myths were a response to and an explana-tion of the growing inequalities of the colonial period. They are first re-corded in the 1920s.

Among the Kaguru

> One of a witch's most feared devices is *musukule* . . . which transforms a victim into a type of zombie . . . which labors for the witch. A victim's relatives are unaware of the tragedy, for the witch charms a banana stem to appear as the victim. This languishes, dies and is buried, deceiving people as to the actual fate of the victim. Kaguru claim that atop the mountains there are entire zombie communities having dances, marriages, circumcision etc.[36]

Both prosperous farmers and shopkeepers were thought to own zom-bies who worked for them at night.[37] Among the Fipa, "Sorcerers are said to have means of turning their victims into zombies (*amasea*) which are then forced to work in their masters' gardens at night, sleeping on top of his hut by day."[38]

Shorter mentions zombie traditions among the Kimbu. "More evil than the forest giants are the zombies or dead people who have been resurrected by witches to work on their behalf and run their errands for them."[39]

An account of the Sukuma, published in 1956, described

> a combination of ghost story and legend in which the newly dead . . . are resurrected to work for the sorcerer. . . . The sorcerer uses no special killing medicines but possesses the spirit of the man before burial so that the corpse is only a representation of the man. The spirit remains with the sorcerer for an indefinite period, being fed by him and living in his roof and coming out to work at night. . . . In the early '20s there were two well known cases. . . .[40]

In Uluguru, a different mythical complex attributed the success of prosperous farmers to another form of witchcraft, *bukula,* which sucked the productivity from one's neighbors' fields.[41] It is yet another form of the zero-sum game.

Zombie rumors were clearly more widespread than these examples suggest. Zambian zombies were thought to be exported to the Congo, and their Congo counterparts to Angola.[42]

The Zombie in South Africa

In the late 1980s and early 1990s, accusations of zombie sorcery expanded in Northern Province (formerly Venda), and seem to have declined thereafter, though they did not disappear. Those most commonly accused were older women, targeted because they received remittances from absent children. Where Cameroon zombies work on plantations, their Venda counterparts are often gold miners.

> Witchcraft in this area is usually associated with the keeping of zombies. These zombies work for the *muloi* [witches], often at night or in the gold mines on the Rand. A person who does better than others (for instance, whose fields produce more than others) or who receives money from sources not readily identifiable stands an increased risk of being accused of witchcraft. Old people who receive money through the post from children who are migrant laborers or who receive their pensions from a source other than the government fall into this category. Because of the fact that they often live longer than men, there are more women than men who receive money from hidden sources.[43]

Zombie beliefs have also been recorded in Kwa-Zulu.[44]

Conclusion

The slave's commodified body is an enduring African image for exploitation, and slavery was a recurrent metaphor for the colonial experience. "[T]he Whites came and subjected us all to their laws. Now all Blacks are slaves of the Whites."[45] "The white man persecutes us, we are slaves."[46] Statements of this kind reflect the powerlessness of the colonized subject, and the perceived violence and rapacity of the state.

The zombie is a metaphor for alienation, as well as exploitation, for the pursuit of wealth and growing economic inequality undermine community relations. In a study of the Tswana published in 1926, Brown wrote with much insight of the social death which results from their disruption.

> When a man's relatives notice that his whole nature is changed . . . so that it may be said that the real manhood is dead, though the body still lives; when they realize that to that to all intents and purposes the human is alienated from fellowship with his kith and kin, they apply to him a name . . . which signifies that though the body lives and moves, it is only a grave. . . .It is no uncommon thing to hear a person spoken of as being dead when he stands before you visibly alive. When this takes place it always means that there has been an overshadowing of the true relationships of life.[47]

Zombies never speak for themselves, but are always anonymous and silent. Zombie stories have been interpreted in different ways. In Haiti, writes Dayan, they "produce and capitalize on an internalization of slavery and passivity, making the victims of an oppressive economic and social system the cause."[48] Fanon, remembering black society in Martinique, suggested that zombies and other supernatural terrors diminished the authority of the settler state. "The zombies are more terrifying than the settlers. . . . the settler's powers are infinitely shrunken. . . ."[49]

In twentieth-century Cameroon and Tanzania, zombie beliefs formed part of a populist discourse on economic inequality. They suggest that some are more successful than others because they are aided by invisible workers. Among the Bakweri, the belief in ekong discouraged "progress" in the form of cash crop cultivation.

This has many parallels at other places and times.. Bentley wrote of Congo at the turn of the century, "When the india-rubber trade commenced, the first to sell were killed as witches; so, too, with every innovation."[50] In Zambia, in the 1950s, young men sang

> "Why don't you build better houses? Speak."
> "It's because we are afraid,
> Afraid of jealousy and witchcraft."[51]

In Ghana, at much the same time, a researcher was told:

> It is only since Tigari [a network of anti-witchcraft shrines] and the other protectors came that rich men in Akwapim have dared to show their riches by building big houses. Before that, if they did anything to show their wealth, they were sure to be killed.[52]

Entrepreneurs of various kinds have often concealed their prosperity for fear of being called witches; since there was a limited amount of wealth in existence, individual enrichment was attributed to astral theft. In a LoDagaa (northern Ghana) version of the life to come, a rich man suffers for the same period as a witch: "the implication here is that you must have treated others badly in order to be well-off yourself."[53] At the heart of these images is a profoundly egalitarian discourse. A different version of the model is often applied to the Big Men who steal the resources of the state and whose continuing hold on power is attributed to their employment of technical experts in the persons of diviners. Again, their apparent invulnerability and obscene wealth are explicable only through magic (see p. 143–9).

Successful entrepreneurs were sometimes accused of witchcraft, but paradoxically, witch-finding and witchcraft eradication have often proved profitable activities for the enterprising, who supply a desired commodity, frequently imported from a distance, at an often considerable price.[54]

Colonial officials, by persecuting witch-finders rather than witches, were thought to be the associates of the latter. In independent African states, the appropriate policy towards witchcraft accusations is a matter for ongoing debate. In Cameroon, alleged zombie sorcerers have been tried and sentenced to imprisonment and massive fines, while diviners give evidence as expert witnesses.[55] Signs become reality in harmful and oppressive ways.

Notes

1. Esteban Montejo, *The Autobiography of a Runaway Slave,* trans. J. Innes (New York, 1968), 128.

2. Eric de Rosny, *Healers in the Night,* trans. R. R. Barr (Maryknoll, NY, 1985), 283 n.66.

3. R. Bureau, *Ethno-sociologie religieuse des Duala et apparenté* (Yaoundé, 1962), 141 n.9 Ardener describes the same pattern among the Bakweri. (I follow the conventional practice of calling the people Duala, the city Douala.)

4. H. Balz, *Where the Faith Has to Live: Studies in Bakossi Society and Religion* (Basel, 1984), 326.

5. E. Ardener, "Some Outstanding Problems in the Analysis of Events," in E. Schwimmer(ed), *The Yearbook of Symbolic Anthropology* (London, 1978), 108.

6. de Rosny, *Healers in the Night,* 278 n.24.

7. Bureau, *Ethno-sociologie religieuse des Duala,* 141–42. Much of his ethnographic data was obtained from indigenous Catholic priests and catechists.

8. de Rosny, *Healers in the Night,* 59–60. Ralph Austen questions this earlier form of ekong, which is not, he informs me, supported by the documentary evidence (personal communication).

9. Ibid., 58–9.

10. Ibid., 3.

11. Bureau, *Ethno-sociologie religieuse des Duala,* 143.

12. Balz, *Where the Faith Has to Live,* 326.

13. F. Autenrieth, *Ins Inner-Hochland von Kamerun* (Stuttgart-Basel, 1900), 40, quoted in Balz, *Where the Faith Has to Live,* 328 (Balz's translation); on the carriers, see 327.

14. J. Gutekunst, *Am Fusse des Kupe, Skizzen über Land,Leute und Missionsarbeit in Nkosiland in Kamerun* (Basel, 1913), 32, quoted in Balz, *Where the Faith Has to Live,* 329.

15. B. G. Stone, "Notes on the Buea District " (unpublished ms., Victoria, Cameroon), quoted in E. Ardener, "Witchcraft, Economics and the Continuity of Belief," in M. Douglas, *Witchcraft Confessions and Accusations* (London, 1970), 158 n.12. Ardener's italics.

16. J. Ittmann, "Der Kupe in Aberglauben der Kameruner," *Der Evangelische Heidenbote* (Basel, 1930), 77, 78, 80, 111–12.

17. G. Y. Nicol, *La Tribu des Bakoko* (Larose, 1929), extract in Bureau, *Ethno-sociologie religieuse des Duala,* 142 n.10.

18. S. N. Ejedepang-Koge, *The Tradition of a People, Bakossi* (1971), quoted in C. Fisiy and P. Geschiere, "Sorcery, Witchcraft and Accumulation: Regional Variations in South and West Cameroon," *Critique of Anthropology* (1991): 263.

19. Ardener, "Witchcraft, Economics and the Continuity of Belief," 147.

20. Ardener, "Some Outstanding Problems in the Analysis of Events," 110–111.

21. Ardener, "Witchcraft, Economics and the Continuity of Belief," p.154. The idea that witches left money on the ground as a bait was also prevalent in Nigeria. Cf. also p. 70 above.

22. Fisiy and Geschiere, "Sorcery, Witchcraft and Accumulation," 256.

23. M. Ruel, *Leopards and Leaders* (London, 1969), 210. Cf. P. A. Talbot, *In the Shadow of the Bush* (London, 1912), 52–4, and plate facing 198.

24. Balz, *Where the Faith Has to Live,* 326

25. P. Geschiere, "Witchcraft, Kinship and the Moral Economy of Ethnicity," paper presented to the Conference on Ethnicity in Africa, Edinburgh, 1995, 3–4.

26. Fisiy and Geschiere, "Sorcery, Witchcraft and Accumulation," 265–66; they provide a very interesting first-hand account of an attempt to introduce *famla* in 1975–76 (267–68).

27. Geschiere, "Witchcraft, Kinship and the Moral Economy of Ethnicity," 8; this varies slightly from the account in "Sorcery, Witchcraft and Accumulation," 263, where it is described as reaching the Beti of the Yaoundé area in the 1930s, after the spread of cash crop cultivation, and as attributed to civil servants and *grand planteurs.*

28. Fisiy and Geschiere, "Sorcery, Witchcraft and Accumulation," 263.

29. Bureau, *Ethno-sociologie religieuse des Duala,* 149.

30. Balz, *Where the Faith Has to Live,* 326.

31. Bureau, *Ethno-sociologie religieuse des Duala,* 143–44.

32. Quoted in S. Drucker-Brown, "Mamprusi Witchcraft, Subversion and Changing Gender Relations," *Africa* (1993): 540.

33. Quoted in Drucker-Brown, "Mamprusi Witchcraft," 539.

34. Ibid.

35. Y. Ouologuem, Bound to Violence [Le Devoir de Violence], trans. R. Manheim (Oxford, 1971), 9.

36. T. Beidelman, "Witchcraft in Ukaguru," in J. Middleton and E. H. Winter, *Witchcraft and Sorcery in East Africa* (London, 1963), 66.

37. Beidelman, "Witchcraft in Ukaguru," 93.

38. R. G. Willis, "Kamcape: An Anti-Sorcery Movement," *Africa* (1968): 4.

39. A. Shorter, "Creative Imagination and the Language of Religious Traditions in Africa," *Kergygma* (1980): 192; see also his *Jesus and the Witchdoctor: An Approach to Healing and Wholeness* (London, 1985), 23.

40. R. E. S. Tanner, "The Sorcerer in Northern Sukumaland," *Southwestern Journal of Anthropology* (1956): 439.

41. J. Brain, "Witchcraft and Development," *African Affairs* (1982): 379.

42. M. Musambachime, "The Impact of Rumor: The Case of the Banyama (Vampire Men) Scare in Northern Rhodesia," *The International Journal of African Historical Studies* (1988): 211.

43. Alan Kirkaldy, e-mail communication, H-Africa, 28 Jan. 1998.

44. Reuters report in [Auckland, New Zealand] *Sunday Star-Times,* 10 Nov. 1995.

45. Quoted in B. Jewsiewicki and Mumbanza mwa Bawele, "The Social Context of Slavery in Equatorial Africa During the 19th and 20th Centuries," in P. Lovejoy (ed.), *The Ideology of Slavery in Africa,*(London, 1981), 96, from E. de Jonghe, *Les formes d'asservissement dans les sociétés indigènes du Congo belge* (Brussels, 1949); on Zaire.

46. H. Meebelo, *Reaction to Colonialism: A Prelude to the Politics of Independence in Northern Zambia 1893–1939* (Manchester, 1971), 148. (Watch Tower members in Northern Rhodesia in 1919–20.)

47. J.Tom Brown, Among the Bantu Nomads (London, 1926), 137–38. The examples he gives include a child who neglects his duty to his parents or vice versa, and a subject who disregards his allegiance to a chief.

48. Joan Dayan, "Vodoun, or the Voice of the Gods," *Raritan* (1991): 54–5.

49. Frantz Fanon, *The Wretched of the Earth,* trans. C. Farrington (Harmondsworth, 1970), 43.

50. W. H. Bentley, *Pioneering on the Congo*(London, 1900), I: 278.

51. P. Fraenkel, *Wayaleshi* (London, 1959), 121.

52. M. Field, *Search for Security:An Ethno-Psychiatric Study of Rural Ghana* (London, 1960), 112 .

53. Jack Goody, *Death, Property and the Ancestors* (London, 1962), 373 n.2.

54. See for example, T. McCaskie, "Anti-Witchcraft Cults in Asante," *History in Africa* (1981): 139.

55. C. Fisiy and P. Geschiere, "Judges and Witches, or How is the State to Deal with Witchcraft?" *Cahiers d' Études africaines* (1990):135–36

9

COLONIAL VAMPIRES:
THE THEFT OF LIFE AND RESOURCES

[T]here are monsters on the prowl, however, whose forms alter with the history of knowledge.

Michel Foucault, "The Discourse on Language"[1]

More than one East African prophet is said to have foretold the colonial era, and called it an age of cannibals. A prophet from southern Tanzania, his words perhaps amplified by those who came later, is said to have prophesied invasion by cannibals from the East.[2] In Kenya, a Kikuyu seer made a curiously similar forecast, "That the nations would mingle with a merciless attitude towards each other, and the result would seem as though they were eating one another."[3]

Rumors of vampires thread their way through the colonial records of Kenya, Uganda, Tanzania, Zambia, Malawi, and the Congo. They are documented in the memoirs of colonial officials and in academic studies by at least four scholars.

There are striking similarities between the sorcerer who exploits the labor of enslaved souls and the vampire, and both myths are sometimes found together (see p. 117–8). In each instance, the life force of the victim is stolen, whether in the form of labor or of blood. Each myth was elaborated during the colonial period, but outlived it. Each has clearly grown out of a vision of moral economy rooted in witchcraft beliefs, and an understanding of life as a zero-sum game. All this is equally true of money magic, the postcolonial myth par excellence. There, is however, one great difference between myths of zombie sorcery and vampirism. The former explains why, in village life where all seem to work equally hard, some attain a relative prosperity. The latter, at one level at least, is a parody of the colonial state, where its employees, such as firemen, steal the blood of their victims to enhance the life force of Europeans, or, in the post-colony, of indigenous Big Men. Like ekoneurs, colonial vampires are anonymous male predators. But whereas ekoneurs enslave zombies to enrich themselves, the activities of vampires are more complex and mysterious, and academic interpretations vary considerably. "If symbols and metaphors are indeed complex, layered, and polysemic, how do we write about them?"[4]

White has suggested specific interpretations of particular versions of the myth, so that the vampires of Nairobi, for instance, shed light on solitary women and inheritance issues.[5] I see them rather as local contextualizations of widespread perceptions of the predatory nature of the colonial or postcolonial state, the illegitimate transfer of resources, the vulnerability and powerlessness of the migrant, and of rural and urban poor in general. Not all these insights, of course, are articulated in any given instance. But always, social meanings are condensed in the metaphor of the abused body, and the theft of its life force. Marx wrote that "Capital is dead labor which, vampire-like, lives only by sucking living labor, and lives the more, the more labor it sucks."[6]

Like Count Dracula, Africa's imagined vampires tended to belong to a world of relative or absolute economic privilege. In Transylvania, vampires remain alive and reproduce by feeding on the blood of their victims. In colonial Africa it was thought that blood was used, not to keep the dead alive, but to enhance the life force of the living.

The vampire, like the cannibal or witch, embodies in an extreme form the idea of life as a zero-sum game. The myth is a True Fiction, for the power and vitality of the colonial state was derived from its appropriation of the meager resources of its subjects, who often perceived it as both violent and predatory. When taxes were first introduced among the Lala of western Zambia,

> one of the princesses proved obdurate. She said she saw no reason on earth why she should give me money: and I said I would burn her hut down if she didn't . . . the firebrand was laid to the thatch. . . .
> "Why," she exclaimed, "this is just like war."[7]

The colonial state outlawed the ordeals by means of which witches were detected and punished. It was easy to believe that the Europeans themselves were witches or the friends of witches, complicit in their astral cannibalism. In the 1940s, in Zambia, a sorcerer was brought before a District Commissioner who promptly imprisoned the accuser. In the poetics of memory,

> turning to the sorcerer, he discharged him and presented him with a bag of salt and a large knife, telling him to go back to the corpse he had been eating. "This is one of the reasons why the Europeans forbade the poison ordeal; so that they could sell salt to people." Another reason is that "the Europeans are afraid of being detected themselves if the ordeal is used; for they, too, are proprietors of sorcery just as they are of whiskey."[8]

The terminology employed for vampires varied. On the Swahili coast, people spoke of *Mumiani,* a word cognate with Arabic and Persian terms for mummies and embalming.[9] *Chifwamba,* a term used in colonial and postcolonial Malawi, originally referred to those who captured slaves (p. 31).Vampirism was sometimes called *chinja-chinja,* from the Swahili verb *kuchinja,* to slaughter (animals for food). In Madagascar, people spoke fearfully of heart thieves.

Mumiani had its origins in the precolonial period, when the dominance of those generically if inaccurately called Arabs was attributed to their magical use of African blood and body parts.

> The blood was made into medicine. . . . It was this that gave them power over the African. . . . As the power of the Arabs declined the theory declined. And as the power of the Europeans increased so was the theory applied in men's mind to them too.[10]

Despite local differences, vampire rumors formed a single, highly distinctive corpus of thought. They spread inland from the Swahili coast and were frequently carried by labor migrants—by Bemba, for instance, returning from Tanzanian sisal plantations. In Zambia, they were called by a Swahili term, with a Bemba prefix, *banyama,* meat or game people, a linguistic footprint of patterns of diffusion. Their rapid spread has been compared with the dissemination of Watchtower teachings, and of the witchcraft eradication ritual, *mchape.* For a variety of reasons, labor migrants often failed to return, and vampire stories explained their disappearance.[11] A Mumiani riot broke out in colonial Mombasa, when the roof of a European's home was being mended with tar. This account illustrates both the belief that Europeans practiced blood magic, and the recurrent theme of the migrant who disappears.

> Some women were watching. . . . They had come in from the country. One of the women said, "That dark stuff. It looks as if it has been mixed with blood. With the blood of our people. Men have been killed and cut up for that blood. My brother perhaps. He went away many years ago and disappeared. . . ."
> "It is done to protect the European's house," another woman said. "To protect it against lightning and thieves."[12]

Vampire rumors gave form to the fears of women left behind, as they worked in isolated fields, or to the vulnerability of other women who earned their living as prostitutes in the new cities.

In a book published in 1948, Elspeth Huxley described a visit to Lamu, an ancient Swahili settlement on the coast. A local boy said that he would be afraid to visit Nairobi, because of Mumiani. She explained:

> This apparition is feared not only in Lamu but all down the coast and indeed up-country. It is a sort of bloodsucker that can take on many guises: in this case, it patrols the streets at dead of night in a truck belonging to the Medical department, and should it come upon a straggler, draws from his vein all his blood with a rubbber pump, leaving his body in the gutter limp and drained.[13]

This text reflects, not only the dangers of city life, but also the way in which the vampire or heart thief benefits from the technology of the modern world—a motor vehicle, or the equipment of western medicine. The products of the west are incorporated in a neo-traditional world view which sees the colony—or its independent successor state—and its employees as violent and predatory.

Arens began his fieldwork in Tanzania in 1968, and wrote later:

> I learned early on that the majority of the inhabitants either had suspicions or were convinced that I consumed human blood. . . . Some time later . . . I collected bizarre stories about these blood-suckers. The tales vividly depicted how a victim would be rendered unconscious and then hung head downward in order to let the blood from the slit jugular drain into a bucket. The fluid was then transported by a fire engine to an urban hospital, where it was converted into red capsules. These pills were taken on a regular basis by Europeans who, I was informed, needed these potations to stay alive in Africa.[14]

In Madagascar, the belief in "heart thieves" or "blood thieves" seems to go through phases of decline and resurgence. During the Second World War, the French were thought to buy children's hearts. Bloch documented *mpakafo,* among the Merina, in a study published in 1971. He is explicit about the underlying concept of life as a zero-sum game. Hospitals are particularly dangerous, and the patient must be accompanied by numerous kin, for protection.

> Europeans are typically heart thieves. At night they suddenly steal the heart or blood of any person, preferably a child, to feed themselves . . . the European increases his own power by dreadful means at the expense of the Merina.[15]

In a different account, it is Malagasy civil servants who obtain hearts for their colonial masters.

> Europeans need, for mysterious ceremonies from which they derive their power, to feed some fabulous animals with hearts torn from young children; Malagasy civil servants rapt [seize] the victims, and bring them to their foreign masters.[16]

In independent Africa, the role of Europeans in vampire stories has diminished, for obvious reasons. In rural Kenya in the 1950s, the vampires were already prosperous Africans.

> The story was that there were motor vehicles painted red that plied along the Kisumu to Busia highway every evening, apprehending the lone pedestrians, taking their victims to some place in the direction of Kisumu, draining their blood and leaving them dead. This blood was then taken to the blood banks in hospitals. Certain prominent people were in local rumor named as *Kachinja.*[17]

In a book based on fieldwork in 1988–90, Weiss analyzed vampire fears in contemporary Buhaya. Blood sellers (*Matende,* evil-doers) are thought to live in towns and to be closely associated with electricity.[18] Vampirism explains why some rural individuals prosper more than others.

> You can see a person who has a brick house, a store, cars. And you think a year ago he was the same as me, but he hasn't done any work. How did he get these things? You know he has been selling people's blood.[19]

Western educated Malagasy have also come to be considered heart thieves.

> The signs which distinguish the heart thieves are revealing; black beard, blue eyes, large dogs. . . . There are also such things as Western suits, homberg hats, glasses, cameras, motor-cars, tape recorders, which . . . are more typical of the Malagasy heart thief.[20]

Heart theft, like vampirism, explains why some individuals prospered in the colony or post-colony, while others remained poor.

Unlike their counterparts in the western film or novel, the vampires of Africa are a nameless collectivity. As Moretti writes, in a different connection:

> Like the proletariat, the monster is denied a name and an individuality. . . . Like the proletariat, he is a *collective* and *artificial* creature. He is not found in nature.[21]

Vampire stories embody a critique of colonial and postcolonial medicine and are clearly linked with the practice of blood transfusion. In distant Niger, the dangerous violent Hauka spirits include a doctor, complete with needle and syringe.[22] Many Africans who were admitted to colonial hospitals did not return home alive, and it seemed probable that they had fallen victim to the European's witchcraft. The anthropologist John Middleton first visited the Lugbara, on the Uganda-Congo borderland, in late 1949, and discovered that one of the words for a European was the name of a cannibal bush spirit.

> Europeans were considered to eat people, because they had the power of taking them to jail or of treating them in hospital, and as all Lugbara knew, some people who went to jail or to hospital never returned.[23]

Vampire rumors were often linked with motor transport—"a truck belonging to the Medical department," "motor vehicles painted red." The driver is powerful, invulnerable even, vis-à-vis the pedestrian. Car ownership is a mirror of access to resources, and the car, an enclosed moving space from which escape was difficult, lent itself to vampire rumors. Fire engines were linked with blood theft, perhaps simply because both were red. Motor transport was a visible symbol of a changing world, and the products of modernity were appropriated to critique it—a process to which we will return in chapter 15.

One of the most striking aspects of vampire rumors was their association with specific government departments. Nairobi traditions identified vampires with the African staff of the Nairobi Fire Brigade.[24] Vampire fears were often linked with game wardens—both, in Zambia, were called Banyama. Africans and Europeans working in tsetse fly eradication programs diagnosed sleeping sickness by taking samples from the lymph glands.[25] Like the collection of blood for transfusions and blood banks, the practice fostered vampire rumors. In Tanzania, solitary European locust officers, geologists, or surveyors, camping in their vehicles in the bush, were often thought to be vampires.[26] In Northern Zambia, it was Catholic missionaries who were thought to be vampires, apparently because of the words of the Mass ("This is my body. . . . Eat this . . . .") Local Watchtower adherents insisted that "Catholics eat people," and in 1932 a White Father received a letter which called him "a prince of demons a serpent and sorcerer" and was signed "your good roast mutton captivity, imprisonment and bandages."[27]

Vampire rumors coalesced with other collective terrors, and in particular, with zombie narratives. Mutumbula—the term for vampire used in the Congo—means a ghost who leaves the world of the dead and carries out the nefarious purposes of a sorcerer. In Zambia and Malawi, it was often thought that banyama took their victims to the Congo, in complex geographies of supernatural and class relations.

> Whenever a person was caught by a crocodile, the assumption was that it was pre-arranged with Banyama to have the body taken across the Luapala to the Congo bank where either the blood was drained and the brain removed, or, if still alive, the victim was taken to a slave farm deep into the Belgian Congo.[28]

Fraenkel worked in radio in post-war Zambia, and wrote,

> Several times during my years in Africa it had come up, the story that there were vampire-men abroad, that they caught children and gave them an injection so that they lost the power of speech and became docile creatures of their captors who led them away to some far-off place, then sucked their blood and feasted on their flesh. Other variants had it that adults too, were caught, that a rubber ball was forced into their mouths so that they could not shout and they were marched off to the Belgian Congo for slave-labor.[29]

In this source—where the silence of the captive is explicit—the Congo is the sinister destination for victim Zambians. The Congo, however, had

its own traditions of vampires, rooted in older narratives of white cannibals. A late nineteenth-century missionary, writing of the ancient Kongo
capital of Sao Salvador, noted that school pupils were cautioned by their
mothers to avoid tinned meat, which was thought to be human flesh.[30] The
rumor was widespread and enduring.

In 1944, the army garrison at Elisabethville (now Lubumbashi) re-
volted, partly because of discontent over their terms of service, and partly
because of fears of white cannibalism, after conscripts died from faulty
smallpox vaccine. "A few weeks later, the survivors were served meat from
cans whose trademark was a smiling African. They concluded that the Europeans had killed their comrades for meat."[31] At much the same time, a
Belgian official noted that Mutumbula were

> blacks engaged by the whites . . . to capture women, kill them and carry their
> flesh to the European, who makes them into tinned meat.[32]

There are many local variations. One incorporates a version of the
hierarchy that was so much part of the colonial experience.

> [T]he Yombe affirm that prisoners "of the first quality" are changed into
> Europeans and redeployed to the place of their birth, that those "of second
> quality" find their way to Europe as white labourers and that the rest are
> changed to pigs and guard dogs. The white does not necessarily *eat* the vic-
> tim; he may just bleed the African, and send the blood to his cannibal col-
> laborator. Captives may serve as medical guinea pigs, or they can be sent as a
> labor force to Angola.[33]

In some accounts, Europeans perch like birds in the trees to watch for
their prey; sometimes, they blind their victims with their car lights.[34] Their
black associates capture their victims with a variety of non-traditional weapons. The text parodies the violence of the colonial state, which later became
a major theme in Zaire's urban art (see p. 91).

> He can stun them with a rubber truncheon or with a belt, sometimes he
> blinds them with his torch or the headlights of a car, sometimes he attacks
> them with his dog or picks them up in a whirlwind or immobilises them
> with a jet of liquid or a paralysing injection.[35]

They prey especially on women, children and the isolated, and prefer
the night.

Vampire stories merge, not only with zombie narratives, but with accounts of blood magic. During the terrible famine which afflicted Malawi in 1949, it was said "that small children were being taken and retailed by Indian shopkeepers to Europeans who used them for food and for the preparation of 'powerful medicines.'"[36]

Vampires, Rumors, and the State

Patterns of witchcraft, vampire, or shapeshifter accusations form intricate themes in counterpoint with the policies of colonial and postcolonial governments. While some—not all—of the colonized believed vampire rumors to be literally true, European officials regarded them as untrue (though in the Belgian Congo, they filed them under the heading of secret societies).[37] Accordingly, vampirism was not banned by law. Colonial authorities considered vampire rumors bizarre and naive, but took them seriously, keeping extensive records, and discouraging the visit of a medical researcher to Zambia in 1945, lest his taking of blood samples encourage an outbreak of these fears.[38]

In the 1950s, in Zambia, vampire stories became politicized, and *banyama* were identified with the Capricorn Africa Society, which supported the Central African Federation, which most Africans opposed as the vehicle of continuing white domination.[39] African radio announcers were attacked as banyama—it was thought that they broadcast Federation propaganda because their wills had been destroyed.[40] Zambians sang a song composed by Kaunda, in which the Europeans are not vampires but vultures, feeding not on the living, but on the dead.

> They are cunning and armed with sharp beaks
> to frighten the live
> and to feast on the dead.[41]

This is strikingly reminiscent of the legend of King Buzzard.

To colonial officials, or M. P.s in distant Westminster, all this was inexplicable.

> [H]ow could they be expected to see political expression in the symbolism of the voiceless fear of the fish for the circling birds of prey, in the nightmare of the monster that strikes men dumb and sucks their blood, in the dread of sexual impotence?[42]

The terror of the vampire survives in the post-colony. Since the 1960s, spirit possession has spread among the Maasai, among whom it was previously almost unknown. Among the afflicting spirits is Mumiani.[43] In a 1983 doctoral thesis, Anthony called Mumiani "one of the most tenacious elements of urban life in Dar es Salaam."[44]

Emasculating Governments

The poetics of rumor sometimes describes the theft, not of the victim's blood, but of sexual and reproductive powers.

In Nairobi, from 1939 on, there were reports that blankets had been treated with a substance that destroyed men's sexual powers, or alternatively, " that European doctors had perfected injections that would produce 'bottled babies' without women."[45]

In Northern Rhodesia, at the time of Federation discussions, there were rumors that Africans were to be given poisoned sugar that would make women bear stillborn infants and render men impotent.[46] These fears reflect the perceived powerlessness of a subordinated people.

Rumors of emasculation or sterilization have often been documented in the post-colony. In the first years of Zaire's independence, canned chicken from America was called "Adoula's corpses." "As the food of the dead, they were expected to cause sterility."[47]

There have been outbreaks of hysteria and crowd violence in independent Ghana, sparked by rumors that witches were making the penis or breasts disappear (pp. 155–6). In 1981, in Antananarivo (Madagascar), there were rumors of male corpses with their genitals removed for magical purposes; the perpetrators were thought to be North Korean aid workers.[48]

There are striking parallels in an urban legend recorded among African Americans in the early 1980s, attributing the disappearance of young black men in Atlanta to the manufacture of the anti-cancer drug Interferon from their genitals.[49] It was also widely rumored that the Klu Klux Klan owns a fried chicken franchise, and doctors the chicken to sterilize black men.[50]

In the colonial situation, vampire rumors reflected a perception that African resources are drained away for the benefit of foreigners and that this is made possible by their African allies. In the post-colony, African rulers and their associates eat the state, and indirectly, its citizens, by consuming its scarce resources. As in myths of the slave as food or industrial raw material, real or perceived threats to society are expressed as threats to an individual body. The colonial subject is drained of life force, or emasculated, or silenced.

On two occasions, I have experienced for myself the terrifying impact of rumor in Africa. In 1971–72, I lived with my family in Zaria, in Northern Nigeria, soon after the end of the Civil War. Periodically, rumors would sweep the Igbo community: "The killings have started again." They were false, but one could not know this. In 1985, when we lived in Jos, there was a sudden rumor that the Muslim insurgents generically known as Maitatsine had come to a specific point in the city, and were burning families alive in their homes. Again, this proved untrue, but I can readily empathize with those who feared vampires. Because these beliefs were so widespread, they seemed mutually confirming. Once the postulate was accepted, local experience seemed to confirm it further—the words of the Catholic Mass ("This is my blood"), researchers who collected specimens of blood or lymph, bottles of (unfamiliar) red wine at European dinner tables, and so on.

The vampire myths of East and Central Africa are not the only twentieth-century symbolic complexes that condemn oppression by identifying it symbolically with cannibalism. It has been an enduring political metaphor in Southern Africa, where it was applied, in the poetics of memory, to the Mfecane, and later, in the poetics of rumor, to the sufferings of present-day African miners. Apparently similar symbols, rooted in the idea of life as a zero-sum game, and focusing on the cannibal or vampire as the quintessence of violent predation, are worked out quite differently in different cultural contexts. Cannibalism is also a recurrent leitmotif in the postcolonial African novel, where it becomes a metaphor for the exploitation and avarice of independent Africa's ruling elites.

The Cannibal Motif in Southern Africa

Cannibalism has proved to be an enduring image in South Africa's political discourse. It is a powerful and familiar metaphor for the phase of the historical experience of Southern Africa usually termed the Mfecane.[51] To Thomas Mofolo, who completed his historical novel, *Chaka,* in seSotho in 1909, "It was Chaka who caused the introduction of cannibalism, that vilest of all practices when men hunt each other like animals—for food."[52] The image has had enduring significance for the Sotho; in the words of a modern singer, "It was in those times when cannibals ate people."[53]

Later, it was the mines that were cannibals, and death itself a welcome release.

> I once went travelling thoughtlessly—
> When I was above the gorge of the Caledon,
> I met them, the cannibals of war.
> I kept quiet and brought down my prayers.
> When I said, Let the earth swallow me up . . .[54]

In Mefikeng, the Comaroffs spoke to a man who had worked in the gold mines when he was young. He used much the same imagery—the mine as a devourer and a grave: "the mine like the grave, has use only for your body. When it has done with you it spits you out, and you are finished!"[55] The Zulu called South Africa *Ningizimu,* Cannibals' Africa.[56]

At Zimbabwe's independence celebrations in 1980, the Zanu-PF Ideological Choir broadcast a song identifying white minority rule with cannibalism:

> The exploiters of Zimbabwe
> Were cannibals drinking the masses' blood,
> Sucking and sapping their energy.
> The gun stopped all this.[57]

This, of course, is political propaganda, very different from the terrors of vampire rumors.

A Motif in the Postcolonial African Novel

Both Ngugi, writing of Kenya, and Okri, writing of Nigeria, employ cannibal images to symbolize the gluttonous rapacity not of a colonial regime, but of postcolonial African elites.

Ngugi's novel, *Petals of Blood,* was written between 1970 and 1975. It ends with a denunciation of a

> system . . . with parasitism and cannibalism as the highest goal in society. . . .
> Tomorrow it would be the workers and the peasants leading the struggle . . .
> bringing to an end the reign of the few over the many and the era of drinking
> blood and feasting on human flesh.[58]

Three years later, Ngugi was a political prisoner in a Kenyan jail, where he wrote *Devil on the Cross* on toilet paper in Kikuyu. Again, cannibalism is a

metaphor for oppression, not by colonial powers, but by Kenyan capital-
ists.

> Two bourgeois women
> Ate the flesh of the children of the poor,
> They could not see the humanity of the children
> Because their hearts were empty. . . .
> Muturi said: "The rich stagger because they over-eat."
> Wangari added: "And the poor because they are starving."[59]

Okri's *Songs of Enchantment* (1993), set in Nigeria, also describes the
rich as cannibals.

> I flew into a world of violence, of famine, of pullulating hunger, with beggars
> swarming the city centre, with maggots devouring the inhabitants, with flies
> eating the eyeballs of the children who were half-dead with starvation . . . with
> the rich and powerful gorging themselves at their bacchanalias, . . . while the
> food spilled on the polished floors and the guests trod on them, while the
> choice delicacies changed into the writhing savoury intestines of the dying chil-
> dren and women, which were gobbled up in celebrations without end.[60]

Okri's and Ngugi's despair make an ironic contrast with the optimism of the Zimbabwe song quoted above. At the moment of Zimbabwe's
independence, it seemed that the age of cannibals had ended. To Okri in
Kenya or Ngugi, writing of Nigeria, it had just begun.

All this is not peculiar to Africa. The greatest of New Zealand's poets,
writing of his own society just before his death in 1972, used the same
imagery, asking

> How can I live in a country where the towns are made like coffins
> And the rich are eating the poor
> Without even knowing it?[61]

Notes

1. Michel Foucault, "The Discourse on Language," appendix to *The Archaeology of Knowledge,* trans. A. M. Sheridan Smith (New York, 1972), 224.

2. R. Willis, "Kaswa: Oral Traditions of a Fipa Prophet," *Africa* (1970): 253, 230. The invaders were *ifituumbu,* a word with associations of cannibalism.

3. J. Kenyatta, *Facing Mount Kenya: The Tribal Life of the Gikuyu* (1938; reprint, London, 1953), 43.

4. L. White, "Vampire Priests of Central Africa: African Debates about Labor and Religion in Colonial Northern Zambia," *Comparative Studies in Society and History* (1993): 756.

5. L. White, "Bodily Fluids and Usufruct: Controlling Property in Nairobi, 1917–1939," *Canadian Journal of African Studies* (1990): 418–38.

6. K. Marx, *Capital,* trans. B. Fowkes (Penguin edition), I: 342.

7. E. Stephenson, *Chirupula's Tale* (London, 1937), 227–28.

8. M. G. Marwick, *Sorcery in Its Social Setting: A Study of the Northern Rhodesian Cewa* (Manchester, 1965), 92.

9. D. H. Anthony, "Culture and Society in a Town in Transition: A People's History of Dar es Salaam 1865–1939" (Ph.D. diss., University of Wisconsin, 1983), 141.

10. D. Bates, *The Mango and the Palm* (London, 1962), 52; on "Arab", see, for instance, G. Shepperson, "The Jumbe of Kota Kota . . . " in I. Lewis (ed.), *Islam in Tropical Africa* (London, 1966), 194.

11. M. Musambachime, "The Impact of Rumor: The Case of the Banyama (Vampire Men) Scare in Northern Rhodesia," *The International Journal of African Historical Studies* (1988): 208.

12. Bates, *The Mango and the Palm,* 55.

13. Elspeth Huxley, *The Sorcerer's Apprentice* (London, 1948), 23.

14. W. Arens, *The Man-Eating Myth: Anthropology and Anthropophagy* (New York, 1979), 12.

15. M. Bloch, *Placing the Dead* (London and New York, 1971), 32, 59.

16. Quoted in A. Ginzberger, "Accommodation to Poverty: The Case of the Malagasy Peasant Communities," *Cahiers d'Études africaines* (1983), 420; he adds his own documentation of the phenomenon.

17. E. S. A. Odhiambo, "The Movement of Ideas: A Case Study of Intellectual Reponses to Colonialism Among the Liganua Peasants," in B. A. Ogot (ed.), *History and Social Change* (Hadith 6, Nairobi, 1976), 172.

18. Brad Weiss, *The Making and Unmaking of the Haya Lived World* (Durham, NC, and London, 1996), 202.

19. Ibid.

20. Bloch, *Placing the Dead,* 32.

21. F. Moretti, "The Dialectic of Fear," in *Signs Taken for Wonders* (London, 1983), 85. (He writes with reference to Frankenstein.)

22. P. Stoller, *Fusion of the Worlds: An Ethnography of Possession among the Songhay of Niger* (Chicago, 1989), 153.

23. J. Middleton, *The Study of the Lugbara* (New York, 1970), 14; the other names for European meant rifle and axe-man.

24. White, "Bodily Fluids and Usufruct," 418–38

25. L. White, "Tsetse Visions: Narratives of Blood and Bugs in Colonial Northern Rhodesia, 1931–9," *Journal of African History* (1995): 236, 237.

26. Extract in A. Dubb (ed.), *Myth in Modern Africa* (Rhodes Livingstone Institute, Lusaka, 1960), 146–47; Bates, *The Mango and the Palm,* 52.

27. Quoted in White, "Vampire Priests of Central Africa," 751–52. She locates these images less in the context of the Mass than in conflicts between the white missionaries and their irregularly paid employees.

28. Musambachime, "The Impact of Rumor," 211.

29. P. Fraenkel, *Wayaleshi* (London, 1959), 200.

30. W. H. Bentley, *Pioneering on the Congo* (London, 1900), I: 252–53.

31. B. Fetter, "The Luluabourg Revolt at Elisabethville," *African Historical Studies* (1969): 273.

32. R. Ceyssens, "Mutumbula, Mythe de l'Opprime," *Cultures et Development* (1975): 486.

33. Ceyssens, "Mutumbula, Mythe de l'Opprime," 487.

34. Ibid., 487–8; the tree-top reference may refer to surveying beacons on hills.

35. Ibid., 491.

36. Megan Vaughan, *The Story of an African Famine* (Cambridge, 1987), 41.

37. Ceyssens, "Mutumbula, Mythe de l'Opprime," 531.

38. Musambachime, "The Impact of Rumor," 209–10.

39. Fraenkel, *Wayaleshi,* 201.

40. Ibid., 202.

41. Ibid., 174.

42. Ibid., 206.

43. A. Hurskainen, "The Epidemiological Aspect of Spirit Possession Among the Maasai of Tanzania," in A. Jacobson-Widding and D. Westerlund (eds.), *Culture, Experience and Pluralism: Essays on African Ideas of illness and Healing* (Uppsala, 1989), 145.

44. Anthony, "Culture and Society," 141.

45. White, "Bodily Fluids," 421.

46. Fraenkel, *Wayaleshi,* 196.

47. W. MacGaffey, "Kongo and the King of the Americans," *The Journal of Modern African Studies* (1968): 178. Adoula arranged this aid during a visit to America, when Prime Minister.

48. S. Ellis, "Tuning in to Pavement Radio," *African Affairs* (1989): 324.

49. Patricia A. Turner, *I Heard it Through the Grapevine: Rumor in African-American Culture* (Berkeley, 1993), 148.

50. Ibid., 82–92.

51. The appropriateness of the label and the precise nature of the phenomenon have been much debated—this lies outside the sphere of this book, but see Isichei, *A History of African Societies* (Cambridge, 1997), 422–24, and sources cited there.

52. T. Mofolo, *Chaka,* trans. F. H. Dutton (1931; reprint, London, 1981), 137.

53. Letsema Matsela, in D. Coplan, *In the Time of Cannibals* (Chicago, 1994), 1–3. The song includes the story about Moshoehoe and the cannibals.

54. Song recorded in 1988, in Coplan, *In the Time of Cannibals,* 7.

55. J. L. and J. Comaroff, "The Madman and the Migrant: Work and Labor in the Historical Consciousness of a South African People," *American Ethnologist* (1987): 192.

56. Coplan, *In the Time of Cannibals,* 2.

57. Quoted in J. Ferguson, "De-Moralizing Economies: African Socialism, Scientific Capitalism and the Moral Politics of '"Structural Adjustment,"'" in S. F. Moore (ed.), *Moralizing States and the Ethnography of the Present* (Arlington, Va., 1993), 78.

58. Ngugi wa Thiong'o, *Petals of Blood* (London, 1977), 344.

59. Ngugi wa Thiong'o, *Devil on the Cross* (London, 1982), 50–1.

60. Ben Okri, *Songs of Enchantment* (London, 1993), 89.

61. James K. Baxter, "Ode to Auckland," in *Collected Poems* (Oxford, 1988), 600.

10

CHANGING BODIES, CHANGING WORLDS

"I have never felt more awake, but I see a leopard coming towards me. Am I a leopard? Is the leopard my dream?"

Azaro's father in Ben Okri, *Infinite Riches*[1]

Traditions still current in Ukerewe, an island community in Lake Victoria Nyanza, tell of a werelion called Butamile, whose ferocity caused its partial depopulation. He is said to have lived at the beginning of the nineteenth century, when the Kerebe were first involved in long-distance trade and exposed to new and fearsome diseases, and to have been created by the king's curse, to strike his enemies. At one level, he is a personification of a time of danger, stress, and transition. Beyond this, in the words of Ukerewe's historian, "Whether he was a demented individual assuming a lion's character . . . or whether he was in fact a man-eating lion, we can never know."[2]

Secret societies of male shapeshifters, such as leopard men, were first recorded in the latter part of the nineteenth century (later, in some regions), and constituted a large number of clearly independent responses to the imposition of conquest states and the experience of early colonial rule. Butamile is an earlier figure, a named individual, contextualized in a different situation of crisis.

Shapeshifting—the metamorphosis from human to animal form—is one of the sinister characteristics of the witch. Witches prey on people and are closely associated with snakes and other familiars from the wild. "They treat humans like animals, killing and eating them. They treat wild animals like people, cooperating to gain and share food."[3] They readily change their form, often to that of a nocturnal bird, or python. In a different sinister transformation human predators are almost always seen specifically as male and typically, in a secret society, take the form of ferocious carnivores, lions, leopards, chimpanzees, or crocodiles, any and all of which it is convenient to refer to as shapeshifters or theriomorphs.

"A candidate for initiation into the Leopard society must be a man."[4] "Among the Kuranko, witches are usually women, the [shapeshifters] invariably men."[5] Shapeshifters become assassins who prey on their fellow human beings and are, in some ways, comparable with the anonymous male predators, the zombie-owning sorcerers and vampires discussed in the preceding two chapters. But they differ from them in one crucial respect.

This book is largely concerned with phenomena that at least some Africans have perceived as real, and Westerners as imaginary. Vampires and zombies belong to the poetics of rumor. Shapeshifting, however, may have been translated, in times of social disruption and angst, into actual behavior—murderers wielding metal claws. Both academics and local African communities have been divided and uncertain on this issue. Hartwig's account of Butamile shows the same hesitations.

Africans sometimes described shapeshifting as a real supernatural transformation. Alternatively, it was thought that at least some predators were men who put on animal skins and killed their victims with iron claws. European officials or missionaries sometimes accepted this, and sometimes attributed such deaths to real lions. When there was an outbreak of lion/lion men killings in Singida, in Tanzania, in the 1940s, colonial officials hedged their bets and sent both professional hunters and an anthropologist to the area![6] Roberts, writing of the Tabwa of eastern Congo/Zaire, considered missionaries who attributed lion killings to real lions "singularly even sublimely obtuse."[7] But the truth is, as we shall see, by no means self-evident. Gittens, writing of the Mende of Sierra Leone, observes:

> There is no conclusive proof that there actually existed a "Secret-Society" composed of men acting as leopards, alligators or baboons and engaging in concerted murder and cannibalism. . . . It is . . . important for us to bear in mind the distinction between "what actually happens" and "what people believe happens."[8]

In popular sensibility, the witch was and is as real as the theriomorph. Many Mende also believed in *ndilei,* a witch familiar in the form of a python ("boa constrictor"), which sucks the blood of the living.[9] Colonial governments never made ndilei illegal, because it was never thought of as "real." Does this suggest questions about the ontological existence of murderous shapeshifter societies?

In African communities, these modes of explanation are not necessarily mutually exclusive. Richards states that some Mende believe in genuine shapeshifting, other in killers in leopard costume.[10] In Tanzania, Schneider describes "three forms, normally interchangeable in Turu thought"—a man disguised as a lion, a real lion subject to a human will, and an apparent lion who reveals his true identity by, for instance, talking or smoking.[11]

In vampire beliefs, in my interpretation, a closely comparable set of symbolic meanings is contextualized in very different ways—vampires are firemen in Nairobi or tsetse fly eradicators in Zambia. The opposite is true of shapeshifter stories; apparently similar lion or leopard men narratives must be interpreted, in varying ethnic settings, in quite different ways. My study of colonial vampires focused on East Africa, and of zombie owners on Cameroon, with some comparative data from elsewhere. Here, I explore the rich material from Sierra Leone, again, with a brief comparison with other case studies.

Many—perhaps all—shapeshifter accusations were as groundless as charges of zombie sorcery or vampirism. This is most evident in the case of Sierra Leone's crocodile men, who were thought to travel under the water "in a self propelled submarine canoe with the appearance of a crocodile."[12] In 1912, it was claimed that this was made by lashing two canoes together. "The lower canoe acts as a sort of diving bell."[13]

A man from the Sherbro who had been educated by missionaries in America and returned to work for the mission became the chief of Imperi, and later stood trial and was acquitted on Leopard Society charges. While not denying the existence of alligator societies, he pointed out the practical difficulties. "How air is supplied, or how the hinged door can be opened and closed when the canoe is under water, I cannot attempt to explain."[14] Colonial officials who dismissed witchcraft beliefs as superstition accepted the ontological reality of men disguised as crocodiles who traveled in locally made submarines. Examples of iron claws and leopard costumes are to be found in museum collections and have often been photographed.[15] But it is likely that many of those who died were the victims of real wild animals or of men trying to convict an enemy of leopard-style killings.

Because colonial officials looked on shapeshifters as "real," those who were the subject of such accusations were tried, and on occasion, executed. Lindskog's exhaustive continent-wide research revealed an approximate total of 1150 victims of murders attributed to lion or leopard men and 1125 convictions for such crimes, over a period of eighty years, in the whole of West and Central Africa.[16]

In Sierra Leone, those accused of leopard crimes often responded to the demand to identify their associates by providing names at random. "I did not know whose name to call so named my uncle." "They put medicine in my eyes. . . . My eyes hurt so much that I called peoples names as members of the Society and confessed, but I am innocent and was lying."[17] Sometimes they confessed to what was clearly the astral cannibalism of the witch. "I used to eat little bits of my brother from time to time but did not mean to kill him."[18]

Staring death in the face, men convicted of leopard crimes often protested their innocence.

> I am a fisherman. I was caught as one of the perpetrators but I am not. The people envy me because I was a good fisherman. When they caught me Bobo asked me to confess. He said I must call Chiefs' names.[19]

This is strikingly reminiscent of the way in which Bakweri who could afford iron roofs were thought to be zombie-owning sorcerers.

A considerable amount of evidence suggests that lion and leopard societies, real or imagined, began in the second half of the nineteenth century or later—the 1860s in Sierra Leone, the 1870s in Cameroon and the 1920s in Singida, Tanzania.[20]

The first reference to theriomorphs in Sierra Leone is to (almost certainly metaphysical) werecrocodiles on the Sherbro in the mid eighteenth century, in the years of the Atlantic slave trade.

> It's the method of these me[n] that I am going to spake of to dress themselves up in the bark of a tree untill they resemble an alegator then they lurk in secret places to surprize any innocent person that has the fortune to pass that way in the night. As soon as thier prize is secure, they devour him. . . .[21]

The supposed shapeshifter, like the witch, underwent a poison ordeal. The penalty was "immadate death . . . by drinking red water, and thier bodies burnt to ashes."[22] Both witchcraft and shapeshifter accusations expanded in the era of the slave trade, and in each instance, the accused were often profitably sold.

In a book published in 1788, Matthews noted:

> If an allegator destroys any body when washing or swimming, or a leopard commits depredations on their flocks or poultry . . . it is immediately attrib-

uted to witchcraft: and it rarely hapens that some person or other is not pointed out . . . as the witch and sold.[23]

Zachary Macaulay's journal entries for 1793 reflect the way in which shapeshifter accusations were used to procure slaves, exploited by local rulers.

> Another fruitful source of slavery is the accidental loss of people by Alligators or Tygers. If a Child for instance is devoured by one of these animals the King glad of an opportunity immediately brings a Palaver against the people of the Town to which the Child belongs.[24]

Almost certainly, real leopards and crocodiles caused these deaths; fabricated accusations of shapeshifting were among the ways in which Big Men obtained slaves. Macaulay, like many others after him, asked himself what if any ontological reality underlay these accusations.

> The only feasable account I can procur of the matter is that sometimes men actuated by a desire of resenting some injury do clothe themselves in the skin of a Leopard, and so habited execute some scheme of revenge. The Metamorphosis is supposed real by the superstitious natives.[25]

He went on to explain that rulers encouraged these beliefs, because they enabled them to enslave "an obnoxious individual."

By the late nineteenth century, both African communities and European officials believed in the existence of numerous murderous shapeshifter societies in southern Sierra Leone—leopard, crocodile ("alligator"), or chimpanzee ("baboon") men. They were often called, inaccurately, "cannibals," reflecting the horror with which both were regarded.

Two different sources suggest that these societies developed in the late nineteenth century, in Taiama, a cluster of towns in Imperi, often called the Mende capital. They were linked with *borfina,* a charm thought to confer power and prosperity, which was originally offered animal sacrifices, but later, human ones. They "sought their victims in the bush and seized them by imitating the habits of the leopard."[26]

Apparently mutually confirming, these texts may well be myth, not history, reflecting the centrality of Taiama both to wereleopards and Tongo players. The latter specialized in the detection and execution of shapeshifters. Those they identified were burnt to death, a fate which befell eighty or more supposed theriomorphs in Imperi, in 1891. One of the victims was Gbana Bunje, the chief who had called in the Tongo players in the first place.[27] He was about to alienate land, "and they therefore made arrangements with the Tongo's to have him killed under the pretext of being a cannibal [shapeshifter]."[28] It is a classic instance of the political manipulation of these concepts, of which there is much other evidence. But shapeshifter rumors and accusations were not peculiar to the Mende. "The Sherbros have the Human Leopard society; and the Bulloms . . . the Alligator society."[29]

Real leopard or crocodile deaths continued to provide an excuse for the extortion of Big Men.

> We have got alligators in the river, and if somebody is caught by an alligator and the case is reported to Paramount Chief Yumkella he will say, "Well, I don't believe you people. Now you shall pay a fine of £10 for me to send people with medicine."[30]

Shapeshifter accusations were intricately entwined with power struggles at the local level, and with the strategies of the powerful. Accusations of lion or leopard murders were among the ways in which African notables manipulated the power of the colonial state against their rivals and enemies, a practice which continues in the post-colony. In the late nineteenth century, chiefs often attempted to suppress leopard societies, by calling in Tongo players. In the first decade of the twentieth, they themselves were often accused by rivals or enemies of being leopard men.[31]

The outcomes of local power struggles in the early colonial situation were determined largely by success or failure in manipulating the representatives of colonial government. The Sierra Leone government banned Tongo players in 1892, three years before the Human Leopard Society Ordinance, a sequence which mirrors changing official perceptions of "reality." In 1901 the Ordinance was amended to include alligator costumes.[32]

Between 1903 and 1912, 186 people were charged with murder under these ordinances, of whom 87 were convicted and sentenced to death. In 1894, an informant who was killed six weeks later in the Hut Tax War claimed to have overheard rituals addressed to borfina. They reflect the concerns of the propertied, and especially of slave owners.

> Do not let any trouble come to us. Let us get plenty of slaves. Do not let the Government know how to free them. Let us be rich.[33]

An account published in 1912 was very similar: "[T]hey tie the Borfimor up, and anoint it, and pray to it, asking that they may get power, money, and slaves . . . and that the English may not know what they do."[34]

The rich and powerful, who in an earlier era had obtained slaves for sale by manipulating shapeshifter and witchcraft accusations, now apparently turned to magic to preserve their privileges. Significantly, they sought invisibility from colonial officials.

Accusations, trials, and executions of supposed leopard men thread their way through colonial records. Powerful men not only accused their rivals of "cannibalism" to ensure that they were punished by colonial authorities but may even have had leopard-style killings perpetrated in order to put the blame on their enemies.

Little, who carried out fieldwork among the Mende in 1945–46 wrote of borfina and "political undercurrents," which were similar to those of an earlier day, whereby an individual seeks to acquire money or political power through blood magic, or alternatively, ritual murders are committed to discredit a local notable.[35] His account of the capture of a lone woman or child is strikingly like East African narratives of vampires written at the same time.

In 1976, the Mende historian, Abraham, called borfina "the all-efficacious charm that was believed to bring wealth, power, respect and untold advantage to its possessor."[36] He detailed the way in which accusations of "leopardism" continued to be a powerful political weapon.

> A cabinet minister was deposed in 1973 and charged with ritual murder. Found guilty, he was condemned and hanged the following year. Many accusations are doubtless frivolous and crude political tactics. But it can be asserted without any fear of contradiction that the complex phenomenon of leopardism (and related variants) is far from dead even today.[37]

Gittens tells of meeting a terrified man running down a country road. "He . . . swore that 'the men' were chasing him 'for bofimei'—i.e. to kill him. He explained it by reference to the current political elections, saying big men from Freetown sent raiding parties for *bofimei* to secure their re-election."[38]

Richards wrote recently:

> Fear of *koli-hinda* [leopard killings] peaks in periods of great social, political or economic tension. . . . *Koli-hinda* was particularly marked in many parts of the Mende hinterland during the colonial take-over, as confidence in indigenous political structures crumbled. Today it is a feature of rural communities suffering power struggles among chiefs. Occasionally, it is a charge used to unseat national political figures.[39]

Alternative Transformations

A 1930s' account of inland Liberia gives quite a different description of shapeshifting societies and seems to represent an earlier moral geography of the animal kingdom, which, in many places, became grotesquely distorted during the multifaceted crisis of the late nineteenth century.

> Twelve hours journey to the north lies the country of Toway, who is really an elephant . . . It is said that elephant people live to be very old. They are not wicked like leopard people, not thieving and petty like wild-pig people [who cause harvest failures by devouring the seed] but great and powerful and wise.[40]

The were-elephant is noble, old, and wise. The wereleopard or werecrocodile is a ferocious murderer. Werepigs are thieves, who kill by causing famine. And there was another society, which had fallen into desuetude by the 1930s. "The buffalo people are very strong, very war-like. What use are these qualities nowadays? They were not able to stand up to the magic of the Liberians, which is stronger than ours."[41] Here the contrast is with the power and prosperity, not of the whites, but of black Americo-Liberians.

Jackson's fine study, *Paths Towards a Clearing,* includes a chapter on shapeshifting among an inland Sierra Leone people, the Kuranko, which has much in common with Donner's account of 1930s Liberia. Here, it is an inherited power, and the theriomorph turns into his clan totem, becoming, perhaps, an elephant. It is a transformation that imperils the shapeshifter, who may be blamed for damaging the crops, or killed, while in animal form, by a hunter.[42]

Interpreting Shapeshifting

Real or imagined societies of lion and leopard men had much in common with masking cults; the mask embodies a spirit, which is sometimes that of a wild animal. Most mask societies (with the exception of Sande and related institutions in Liberia and Sierra Leone) were controlled by men acting in concert and in secret. They could and did function as executioners—notably of rejected initiands and witches. Lion and leopard societies inherited the pattern of a secret male cult, which could practice violence in the anonymity bestowed by disguise. The pattern of violence was different.

Masks executed real or imagined social deviants. The violence of human lions was apparently random.

Witchcraft —or shapeshifter—confessions are both tragic and puzzling; they are culturally determined, common in some African cultures and unknown in others. Often, these confessions were made during a mortal illness; sometimes, they clearly embody psychotic delusions. With characteristic insight, Jackson suggests that they can represent an attempt to take control of one's life, just as Jean Genet, called a thief when young, decided to become one.[43]

Contemporaries struggled to understand these events. Will Caulker, a chief from a well-known mètis family of coastal merchants, wrote in 1889 that he "felt compelled to come here, and to ascertain for myself, whether this was the work of Leopard."[44] Even eyewitnesses were unsure what they had seen. "All of a sudden I saw 'something' catch hold of Deceased. . . . I cannot tell whether the things I saw were persons or beasts."[45]

In the poetics of rumor, vampirism was explained in various ways— the theft of the life force of others, or the sale of blood for money. Zombie sorcery was attributed to the desire for wealth. But it is significant that there appeared to be no rationale for the random violence and cruelty ascribed to leopard or lion men, other than its association with blood magic, which promised wealth and power.

Complex and multiple social tensions created the social pathology of real or imagined leopard societies, among them the crisis which the ending, first of the external slave trade and later of domestic slavery created for the propertied. Chiefs sought to maintain as much as possible of their wealth, power, and prestige amid new power equations. Their victims were often, not always, women and children. "[T]he natives say 'that they wanted to catch woman to make medicine in order to get riches.'"[46]

In a sense, the man who becomes a leopard or lion can be understood as another form of the commodified body. The assassin in lion or leopard form is the dark mirror image of the humanized animal world of the storyteller. There is an intrinsic danger in that blurring of categories and boundaries which the theriomorph exemplifies par excellence. "[A]ll margins are dangerous. If they are pulled this way or that the shape of fundamental experience is altered. Any structure of ideas is vulnerable at its margins."[47]

In Sierra Leone, theriomorph accusations sprang from the power struggles, at the local level, of the rich and prominent, and from their attempt to retain their privileges, despite the rapid advance of colonialism. Among the Tabwa, on the Congo shore of Lake Tanganyika, outbursts of "lion" deaths at intervals between 1886 and 1942 been interpreted as an attack on oppressive chiefs. A ruler's power rests on his followers and is effectively destroyed if they move away. The terror of lion attacks achieved this very effectively.[48] Attacks on mission adherents had the same effect, for the survivors fled from the mission station.

Gender hostility is central in Schneider's analysis of shapeshifter killings in the Singida region of Tanzania, which began in the 1920s and peaked in 1946–48. Here, lion men are believed to execute the wishes of women witches.[49] Apparently similar beliefs are in fact quite different, in diverse cultural settings.

The real or supposed transformations and murders of lion or leopard men were metaphors for an age of violence and dislocation, collapsing social change into the microcosm of the transformed body. But we are not dealing only with metaphors. The sinister image of the shapeshifter took on a life of its own; some may have acted out murderous leopard roles, and many were killed because they were thought to have done so—"events becoming signs and signs becoming reality."[50]

Ideas shape human behavior; in this case, they shaped it in profoundly damaging ways, which led both to the execution of supposed theriomorphs, and also, if most academic commentators are correct, to a new kind of assassin.

> The human leopards took out their grievances on their own social body. . . . [The] leopard-men sought control over their own situation by realising the wildest imaginings and worst prejudices of their oppressors, but in the end they were victims of their own rituals and of their own convoluted and clandestine strategies.[51]

Notes

1. Ben Okri, *Infinite Riches* (London, 1998), 7.

2. G. Hartwig, *The Art of Survival in East Africa* (New York, 1976), 74–6.

3. T. Beidelman, *Moral Imagination in Kaguru Modes of Thought* (Washington and London, 1993), 143.

4. R. G. Berry, "The Sierra Leone Cannibals," *Proceedings of the Royal Irish Academy*, 1912, 46.

5. M. Jackson, *Paths Towards a Clearing. Radical Empiricism and Ethnographic Inquiry* (Bloomington, 1989), 102.

6. H. Schneider, "Male-Female Conflict and Lion Men in Singida," in Simon Ottenberg (ed.), *African Religious Groups and Beliefs* (Berkeley, 1982), 97.

7. A. F. Roberts, "'Like a Roaring Lion: Tabwa Terrorism in the Late Nineteenth Century," in D. Crummey (ed.), *Banditry, Rebellion and Social Protest in Africa* (London, 1986), 65.

8. A. J. Gittins, *Mende Religion: Aspects of Belief and Thought in Sierra Leone* (Nettetal, 1987), 131.

9. K. Little, *The Mende of Sierra Leone* (London, 1951), 231. For a much more recent account, see Gittins, *Mende Religion,* 123–27.

10. P. Richards, "Natural Symbols and Natural History: Chimpanzees, Elephants and Experiments in Mende Thought," in K. Milton, *Environmentalism: The View from Anthropology* (London, 1993), 148.

11. Schneider, "Male-Female Conflict," 97.

12. Carol MacCormarck, "Human Leopards and Crocodiles: Political Meanings of Categorical Anomalies," in Paula Brown and Donald Tuzin, *The Ethnography of Cannibalism* (Washington, DC, 1983), 54.

13. Berry, "The Sierra Leone Cannibals," 32.

14. Wilberforce, "The True Verdict or Cannibalism in the Hinterland of Sierra Leone" (Board of Missions Archives, North Carolina), in M. Kalous, *Cannibals and Tongo Players of Sierra Leone* (Auckland, 1974), 58, 73.

15. Roberts, "'Like a Roaring Lion,'" 83 n.19. There are two sketches of "leopard-knives" in Berry, "The Sierra Leone Cannibals," 69.

16. B. Lindskog, *African Leopard Men* (Uppsala, 1954), 206. Even if many cases were never documented, or were not discovered in his research, the order of magnitude is instructive.

17. Confidential Minute papers, 163/1917, S[ierra] L[eone] Archives, in Kalous, *Cannibals and Tongo Players,* 78.

18. Ibid., 79.

19. General Minute papers, 4199/1904, Sheriff to Colonial Secretary, S. L. Archives, in Kalous, *Cannibals and Tongo Players,* 277.

20. Lindskog, *African Leopard Men,* 9ff.

21. Nicholas Owen, *Journal of a Slave Dealer* (London, 1930), 84. Entry for 28 Nov. 1757.

22. Ibid., 85.

23. J. Matthews, *A Voyage to the River Sierra-Leone* (London, 1788), 131–32.

24. Journal of Zachary Macaulay, 18 Nov. 1793, extract in C. Fyfe, *Sierra Leone Inheritance* (London, 1964), 75.

25. Journal of Zachary Macaulay, 1 Oct. 1793, 75.

26. Berry, "The Sierra Leone Cannibals," 53–4.

27. C. Fyfe, *A History of Sierra Leone* (London, 1962), 507; T. J. Alldridge, *A Transformed Colony* (London, 1910), 275.

28. Quoted in Lindskog, *African Leopard Men,* 96.

29. Berry, "The Sierra Leone Cannibals," 32. Sherbro and Bullom are alternative ethnyms for the same people.

30. Draft, Cox Commission of Inquiry Report, Evidence, S. L. Archives, in Kalous, *Cannibals and Tongo Players,* 86.

31. K. J. Beatty, *Human Leopards* (London, 1915), 11. Beatty was a barrister, who sat on a special commission investigating leopard murders in 1912–13.

32. Ibid., 5–6.

33. Eyewitness account by Special Messenger Samuel Parkes, 13 Oct. 1894, S. L. Archives, in Kalous, *Cannibals and Tongo Players,* 112. Much the same statement is given in T. J. Alldridge, *The Shrbro and its Hinterland* (London, 1901), 155.

34. Berry, "The Sierra Leone Cannibals,", 53.

35. Little, *The Mende of Sierra Leone,* 233.

36. A. Abraham, "'Cannibalism' and African Historiography," in *Topics in Sierra Leone History: A Counter-Colonial Interpretation* (Freetown, 1976), 12 6.

37. Ibid., 128–29.

38. Gittens, *Mende Religion,* 133.

39. Richards, "Natural Symbols and Natural History," 147.

40. Etta Donner, *Hinterland Liberia,* trans. W. M. Dean (London and Glasgow, 1939), 174.

41. Ibid., 176.

42. Jackson, *Paths Towards a Clearing,* 103.

43. Ibid., 101.

44. S. L. Archives, Native Affairs 382/1889, Gbannah Will Caulker to Governor, 7 Dec. 1889, in Kalous, *Cannibals and Tongo Players,* 50.

45. S. L. Archives, Native Affairs 435/1890, in Kalous, *Cannibals and Tongo Players,* 51.

46. Berry, "The Sierra Leone Cannibals," 51.

47. Mary Douglas, *Purity and Danger* (1966; reprint, New York, 1979), 121.

48. Roberts, "'Like a Roaring Lion," 68.

49. Schneider, "Male-Female Conflict," passim.

50. Okri, *Infinite Riches,* 112.

51. Jackson, *Paths Towards a Clearing,* 114

11

SYMBOLIC MONEY

Everything will have its price
grass and the very earth itself..

The Fipa prophet, Kaswa[1]

In Africa as elsewhere, money has acquired a symbolic meaning that has often been invisible in conventional economic histories, but that is as much a part of the African past as, for instance, groundnut exports. It is part of a cognitive world often undervalued or ignored. This chapter explores three allied motifs—vanishing money, dangerous money (that is, ill-gotten money that brings only misfortune), and the lethal money acquired through blood magic. The first two are symbolic modes of expression, each of which embodies a particular view of moral economy. The belief in money magic, however, like myths of vampires or shapeshifters, is part of the poetics of rumor, and is enormously widespread in postcolonial Africa.

Vanishing money is introduced through examples drawn mainly though not exclusively from West Africa, especially Nigeria and Ghana (which also provide the case studies for blood or money magic.) The second motif—dangerous money— is developed in terms of a Luo (Kenya) example, and the expression is a translation of a Luo one. There are also arresting parallels with Taussig's work in Latin America.

Vanishing Money

A legend current among the black poor of rural Columbia suggests that at a child's baptism, a godparent can have a peso bill surreptitiously baptized instead. The money acquires a life—and name—of its own and returns to the godparent with many other peso bills, which vanish from their owner's possession.[2] In the 1990s, Ghanaian women traders told strikingly similar stories about "a satanic banknote which, once put into the purse, starts to steal the owner's personal money in a spiritual way until not one cedi is left."[3]

In a sense, the tendency of money to vanish is a human universal. A major recent study of international finance begins with a humorous quatrain:

> That money talks
> I'll not deny
> I heard it once:
> It said "Goodbye."[4]

In Africa, symbolic statements about vanishing money give poignant expression to the pain of poverty. They are found, in varying forms, in widely separated geographic areas, over a time span of a century. In the early colonial situation, these images reflected the extreme difficulty of acquiring cash and the burdensome demands of tax collectors. In the 1930s, an Igbo village group summarized its own history as "a series of public disasters of the greatest magnitude"—foreign conquest, the influenza pandemic, forced labor, taxation.[5] Taxation was a disaster because so little was given in return and because money was so difficult to obtain, and men left home as labor migrants, or sold food that their families needed. Early this century, the Mbulu of Tanganyika believed that a rupee must be placed on a stone or it would sink into the ground.[6]

In colonial and postcolonial Africa, money acquired an overwhelming importance. Villagers and city dwellers alike are driven by the need for a cash income—to pay school fees, and to acquire necessities such as clothes, and kerosene, and, often, food. Wealth in people has come to depend on wealth in money. Schmoll writes of the Hausa of Niger, "A man cannot get or keep a wife without money. One cannot even court a woman without money. . . . [C]urrency is gradually replacing goods in kind . . . as the standard and preferred gift."[7]

In contemporary Africa, the myth of vanishing money continues to mirror the dilemmas of the poor, and now, also, of salaried professionals.

Rampant inflation, recurrent devaluations, falls in the prices of primary produce, and the frequent collapses of banks have all had the effect of making money vanish. It is experienced not as a matter for jocular regret, but as a catastrophe.

Vanishing money is contrasted with the security offered by land, and the food grown on it. The Haya point out that one who sells land "doesn't have anything to eat. This is the foolishness of money. You think you've got a profit but it just finishes. Even 100,000 shillings, after a while you just eat it and it is gone."[8] The Tshidi (Tswana) of South Africa, former pastoralists, make the same point. "Money runs through your pockets and leaves you hungry. Cattle always return to make you fat." But they live in a world where few now own cattle. "Money has eaten our beasts."[9]

As in the story of the baptized peso, money often vanishes because of occult forces. Its disappearance is frequently attributed to the malice of a witch, seen in this context as a woman, a form of gender-based scapegoating, a theme to which we return in the next chapter. The cannibal witch devours the life force of a victim. In a world where the cash nexus has become all-important, the witch devours prosperity, often from ill will rather than avarice. In the Gold Coast, later Ghana, in the 1950s, it was said, "It is only in conversation with semi-educated people that the idea arises of her benefitting materially."[10]

A woman who sought help at a Ghanaian anti-witchcraft shrine in the 1950s had internalized these stereotypes:

> She took away her first husband's prosperity and made him impotent. . . . She killed her uncle and another relative. . . . She spoiled the local diamond industry. . . . A key belonging to her mother she often took with her when she flew to steal away the luck or money of any victim.[11]

Vanishing money was the most frequent complaint made at the shrine.

> "My hand has become a sieve. Money does not stay with me; it becomes disorderly and I do not know how it goes." A workman came saying that he earned very high wages but witches had made his hand into a sieve and every week the money "got finished" with nothing to show for it, and he remained in poverty.[12]

The hand that becomes a sieve is a recurrent metaphor.

> A poor man, needy and forlorn, was told by a juju man that the witches in the family had perforated his pockets, so that any coin that was dropped in was sure to vanish miraculously. . . . A man was told by a fetish priest that a witch took

him to a place where she perforated his hands which thus became something like a sieve, letting all his money slip through and impoverishing him.[13]

Significantly, in Osei-Poku's 1989 novel *Blood for Money,* the victim is a well-educated professional man.

> Amma Prekese . . . had recently returned from a shrine where she admitted that every night she set whatever fortunes her brothers had on fire. . . . Even though he earned a high salary as a senior lecturer . . . and as a private consultant . . . he had no savings and had not managed to buy even a single shirt within the past four years.[14]

These beliefs are not peculiar to Ghana. In an account by an Igbo Catholic, vanishing money is the work of evil spirits. "There is today a common complaint of people missing their money. . . . Even if the money is safely kept out of reach of everybody, the whole is found less than the total."[15] In Niger, money which vanishes mysteriously is called wind money, *kudin iska.*[16]

A man in Togo became a devotee of Mami Wata because "his money 'seems to slip through his fingers.'"[17] But a narrative from the Niger Delta suggests that the money she provides will vanish in its turn.

> My grandmother told me some time ago that once she encountered Mami Wata and was given one manilla as a present. She was also given some instructions to observe. She returned home and prepared a part of her room, kept the manilla on a decent furnished table with seven burning candles. At night she discovered that the manilla had miraculously increased into hundreds of manillas. . . . She invited my grandfather to the scene. . . . No sooner had my grandfather appeared, the manillas disappeared. . . . She.wept bitterly for the great loss.[18]

Vanishing money is a motif in Babarinsa's novel *Anything for Money,* set in Nigeria. The currency apparently created by money magic has actually vanished elsewhere.

> [T]he head has great powers. It mystically draws money from here and there. There are large sums that simply go missing . . . small sums of cash that we think we have misplaced but never see again."[19]

Money acquired by magic has its own tendency to vanish. "The sum realized . . . continuously and mystically halved hour by hour until the money changed hands."[20]

Dangerous Money

Vanishing money disappears either because it has been stolen by occult means, or because it has been obtained in forbidden ways, such as blood magic. Money obtained in morally unacceptable ways will prove not only useless but dangerous.

Poor peasants in Colombia believe that a pact can be made with the Devil, in return for greater productivity, hence higher wages. But "these wages are inherently barren: the land will become sterile, and the animals will not thrive and will die."[21] The Faustian pact applies to wage labor, such as cutting sugar cane, and not to peasant cultivation or to work on other peasant plots. "[S]uch a practice would damage the peasant plot and . . . the money gained could not be used to maintain equipment or land."[22] For this reason, the money can only be spent on consumables. Only men are thought to make a pact of this kind. "Since the 'wages of the devil' are inherently destructive and barren, and since women assume almost all the obligation of raising children, it would be devastatingly counter-productive for them to raise a family with such money."[23] One who makes such a pact dies prematurely.

This account of the dangerous nature of money obtained in morally unacceptable ways has many parallels in Africa. In 1983, survivors of the 1949–50 Malawi famine related that "the goats sold by famine victims changed into snakes when taken home by their new owners."[24] Profits won from the plight of the starving are deadly.

Gambian Muslims believe that charitable gifts or a pilgrimage financed by money gained as interest will yield no spiritual fruit. Usury will lead, indeed, to a sinister form of consumption, and one who "eats" it will end up food for vultures.[25]

Shipton has analyzed the concept of *Pesa Makech* among the Luo of western Kenya. *Pesa* means money, and English speaking Luo translate *makech* as bitter, but it can also mean evil or dangerous.[26] Pesa Makech takes many different forms, among them the proceeds of crime, lottery winnings, or money found by chance. It also includes money obtained through the sale of "land, gold, tobacco, and cannabis—a list to which many add the homestead rooster."[27] The ancestors disapprove of the sale of land, and animals purchased in this way die; if money from land sales is used for bridewealth, the bride will die. The rooster is symbolically linked with the homestead and male identity. Tobacco and cannabis were traditionally cultivated at abandoned homesteads, where ancestors are buried.

Pesa Makech causes sterility or death to people and animals, and is dangerous and useless unless ritually cleansed—the fact that this is possible suggests a certain ambivalence. Women's earnings from distilling, prostitution, or smuggling are not viewed as Pesa Makech. Money from the sale of sugar cane and cotton is not bitter—so the concept is not simply a response to foreign exploitation (nor indeed would this explain some variables, such as roosters). No single explanation fits all the facts, but the concept of bitter or dangerous money clearly implies that moral concepts—largely rooted in respect for the past—are more important than profit.

Money obtained in morally unacceptable ways will lead only to disaster. However desirable it may be, it should not be pursued at any cost. These myths are essays in moral economy, articulated in symbolic terms.

Lethal Money

In Zambia and Zimbabwe in the 1990s, urban legends have been recorded that are strikingly similar to West African stories of vampire cowries. According to a report in the Zambian press,

> The talk among Livingstone residents was that the stolen children were being thrown into the sea along the Namibian coast to attract sea animals suspected to have swallowed some diamonds. Once the animals resurface from the sea they are shot at. There was also the story that the children were being transported to the Middle East and Europe where they were been sold for US$30,000.[28]

And Luise White writes that in Harare border crossings are said to be

> places where entrepreneurs can exchange the heads of abducted children . . . for some pretty precious commodities like Kombis. The heads are then sold to South Africans who use them as bait to attract fish who have swallowed gemstones. I asked people how come they couldn't get gems out of the ground. I was told that mine owners got all that, the only way for ordinary people to get gems was to fish with heads.[29]

These mysterious stories of marine creatures who swallow diamonds and can be lured only with human bait represent a (clearly mythical) form of money magic, and condemn those who seek wealth at a human cost.

Money or blood magic is a dominant motif in the poetics of rumor in contemporary Africa. It is a recurrent theme in the African press, and provides an explanation for the immense power and wealth a small minority have acquired in the postcolonial situation. Its hold over the popular imagination is reflected in its prominence in contemporary West African fiction. In some versions, the protagonist, like the witch, grows rich when he makes an astral sacrifice of a loved member of his family; in others, hired assassins murder the powerless—often, children—to acquire human body parts to use in rituals that produce actual currency. As with vampire cowries, the human body is commodified and money is alive and feeds on people. In both creative literature and the poetics of rumor, money magic invariably leads those who practice it to ruin. Accounts of it are moral fables denouncing those who sacrifice people to things and foretelling their inevitable downfall.

Money magic differs from earlier forms of sacrifice in that it has parted company both with communal ritual and with the sacred, and become a form of commercial and even industrial transaction. Many sources refer to "human spare parts," an analogy with the motor trade, and a classic example of the commodified body. "The world has now got to a stage where many people believe that the surest way to make money is to kill. Haven't you heard of human spare parts on sale in some parts of the world, Ghana included?"[30] Money magic requires "spare parts" and a technical expert (a sorcerer). Ironically, human spare parts abound, while spare motor parts are unobtainable. The very fragmentation of the body is profoundly dehumanizing, and a fragmented human body symbolizes a divided body politic. Once more, social dangers are expressed in terms of threats to the individual.

These rumors reflect a widespread and deeply held perception of corruption and ill-gotten wealth, which is contrasted with the sufferings of the poor. In a fictional account from Kenya, published in 1982,

> Mwaura was one of those who worshipped at the shrine of the god of money. He used to say that there was no universe he would not visit . . . no crime that he would not commit in loyal obedience to the molten god of money. . . . Mwaura would tell people, "This money that has been brought here by Europeans is wholly evil. . . . As for me, I would sell my own mother if I thought she would fetch a good price." People used to think that this was the idle boast of a light-hearted businessman. Only one man knew that Mwaura never joked where money was concerned, but he never came back to tell the tale.[31]

Stories of money magic articulate a subversive commentary on the greed and power lust of Big Men. They have, understandably, been little studied by academics.[32] Here, from an abundance of material, I have chosen two case studies. The account that follows is based on both the ethnographic and the literary source material for Ghana and Nigeria.

Money Magic in Postcolonial Nigeria

A belief in the existence of blood or money magic was already well established when a psychiatrist carried out research in four Yoruba cities in 1961–62.[33] In a paper published in 1982, Barber, a specialist in Yoruba oral literature, wrote:

> It is widely believed that there are people who abduct children—in one version by turning them into goats—confine them in a secret room, make medicine from their blood, and then by uttering the right incantations, cause unlimited quantities of naira to shower down into a calabash placed on the child's head."[34]

Matory, an ethnographer who carried out fieldwork in Yorubaland in the 1980s, described in a 1993 study

> a ritual complex, reported by respected Nigerian newspapers and television stations, in which women are murdered and their excised vulvas, breasts, and heads are used in money making magic. . . . An alternative technology requires the juxtaposition of the victim's head with a calabash. . . . When the descriptive poetry (*oriki*) of money or of the victim is spoken, money comes out of the calabash or the victim's mouth. Some rural people believe these atrocities to be common among urban elites— "the rich Alhajis, Alhajiyas, and ministers" whose mansions are full of bodies.[35]

One of these texts identifies the victims as children, and one as women. The association of blood magic with Muslims is significant, and has parallels in other sources. In the colonial era and during the First Republic, "the North" was perceived, by southerners and colonial officials alike, as "traditional." Southerners saw the North as "backward," the South as "progressive." It is now the North that is linked with wealth and power, and urban legends reflect southern perceptions of northern domination of government and its financial rewards.

The belief in blood or money magic is not, of course, peculiar to the Yoruba. In 1982, the Nigerian novelist, Amadi, who comes from the northern edge of the Niger Delta, noted in a non-fictional context:

This class of murders is committed by people who use parts of the human body for rituals aimed at making them richer, stronger, healthier, longer-lived, invulnerable to bullets and other weapons, or merely to absolve them from abominations that they may have committed.[36]

Ludwar-Ene has described the belief in money magic in Calabar, where it is called *unam okuk* ("meat of money").[37] In some Igbo communities, new rituals have been introduced in the quest for protection against it.[38]

Frank has analyzed the way in which older beliefs in exchanges with water spirits have grown into a belief in money magic among the Ron of central Nigeria, a good example of the way in which community rituals are thought to be replaced by the cruel anti-social magic of individuals. In the past, it was acceptable for women, acting collectively, to seek magic seeds from water spirits to improve the harvest, if hunger threatened. But if an individual stole from the spirits, they would demand a high price or kill the thief. Now it is thought that one can obtain money from the water spirits, and place it in a box that becomes full of money. For a small sum, an animal sacrifice is required, and for a large one, a human being; the spirits would use the human body parts provided for magical purposes. If no victim is forthcoming, the sorcerer's own life or that of his or her child is forfeit.[39]

The notorious longevity of some of Africa's politicians—which contrasts with the short lives of many of their subjects—has often been attributed to occult powers obtained through human sacrifice. But popular stories of money magic suggest that the perpetrator does not live to be old.[40]

In 1982, two Nigerian novels dealing with money magic appeared— Emecheta's *Naira Power* and Oyegoke's *Cowrie Tears*. A third, Akinbolu Babarinsa's *Anything for Money,* was published three years later.

In *Cowrie Tears,* set in a western Nigerian city in c.1980, the hero experiments with religio-magical techniques to escape from poverty. At the instigation of his (suddenly rich) girl friend, he consults a sorcerer who tells him about various forms of money magic—the most profitable requires a human head."[41] He buys what he believes to be a newly decapitated human head, in a parcel, but throws himself to his death from a bridge to escape being searched at a police road block. The head proves to be that of a goat, minus its horns.[42] His friend, who becomes rich suddenly and mysteriously, dies of cholera on the pilgrimage to Mecca.[43]

Emecheta's *Naira Power* is set in the Muslim Hausa community in Lagos, and makes several references to blood magic.

[It] was the time of that big scandal concerning Baleodo, the politician. . . . Baleodo involved himself in all sorts of terrible practices, including ritual killings, to win the election. The whole business was made public in the end—he lost the election. It cost him seven male heads obtained from ritual murders and well over a hundred thousand naira.[44]

Baleodo's crimes come to light and he is hanged. The novel's protagonist, Ramonu, becomes a rich drug smuggler; he is caught in a vehicle with five human heads in it—"he was to sell the heads for the get-rich business people we have in our country."[45] He escapes from prison, but is later burnt to death by a lynch mob as a pickpocket —a crime of which he is innocent.[46]

In Akinbolu Babanrinsa's novel *Anything for Money,* it is a Lagos magistrate, Kadara, who practices money magic, using a head obtained in a car accident, which vomits money after appropriate incantations. Again, this leads only to disaster: the head (in a box) falls into the hands of robbers, and Kadara makes desperate attempts to recover it. Finally, in his panic, he falls to his death from a tall building. Ironically, the box had been exchanged for another, which contained nothing of importance.

Money magic in Ghana

In Field's 1940 study of the Ga, she described a form of money magic based on the idea of life as a zero-sum game. The witch would "'suck' out the essence" of a sum of money, the victim would have that sum mulcted from him in fines or expenses and the owner of the charm would have a windfall of the same sum.

> He must not "eat" (enjoy or spend) any of this windfall, but must treat it as capital and invest or trade with it. With its profits he must be generous. . . . If he were to "eat" any of the original twenty pounds "sucked" from the stranger, he would become an *obeyefo* (a killer—witch who cannot stop killing) and would have to join flesh-feasting bands of other wicked killers.[47]

Although the charm is an astral form of theft, the "good" use of the proceeds avoids the absolute evil of witchcraft.

By 1961, the poetics of rumor linked money magic with the (astral) sacrifice of the living. These charms were thought to be purchased in Nzima, a remote coastal area in western Ghana, and were called Nzima-bayi. The one involved must name the one he loves best, who dies mysteriously. The protagonist also pays a price in his own body, for instance, a chronic ulcer. In return, he acquires a magic snake, which must be fed regularly and secretly, and will vomit money. Money acquired in this way must not be spent for three years. The pact maker dies prematurely, his years determined by the number of grains eaten by a fowl during the initial ritual. Nzima informants agreed that they sold charms but indignantly rejected the suggestion that human sacrifice was involved.[48]

A book by a Ghanaian author, published in 1982, referring specifically to the Akan, goes into considerable detail about the acquisition of wealth through sorcery and about the moral geography linking witchcraft with distant places.

> [M]ost of those who purchase it do so with the sole aim of amassing wealth with it. And such is the greed of some traders that they travel to as far away as Niamey in Guinea to buy witch-spirits to help them in their trading business. . . . Among the many clients of this oracle are politicians seeking political power, civil servants seeking promotions, and money-hungry traders.[49]

Those who cannot afford this journey go to Togo, Nzima or to northern Ghana—another supernatural version of long-distance trade.

In 1995, a study of witchcraft among the Ewe of southern Ghana documented the transition from the belief in astral cannibalism to urban legends of money magic.[50]

> People who want to get rich quickly will consult a priest in the countryside. However they will achieve the desired wealth only in exchange for a blood relation, their spouse, their fertility or a part of their own body. . . . [A] lot of money can be gained only by sacrificing a beloved, closely related person.[51]

Osei-Poku's novel *Blood for Money,* published in Ghana in 1989, offers a fascinating contrast to its Nigerian counterparts. When Diawuo is still hesitating about money magic, he speaks with Ansah, who has already taken the plunge. They discuss the relative merits of wealth in people and wealth in things.

> "Diawuo, you are making a serious mistake. In this world nothing can be substituted for riches. Have you forgotten the Akan proverb that no rich man is ever lonely . . . ?"
>
> "But isn't it true that if you have people, you can be sure of assistance should the need arise?" Diawuo demanded.
>
> "Perhaps that was true in Ghana when Peugeot 404 estates plying Accra-Kumasi road were appropriately nicknamed one-pound-one-pound."[52]

Diawuo's history encapsulates the tragedy of many Ghanaians in real life. He does well at school, but cannot continue with his studies for lack of financial support. He becomes a skilled furniture maker, but finds that he cannot compete with large firms. His first wife trades in yams, but loses much of her stock in a lorry accident. He marries a second wife because of her financial resources, but she does not respect him, because of his poverty. It is part of the tragic irony of the novel that neither Diawuo nor Ansah, a skilled mechanic, is destitute.

Diawuo follows Ansah's example, sacrifices his wife by astral means, and is given magical snakes that regularly manufacture a large amount of paper money. Like Ansah, he invests his capital and becomes a successful businessman. But he has only three years to live (since only three grains were consumed by the cock). Both men are haunted by the ghost of a dead wife. When the time of his death is near, Diawuo kills himself and Ansah.

Like *Cowrie Tears* and *Anything for Money*, the novel is a moral fable; its message is that the promise of wealth through magic leads only to destruction. In these stories, those who make these sinister pacts are not witches or sorcerers. The sorcerer is essentially a technical adviser who provides detailed instructions about the techniques of money magic. Diauwo is as much victim as villain; crucial pieces of information—the shortening of his own life and the fact that his dead wife would haunt him—are withheld from him. His friend urges him to practice money magic because he wants a companion in misery.

There are comparable fictional accounts of money and blood magic elsewhere in Africa.

Rumor and Event

Rumors of money magic often lead to mob violence. The murder of a child groundnut seller, supposedly as a ritual victim, led to riots in Owerri, Nigeria, in 1996. The alleged killer died mysteriously in prison soon after his arrest.[53]

African vampire stories are True Fictions, essentially statements about social relations. Is this also true of money magic, or have the abstract concepts of witchcraft been translated into practice? Have signs become reality? As with leopard men, the evidence is ambiguous and differently interpreted.

As folklorists point out, modern urban legends in the United States, such as stories of alligators in New York sewers, are related as if true, with an accretion of believable detail. Sanderson says of Western urban legends about cars, "They are almost invariably told for true, and they are supplied with such supporting credentials as details of places, names and dates."[54] An illuminating comparison has been made between money magic stories in Africa and (baseless) rumors, both in Britain and North America, of children sacrificed in Satanic rituals.[55] The West African press carries detailed accounts of ritual sacrifices, with names of both victims and killers and, on occasion, photographs. But there are equally specific and detailed narratives about ghosts who return to earth and acquire a new spouse.[56]

We have seen how the Nzima people, while agreeing that they sold charms, were horrified by the suggestion that loss of life was involved. The diviners of Douala saw themselves as healers, doing battle with evil sorcerers. A Muslim Temne diviner believed that blood magic existed, but was the work of ritual specialists from abroad. "Some come from Guinea, some from other countries. This work, I don't want it. It's the money of Hell.[57] Like cannibalism, blood or money magic is attributed to those far away. Is money magic merely a motif in the poetics of rumor, or has it also entered the realm of social history? This is a book about the history of ideas; on the ontological reality of money magic—or of murderous leopard men—I am inclined to the Scottish verdict of Not Proven.

This account does not, of course, exhaust symbolic accounts of money. There is an extensive discourse on indebtedness—Anansi, the Akan Trickster, brings debt into the world and "the Ashanti say that what joins them together, makes them Ashanti, is debt."[58] Much popular imagery utilizes new forms of ancient metaphors of improper consumption—"chopping bribes"—a theme to which we return in a later chapter.

Notes

1. R. Willis, "Kaswa: Oral Traditions of a Fipa Prophet," *Africa* (1970): 253.

2. M. Taussig, "The Genesis of Capitalism Amongst a South American Peasantry: Devil's Labour and the Baptism of Money," *Comparative Studies in Society and History* (1977): 137–38 .

3. B. Meyer, "Delivered from the Powers of Darkness: Confessions of Satanic Riches in Christian Ghana," *Africa* (1995): 238.

4. A. Leyshon, and N. Thrift, *Money/Space, Geographies of Monetary Transformation* (London and New York, 1997), epigraph, quoting Richard Armour.

5. National Archives, Nigeria, Enugu. CSO 26/211, Clark, Intelligence Report on Nkanu (North) Villages of Udi Division (1932), 5.

6. J. Iliffe, *The African Poor: A History* (Cambridge, 1987), 154.

7. P. Schmoll, "Black Stomachs, Beautiful Stones," in J. and J. Comaroff, *Modernity and Its Malcontents* (Chicago and London, 1993), 197.

8. B. Weiss, *The Making and Unmaking of the Haya Lived World* (Durham and London, 1996), 136–37.

9. J. and J. L. Comaroff, "Goodly Beasts, Beastly Goods: Cattle and Commodities in a South African Context," *American Ethnologist* (1990): 209–11.

10. H. Debrunner, *Witchcraft in Ghana,* 2nd ed. (Accra, 1961), 182.

11. M. Field, *Search for Security: An Ethno-Psychiatric Study of Rural Ghana* (London, 1960), 262–63.

12. Field, *Search for Security,* 109–10.

13. Debrunner, *Witchcraft in Ghana,* 40.

14. K. Osei-Poku, *Blood for Money* (Accra, 1989), 6.

15. Luke M. Odinkemelu, *The Problem of Mammy Water: Mammy Water in the Society* (Nigeria, 1988), 34.

16. Schmoll, "Black Stomachs, Beautiful Stones," 198.

17. S. L. Kasfir, review of *"Mami Wata, Der Geist der Weissen Frau"* (film by T. Wendl and D. Weise, Göttingen, 1988), *African Arts* (1994): 81.

18. John Obele (b. 1942) of Eleme, in June, 1972. (I owe this source to David Dorward).

19. Akinbolu Babanrinsa, *Anything for Money* (London and Basingstoke, 1985), 28.

20. Ibid., 83.

21. M. T. Taussig, *The Devil and Commodity Fetishism in South America* (Chapel Hill, NC, 1980), 13.

22. Taussig, "The Genesis of Capitalism," 136.

23. Ibid., 136–37 n.7.

24. Megan Vaughan, *The Story of an African Famine* (Cambridge, 1987), viii.

25. P. Shipton, *Bitter Money: Cultural Economy and Some African Meanings of Forbidden Commodities* (Washington, 1989), 72–3.

26. Ibid., 28. Shipton's study is the source for the account that follows.

27. Ibid., 28.

28. Moses Bwalya, "Child Abductor Arrested," *The Post* (Zambia), 26 Oct. 1995 (no. 330). (I owe this reference to Owen Sichone).

29. Luise White, e-mail communication, 26 Oct. 1995.

30. Osei-Poku, *Blood for Money,* 67.

31. Ngugi wa Thiong'o, *Devil on the Cross* (London, 1982), 32–3.

32. But cf. M. Bastian, "My Head Was Too Strong! Body Parts and Money Magic in Nigerian Popular Discourse" (unpublished ms.) and the articles by Frank and Ludwar-Ene cited below.

33. R. Prince, "Indigenous Yoruba Psychiatry," in Ari Kiev (ed.), *Magic, Faith and Healing* (New York, 1964), 89.

34. K. Barber, "Popular Reactions to the Petro-Naira," *Journal of Modern African Studies* (1982): 438.

35. J. L. Matory, "Government by Seduction: History and the Tropes of 'Mounting' in Oyo-Yoruba Religion," in J. and J. Comaroff, *Modernity and Its Malcontents,* 81. This passage occurs in the context of a very valuable discussion of changing gender roles.

36. Elechi Amadi, *Ethics in Nigerian Culture* (Ibadan, 1982), 19.

37. G. Ludwar-Ene, "Explanatory and Remedial Modalities for Personal Misfortune in a West African Society with Special Reference to Witchcraft," *Anthropos* (1986): 558.

38. N. Onwu, "Igbo Religion: Its Present Situation," *Africana Marburgensia* (1985): 27.

39. B. Frank, "Permitted and Prohibited Wealth: Commodity Possessing Spirits, Economic Morals and the Goddess Mami Wata in West Africa," *Ethnology* (1995): 335–36, 339.

40. Barber, "Popular Reactions to the Petro-Naira," 443 n.1.

41. L. Oyegoke, *Cowrie Tears* (Harlow, 1982), 169.

42. Ibid., 187ff.

43. Ibid., 155.

44. Buchi Emecheta, *Naira Power* (London and Basingstoke, 1982) 87. A Western Igbo, she grew up in Lagos, and has lived for many years in England. According to the cover of this book, she "pays regular and long visits to Nigeria."

45. Ibid., 92.

46. Ibid., 12–14, 107.

47. M. Field, *Social Organization of the Ga People* (London, 1940), 218 n.1, 219.

48. Debrunner, *Witchcraft in Ghana* 182–88.

49. G. Bannerman-Richter, *The Practice of Witchcraft in Ghana* (Winona, MN, 1982), 40.

50. B. Meyer, "'If you are a Devil, you are a witch and if you are a witch, you are a devil': The Integration of 'Pagan' Ideas into the Conceptual Universe of Ewe Christians in Southeastern Ghana," *Journal of Religion in Africa* (1992): 117–18.

51. B. Meyer. "'Delivered from the Powers of Darkness': Confessions of Satanic Riches in Christian Ghana," *Africa* (1995): 240.

52. Osei-Poku, *Blood for Money,* 9.

53. Taye Ige, "For the Love of Money," *The Month* (Lagos) 14 Oct. 1996. I owe this source to Misty Bastian.

54. S. Sanderson, "The Folklore of the Motor-car," *Folklore* (1969): 248.

55. J. Comaroff, "Consuming Passions: Child Abuse, Fetishism, and 'The New World Order,'" *Culture* (1997): 13–15.

56. Sam Sarpong, "Ghana: Human Ghosts: Fact or Fiction?" *Africanews,* 15 June 1997 (electronic bulletin, Koinonia Media Centre, Nairobi).

57. R. Shaw, "The Politician and the Diviner: Divination and the Consumption of Power in Sierra Leone," *Journal of Religion in Africa* (1996): 39.

58. C. Vecsey, "The Exception who Proves the Rules: Ananse the Akan Trickster," *Journal of Religion in Africa* (1981): 171.

12

DANGEROUS WOMEN IN AN AGE OF AIDS

> "Do you not know that the Angolan woman is the worst witch in the world? If you look carefully into the eyes of most Angolan women you will see that they resemble the devil."
>
> Carlito in S Jamba, *Patriots* (1990)[1]

In some contexts, as we have seen, the cash nexus has shaped new concepts of the witch as a zombie-owning entrepreneur, or as the consumer of prosperity, rather than of life force. The same pressures, however, can also lead to the supposed expansion of witchcraft seen as astral cannibalism. This has been studied among the Hausa of Niger, where witchcraft is thought to be a physical substance in the body, shining stones, which are alive. Inherited from a parent, they increase and multiply, and clamor to be fed on life force (hence astral cannibalism). It is thought that these stones can now also be purchased, with the result that witchcraft has expanded enormously. The motive for acquiring them is thought to be jealousy of another's prosperity.[2]

> It's you [the whites] who provoked this! [The problem] is that nowadays men and women, old and young, everyone wants to get rich. . . . When I say that soul-eating has spread in the last forty years it's because today there are few people who respect their heritage. . . .[3]

The concept of the witch as astral cannibal is gender-specific in some ethno-linguistic groups, but not in others. Akiga Sai, writing of the Tiv, described the mbtsav as "old men and women."[4] Esther Goody, writing in 1970 of Gonja, in northern Ghana, analyzed a distinction between the legitimate male sorcery of political authority and the illegitimate witchcraft of individual women, who practice astral cannibalism and repay flesh debts with the lives of their relations. "Both men and women may seek and obtain witchcraft powers. But . . . it is women, mostly old women . . . who are the witches who kill." Men are thought to use their occult powers to discern harmful (female) witches and protect others from them.[5] Traditionally, a woman witch was executed in one of several cruel ways that included a grisly piece of gender-specific symbolism, placing a red-hot cooking pot over her head.[6] Gottlieb, writing in 1989 of the Beng of Ivory Coast, described a not dissimilar situation.[7] There is a contrast between the abhorrent witchcraft of individual women and the socially sanctioned witchcraft of authority.

Castrating Witches and Plastic Wombs

The image of the woman as witch and sexually voracious predator is particularly well documented among the Yoruba. In the southwest, members of the Gelede mask society, men dressed as women dance to appease witches. Their invocations are a vivid example of the image of the castrating female.

> Mother whose vagina causes fear to all.
> Mother whose pubic hair bundles up in knots.
> Mother who set a trap, set a trap. . . .[8]

(*Aje* is Yoruba for witch, but the word is avoided, hence the euphemism.) Men tend to join Gelede because of reproductive or sexual problems. They praise the witches as rulers of the world.

In a widely cited paper, "Radical Yoruba Sexuality: The Witch and the Prostitute,"[9] Hoch-Smith explores the way in which gender is depicted in Yoruba plays. In *Sisi Onigarawa,* (*Sixpence Owner of a Suitcase)*, an unsophisticated man is defrauded of his pension by his grasping wife, who feigns pregnancy with a calalabash, the witch's amalgam of greed and infertility. In *Onimoto* (*Car Owner*) a young man acquires a charm from an old witch that makes him rich through fraud. She steals his money and he goes mad.[10]

The fear of witchcraft—and especially the witchcraft of the poor, and of older women—is also deeply embedded in Igbo societies. In 1975, a Western Igbo secondary school teacher explained to me:

> We believe in witchcraft everywhere in Ubulu-Uku and the whole of Aniocha and Ika Divisions. It is believed that witchcraft causes infant mortality, premature death and misfortune. The majority of women are witches. It is believed that the witches "eat" human beings. It is the victim's soul which is stolen and "eaten" and not the physical body itself. They have a gathering. . . . However it is only the witch's soul which attends. . . . In some cases they confess to their crimes. They will admit that they were responsible for killing members of their own family, even their own children whom they love.

This school teacher told me of a male friend who became a witch himself to protect his children, because his wife was killing them (in other words, she was blamed for the tragedy of recurrent infant mortality).

The Ebirra of central Nigeria say, "God made things double; masquerading for men and witchcraft for women."[11] A profound antagonism between the female witch and the anonymous male collectivity of the masking cult is also widely documented elsewhere.

At the Ghanaian anti-witchcraft shrine that Field studied in the mid 1950s, many supplicants complained of childlessness.

> Most commonly the deity diagnoses witchcraft. The witches have stolen away the supplicant's womb or penis—that is the spiritual counterpart of the organ—and have either eaten it (in which case there is no hope) or broken it in pieces, or hidden it in a river.[12]

A Ghanaian author wrote in 1982:

> [F]emale witches are believed to outnumber the males by a wide margin. . . . The commonest human ethereal anatomical parts which witches like to remove are the genitalia . . witches relish human blood. . . .[13]

Since the genitalia are often listed among the human "spare parts" money magic requires, this new form of collective nightmare fits readily into older concepts of the witch as a destroyer of sexual and reproductive powers. In West Africa, in the 1980s and 1990s, recurrent bouts of popular hysteria reflected a fear of castration through witchcraft.

> Residents in Accra . . . recall a similar scare in the early 1980s. They attributed that country's crisis to the fact that genitals are used in certain voodoo

rituals. . . . The scare spread from Accra to country towns and then sub-
sided.[14]

Early in 1997, a dozen lynchings were reported.

"Panic, drama in Accra as men with alleged mystic powers hit the streets,"
screamed the front page of the state-owned *Daily Graphic.* "Seal of Satan
Reaches Accra," declared its sister paper, *the Ghanaian Times.*[15]

By March, the hysteria had spread to Abidjan in Ivory Coast, where
the accused were burnt alive. There have been similar outbreaks of hysteria
and lynchings in Nigeria.

In these scares, both the alleged perpetrators and the supposed victims
could be either male or female. Witches endanger women's fertility as well as
men's virility. In Calabar, in Nigeria, seers in prophetic churches warn of witches
who turn wombs into plastic bags. This modern metaphor for infertility is a
recurrent one, and is yet another variant on the theme of the commodified
body. Money magic employs human "spare parts." Witchcraft turns fertile
wombs to unproductive plastic. "There is in our midst a pregnant woman
whose womb has been transformed into a plastic bag by an evil person."[16]
Witchcraft accusations are often shaped by age, as well as gender. A village for
those accused of witchcraft in the Mamprusi region of Ghana is called "settlement of old ladies." The inhabitants "complain of lack of food and the poor
condition of their housing. Most of them bitterly deny that they are witches."[17]

Women, Death, and the Market

Concepts of dangerous women often reflect an ancient association with the
market, which is thought to be linked with sinister supernatural forces.
Markets were often ruled by a woman official—we have noted an Oyo
example (p. 72). Nadel did research among the Nupe of Central Nigeria in
the mid 1930s and was told that in the past, the Lelu, the woman head of
the market, was thought to be a powerful witch.[18] Henderson studied the
Niger Igbo community of Onitsha between 1960 and 1962 and described
the supernatural presences in Onitsha market, which was recognized as a
women's sphere. They included a werewoman "who, it is said, still appears
in the great market . . . and entices people into it with her magic fan." At
night, witches meet in the places where women trade by day, and the market queen and her advisers turn into occult birds.[19]

Onicha market is a terrible place. A market where you can see all sorts and conditions of men. . . . I am sure that if one looks for a human head, one can easily find it in that market.[20]

A Ghanaian author writes of the witch familiars of market women, and describes an incident "when in 1979 the military regime . . . decided that the only way to relieve the congestion at the Makola Market in Accra was to drop bombs on the market." This was done, after warnings were issued.

]A] large number of witch-pets were seen scurrying round in the debris. One business executive and his wife who were at the scene said they saw mice with pierced ears and wearing gold earrings; they also saw crabs with gold necklaces dangling around their shells.[21]

It was thought that these familiars could force people to buy what they did not need, and thus waste their resources,[22] another version of vanishing money.

The recurrent linkages between witchcraft and market women have multiple roots. Their husbands may well resent their economic independence and the way in which their trading activities take them away from home. As middlemen, they are often blamed for shortages and high prices. There are, of course, more specific factors operative in any given situation. The Atinga anti-witchcraft movement reached western Nigeria in 1949–50. Its agents were the young of both sexes, its victims older women, its sponsors wealthy men.[23] Its success has been linked with resentment at the Cocoa Marketing Boards, which siphoned off much of the farmer's profit, just as the astral cannibalism of the witch siphoned off the victim's life force.

Gender Hostility: Work and Its Rewards

In precolonial African communities, work was gender-specific; the details varied in different societies, especially in the allocation of the various tasks involved in agriculture. During and after the colonial period, the old patterns of work distribution by gender were undermined by labor migration, urbanization, and cash crop cultivation. The buying and selling of land have often disturbed women's rights of usufruct. In different parts of Africa, scholars have described the way in which these changes created new tensions between men and women, which were often articulated in witchcraft accusations.

The quest for a cash income has dislocated the traditional patterns of rural life and created new forms of gender hostility. In Field's *Social Organization of the Ga People,* published in 1940, she quoted men who complained, "The women do not respect us; they have more money than we have. Money always spoils respect." Others said, "It is money that is breaking things down." "It is money that is spoiling our towns."[24]

In a different study, she recorded the case of a woman who

> said she had been resentful towards her husband because she had helped him make a farm and he had given her no share in its profits. She therefore cursed him to a river. . . .[25]

In Sierra Leone, Kono men now work as diamond miners, an activity that for most proves financially unrewarding. They rely on women to grow their food. Women are not allowed to own land and so turn to market activity, which reduces the time available for farming.[26] From a male viewpoint, this endangers the family food supplies and provides women with a threatening economic independence, and is sometimes equated with prostitution.[27] In the past, Kono women were sometimes accused of being witches and driven away. Now they are accused of deviant behavior that makes the household vulnerable to witchcraft. Witchfinders are sponsored by men; their visions are of cannibal witchcraft.

> I have seen a garden filled with witches. They held a small child. The child was dead . . . they said, "we have captured a leopard." I asked what they were going to do with the leopard and they said it would be eaten.[28]

One of the main characters in Okri's *Famished Road* sequence is a Dangerous Woman. His powerful and nuanced portrait leads us far beyond equations of the witch with absolute evil, and disentangles the complexities and ambiguities of lived experience from the polarities of such stereotypes. Madame Koto is the relatively wealthy owner of a palm wine bar. She joins the Party of the Rich, which relies on occult forces.

> They said of Madame Koto that she had buried three husbands and seven children and that she was a witch who ate her babies when they were still in her womb. They said she was the real reason why the children in the area didn't grow, why they were always ill.[29]

Later, she becomes temporarily insane, and with eloquence and insight gives her own account of her life and her predecessors, reclaiming the precedent of ancient water goddesses.

I did not eat your children in the womb of your women. . . . But yes, I sit on the head of my enemies. I take power where I find it. . . . So what if two thousand years ago, when you thought the world the size of your village and your rumors, so what if my crocodiles cried for your flesh . . . ? [The] people I have saved outnumber my enemies by five to one.[30]

Though prosperous and powerful, Madame Koto is fatally flawed, weakened by a phantom pregnancy and agonizing illness. In the end she is assassinated, by those who believe her commitment to the Party of the Rich is weakening. She is buried with pomp and splendor, amid terrifying portents. Those who attend her funeral included elite women who had once worked as prostitutes in her bar. They "determined for her an honorable funeral, because they knew that great old trees are impossible to replace."[31]

The Dangerous Woman and AIDS

The scapegoating of women takes many forms and is ever more widely documented. In 1986, *karuwai* ("prostitutes," but the terms are not identical) in the northern Nigerian city of Katsina were attacked, and their property destroyed, because they were blamed for drought.[32]

Ancient links between female sexuality, witchcraft, and death have been powerfully reinforced by AIDS, which, as a number of observers have pointed out, tends to be blamed on women. Adolescent school pupils in Rakai district in Uganda were asked to write essays on AIDS. Forty of them (out of fifty-five) thought it was primarily spread by women. "It is rumoured that it is from ladies that AIDS has spread to men in the whole world." "So far women are the main spreaders of the disease. Each woman who dies leaves ten men to follow her."[33] Weiss, writing of Buhaya in western Tanzania, notes, "despite the fact that men are engaged in the same actions as women, men are simply *susceptible* to the potential of these actions, while women are *responsible* for their consequences."[34] A Zambian newspaper carried an advertisement: "Avoid AIDS. Take Time To Know Her."[35]

From the 1930s on, many Haya women have resorted to urban prostitution in search of economic independence. Prostitution is often known as *wazi-wazi,* after the waZiba of the Haya kingdom of Kiziba. Weiss recorded a fragment of a (male) Haya conversation about a man's death from AIDS. It is a dialogue about wealth in people and in things.

"All of this trouble is because of money."

"Absolutely," my younger friend replied. "Take a young girl. If she sees those beautiful clothes and dresses do you think she can give them up? She can't!

She'll say 'If I'm going to die, let me die! She doesn't care.' A woman," continued the elder, "she thinks she's getting rich. Goodness! She's buying her grave."[36]

But a group of Ugandan village women said:

We all live in daily fear of the new disease. Women fear what their husbands may bring home. Women are innocent. They are dying for nothing. . . . I wish they would invent a drug for women's protection."[37]

Gender stereotyping is, of course, only one element in the cognitive history of AIDS.

Magical Explanations

The ways in which AIDS is transmitted are well known in Africa. In an 1889 Ugandan sample, 75% understood the medical facts and 4% attributed it to witchcraft.[38] But since Western medicine provides a detailed explanation and palliatives but no cure, AIDS has undoubtedly strengthened the role of traditional healers. Yamba gives a grim picture of a witch finder on the Zambezi, in 1994–95, who caused sixteen deaths in poison ordeals and who by injecting people with the same needle or scarifying them with the same razor may well have contributed to the spread of AIDS.[39]

Even where the physical causes are well known, witchcraft provides an answer to the otherwise insoluble problem of why some but not all of those exposed to infection succumb. The British journalist, Hooper, who wrote with remarkable honesty of his own sexual encounters in East Africa, felt it necessary to be tested eight times for AIDS, but remained unscathed.[40]

AIDS, like cannibalism or money magic, is attributed to the Other. Tanzanians believe that it came from Nairobi and Kampala. Ugandans point out that it began after the 1979 Tanzanian invasion and often associate it with Haya prostitutes, called BK (Bukoba) girls. "Slim had come across from Tanzania—the witches and sorcerers there had conjured it up as a punishment for Ugandan traders who had cheated them in the past. Not true—it had been brought by . . . the heavy field artillery from the civil war of 1979, which had released bad germs into the atmosphere."[41] The cheated individuals came from Keregbe; some who had defrauded them sought their victims out in order to repay them.[42]

Apocalypse Now

The scapegoating of women is one of many threads in the complex fabric of popular discourse about AIDS in Africa. In East Africa, where AIDS typically presents as a wasting disease, it is often called Slim. Euphemism and double entendre help to ameliorate the psychological impact of disaster. (Montaigne described the same thing among the French peasantry of his day, who called consumption a cough). But AIDS has other names in southern Uganda, such as *namuzisa,* the one who causes extinction, or *mubbi,* the robber. "In coming years the country will be dominated by animals and trees."[43]

In the cognitive history of AIDS, class looms large, as well as gender. On one of his visits to Rakai district, Hooper found the police mounting roadblocks in search of a man with a white Mercedes. He was thought to be a rich man who had AIDS, who slept with women, paid them well, and then told them of his condition. "The man didn't want to die alone."[44] The story of the man in the white Mercedes is probably an urban legend, but it is often suggested that the elite are particularly hard hit by AIDS. A teenage essayist in Rakai noted, "The money wasted on educating people who die of AIDS is regretted by their parents. Our parents weep all the time."[45]

In Africa, as elsewhere, AIDS is often surrounded with apparently bizarre rumors. In 1991, a consignment of red oranges was thrown into Durban harbor because they were thought to be injected with infected blood.[46] "Are fish eaters safe from AIDS?" asked an anxious correspondent in the Ugandan press.[47] "On a trip to Rakai . . . peasants told him [Museveni] that AIDS would go soon because they were now good: They had stopped stealing goats."[48] Some Ugandans claimed to have seen visions of the Virgin Mary, who said that AIDS was a punishment for adultery. "The sun moves this way and that. Rosaries fall from the sky."[49] One man grouped AIDS with blood magic and other themes in the poetics of rumor—"the talking tortoise, child abductions, exported skulls and genitals, trees rising from the dead."[50]

Many at risk responded with fatalism and denial. A man in a bar in Rakai said, "People were never meant to be like timber and live forever."[51]

Urban legends also grow up around other deadly diseases. In 1995, it was rumored in Kinshasa that the outbreak of Ebola in Kikwit began when a doctor operated on a woman and found and stole two diamonds in her stomach. "The gems, say many Zaireans, are the cause of the mysterious illness—there is a curse on the doctor who stole the diamonds."[52]

Infect One Infect All

Fifty-one out of the fifty-five Rakai school essays on AIDS described the infection of others, in rage and despair, as a possible response—"I did not bring the virus, why should I die alone?"[53] In the late 1980s, the director of Uganda's AIDS control program argued against informing patients when they tested positive: "he will say let me not die alone, let me use up all my money, and then he will run around spreading the disease."[54]

This response has also been documented in South Africa. As in Uganda, the spread of AIDS is inextricably linked with other aspects of recent history—in this case, with the violence and uncertainties of the last years of apartheid, and with continuing poverty. A young man said, "We thought that with the new government we could relax, study, plan a future. Now AIDS is here to give us no future. Well we'll all just get it and that's life. We're cursed; we really are the lost generation."[55]

In a study of attitudes among young Zulu in Durban, Leclerc-Madlala paints a grim picture of a society where the collective action of the Apartheid era—Pass One, Pass All—has taken a sinister form, Infect One, Infect All. "If I have HIV I can just go out and spread it to 100 people so we'll all go together. Why should they be left behind having fun if I must die?"[56] Some applied to it the concept of *ubuntu,* community. "This disease is horrible. The only good thing would be if we're all together. *Ubuntu,* we share."[57]

Leclerc-Madlala also recorded a sinister myth to the effect that intercourse with a child virgin will rid a man of AIDS. (This was thought to be a cure for syphilis in nineteeenth-century England.)[58]

> I first heard this belief in Soweto in January 1995. . . . Since then I have been told this (and the concomitant story that a small child is less likely than a teenager to carry AIDS) on at least 30 separate occasions. I have also been told (by two quite separate groups of women) that belief about the curative powers of virgins is (in Soweto at least) no more than an extension of an older belief that virgins can cure a number of ailments, most specifically coughing. . . . Both groups of women were intensely cynical about the belief.[59]

A Cuban narrative from a former slave born in 1860 described an earlier form of this myth.

> There was one type of sickness the whites picked up, a sickness of the veins and male organs. It could only be got rid of with black women; if the man who had it slept with a Negress he was cured immediately.[60]

Women are blamed for AIDS, and girl children are sacrificed in pursuit of a cure.

Plastic Teeth: a Mirror Image of AIDS

The sudden spread of AIDS led to rumors about other diseases that had arrived at the same time. In Uganda, there were rumors of "a new sickness causing welts and discolouration of the skin, and affecting all ages, including children."[61] Weiss described, in Buhaya, the phenomenon of "plastic teeth," first reported in 1987.[62] It is a mirror image of AIDS. "Plastic teeth are a kind of children's 'Slim'; but fortunately there are doctors to take care of children. We adults don't have any medicines. We just die."[63] Some Haya thought it had come from Uganda, others from milk from the herds of Rwandan immigrants.

It is believed that a failure to thrive in babies and toddlers is caused by the fact that several of their teeth are made of plastic. The cure is to extract—sometimes from beneath the gums—two or four canines or incisors, gouged out by a local specialist with a hypodermic needle or bicycle spoke. Loving parents embark on this at considerable expense; the medical dangers, and the pain inflicted, need no elaboration here.

The symbolism of "plastic teeth" is polyvalent, as Weiss's complex analysis makes clear. At one level it is a new form of ancient continent-wide anxieties about children who cut their top teeth first or are born with teeth (which is seen as a characteristic of wild animals). At another, it is one more form of symbolic representation of the commodified body, which has a peculiar poignancy in an age when the poor sell their blood and even their kidneys.

The same phenomenon—called false rather than plastic teeth and linked with "worms in the gums"—has been recorded among the Madi, on the Uganda-Sudan border. Certain milk teeth are excised with a nail or razor and the child sometimes dies.[64]

AIDS and Cognitive history

As a number of researchers have pointed out, the success of AIDS prevention programs depends on how successfully they mesh with existing cognitive worlds. The advocated use of condoms runs counter to the emphasis on fertility, a concern widely recorded among African AIDS victims. "I don't mind dying, but to die without a child means that I will have perished without trace. God will have cheated me."[65]A psychiatrist in Zambia told of "a man who already had four children but who was still distraught when he found out that AIDS would prevent him from having more children."[66]

African nations have often been slow to accept the reality of the AIDS threat because it has seemed like one more way of marginalizing both Africans and the black communities of the Diaspora, and it would be naive to suggest that it has not had this effect. Dada quotes an anonymous leaflet distributed in Britain, entitled *Conspiracy*: "AIDS-infected Africans are brought into Britain from AIDS-infested Africa (supposedly to work) to live on the dole and social security etc at our expense."[67] A leading British weekly, the *Sunday Telegraph,* carried the headline in September, 1986, "African AIDS deadly threat to Britain."[68] Tourism is Kenya's largest foreign exchange earner; reports of AIDS cut it by thirty per cent.[69]

Africans passionately resent the suggestion that AIDS originated in Africa; they particularly resent suggestions of a viral transfer from the (African) animal world, and from green monkeys in particular.

Not surprisingly, both Africans and African Americans have welcomed a theory that attributed AIDS to American experiments in viral warfare. This theory was published in a USSR weekly in 1985, and gained international currency—it was given front page coverage in a London Sunday newspaper. Some versions describe experimentation among supposedly expendable populations in Africa and Haiti. Others suggest the aim was to reduce the African population.[70] A letter to a Ugandan newspaper in 1987 suggested that Western scientists and journalists were "missionaries to prepare the ways for the New Colonisation of Africa and possibly genocide on behalf of US and Western imperialists struggling daily to put down the African people."[71] A later letter in a different Ugandan paper suggested that it was introduced by the World Health Organization in vaccines.[72] Hooper described a conversation with journalists in Uganda:

> [The] major ideas that emerged were that AIDS had emanated from America . . . that it had probably originated from a germ-warfare experiment . . . and that a lot of the Africans now being diagnosed with AIDS were . . . sick with other diseases.[73]

Research in the worst-affected part of Uganda had to be stopped because of rumors that American researchers were introducing AIDS.[74]

In the last years of apartheid, South African whites sometimes did suggest that AIDS was a remedy for overpopulation, producing a kind of survival of the fittest. A letter to a South African newspaper said that "nature . . . with an exquisite sense of poetic justice, has chosen the most appropriate scourge with which to cleanse this continent from the blight of over-population."[75] Sontag writes of "the view, increasingly heard, in which AIDS is regarded as a kind of Darwinian test of a society's aptitude for survival."[76]

In 1987 these words appeared in an African American newspaper:

> In 10 years time more African people worldwide will be dead from AIDS than died in the Atlantic slave traffic over a period of 400 years. . . . Where are the demonstrations? . . . Where is our rage?[77]

Conclusion

International differences in AIDS treatment reflect, with brutal clarity, the immense inequities of the global distribution of resources. The United States spent more on its early AIDS cases than the total health budget of several African nations. In the West, its onset is now delayed by powerful drugs, but for financial reasons, these are seldom an option in Africa.

The peculiar horror of AIDS, in the Western world, is that it is incurable. It is assumed that medical science cures diseases, though the resurgence of TB, malaria, and infections resistant to antibiotics shows how fragile and contingent its victories in fact are. In Africa, where medical resources are inadequate, far more diseases are incurable, or at least uncured, and diarrhea is a major killer of children.

Some have seen, in both AIDS and cancer, metaphors for the Lemba sickness of the West. "America is prey to a wasting disease of the spirit. . . . [O]nce a cultural cancer has metastasised, it is exceedingly hard to reverse."[78]

There is no simple equation between gender hostility, witchcraft accusations, and AIDS. In some communities, the tendency to equate witchcraft with women is unequivocal, but there are many exceptions—the archetypal Fipa sorcerer, for instance, is an old man. There is undoubtedly, in Africa, a tendency to blame women for AIDS, but here as elsewhere, popular understandings have many and complex strands. The cognitive history of AIDS determines, in the most literal sense, whether those at risk live or die. There can be no more telling demonstration of the need to "entertain the claims to attention of local, discontinuous, disqualified, illegitimate knowledges."[79]

Notes

1. S. Jamba, *Patriots* (London, 1990), 176.

2. P. Schmoll, "Black Stomachs, Beautiful Stones," in J. and J. L. Comaroff, *Modernity and Its Malcontents* (Chicago and London, 1993), 203–205 and 217 n.8.

3. Quoted in Schmoll, "Black Stomachs, Beautiful Stones," 211.

4. R. East, trans. and ed., *Akiga's Story* (Oxford, 1939), 248.

5. E. Goody, "Legitimate and Illegitimate Aggression," in M. Douglas (ed.), *Witchcraft Confessions and Accusations* (London, 1970), 211.

6. Goody, "Legitimate and Illegitimate Aggression," 213.

7. A. Gottlieb, "Witches, Kings and the Sacrifice of Identity . . . ," in W. Arens and I. Karp, *Creativity of Power: Cosmology and Actions in African Societies* (Washington and London, 1989), 252–54.

8. Quoted in H. J. Drewal, "Efe: Voiced Power and Pageantry," *African Arts* (1974): 60. Some Gelede dancers enact the roles of men, and others of women.

9. J. Hoch-Smith, "Radical Yoruba Sexuality: The Witch and the Prostitute," in Hoch-Smith and A. Spring (eds.), *Women in Ritual and Symbolic Roles* (New York and London, 1978), 245–67. This is the source for the account that follows.

10. Hoch-Smith, "Radical Yoruba Sexuality," 261.

11. J. Picton, "Masks and the Igbirra," *African Arts* (1974): 38. My Igbo informant was J. H. Bardi.

12. M. Field, *Search for Security: An Ethno-Psychiatric Study of Rural Ghana* (London, 1960), 121.

13. G. Bannerman-Richter, *The Practice of Witchcraft in Ghana* (Winona, MN, 1982), 17, 28, 34.

14. [Auckland, New Zealand] *Sunday Star-Times,* 9 Mar. 1997.

15. Ibid., 19 Jan. and 9 Mar. 1997.

16. G. Ludwar-Ene, "Explanatory and Remedial Modalities for Personal Misfortune in a West African Society with Special Reference to Witchcraft," *Anthropos* (1986): 563—64.

17. S. Drucker-Brown, "Mamprusi Witchcraft, Subversion and Changing Gender Relations," *Africa* (1993): 535.

18. S. F. Nadel, *A Black Byzantium: The Kingdom of Nupe in Nigeria* (1942; reprint, London, 1973), 148.

19. R. Henderson, *The King in Every Man* (New Haven and London, 1972), 311.

20. Flora Nwapa, *Efuru* (1966; reprint, Oxford, 1978), 113.

21. Bannerman-Richter, *The Practice of Witchcraft in Ghana,* 41–2.

22. A. Ampofo, "Controlling and Punishing Women in Ghana," *Review of African Political Economy* (1993): 102–10.

23. A. Apter, "Atinga Revisited: Yoruba Witchcraft and the Cocoa Economy," in J. and J. L. Comaroff, *Modernity and Its Malcontents,* 114–15.

24. M. Field, *Social Organization of the Ga People* (London, 1940), 214, 218.

25. Field, *Search for Security,* 268

26. D. Rosen, "Dangerous women: 'Ideology', 'Knowledge' and Ritual Among the Kono of Eastern Sierra Leone," *Dialectical Anthropology* (1981): 162. My chapter title echoes this terminology.

27. Ibid., 158.

28. Ibid., 161.

29. Ben Okri, *The Famished Road* (London, 1991), 100.

30. Ben Okri, *Infinite Riches* (London, 1998), 28–9.

31. Ibid., 312.

32. R. Pittin, "Women, Work and Ideology in Nigeria," *Review of African Political Economy* (1991): 48. She points out the differences between "karuwai" and "prostitute."

33. T. Barnett and P. Blaikie, *AIDS in Africa: Its Present and Future Impact* (London, 1992), 46, 48, 50.

34. Brad Weiss, *The Making and Unmaking of the Haya Lived World* (Durham, NC, and London, 1996), 179; see also C. B. Yamba, "Cosmologies in Turmoil: Witchfinding and AIDS in Chiawa, Zambia," *Africa* (1997): 202.

35. *National Mirror,* 1 Nov. 1986, quoted in C. Bledsoe, "The Politics of AIDS: Condoms, and Heterosexual Relations in Africa: Recent Evidence from the Local Print Media," in W. P. Handwerker (ed.), *Births and Power: Social Changes and the Politics of Reproduction* (Boulder, 1990), 208.

36. Weiss, *The Haya Lived World,* 179. Weiss, it should be emphasized, stresses that this and similar conversations are not primarily about prostitution, and locates them in a wider discourse about gender, land, and money.

37. Barnett and Blaikie, *AIDS in Africa,* 106.

38. Cited in Barnett and Blaikie, *AIDS in Africa,* 44.

39. Yamba, "Cosmologies in Turmoil," 200–23.

40. Ed. Hooper, *Slim: A Reporter's Own Story of AIDS in East Africa* (London, 1990), 343, 350.

41. Ibid., 18; see 246 on BK girls.

42. Ibid., 59–60.

43. Anonymous, Rakai Essays, in Barnett and Blaikie, *AIDS in Africa,* 51–2.

44. Hooper, *Slim,* 241.

45. Barnett and Blaikie, *AIDS in Africa,* 49.

46. S. Leclerc-Madlala, "Infect One, Infect All; Zulu Youth Response to the AIDS Epidemic in South Africa," *Medical Anthropology* (1997): 364.

47. *Focus,* cited in Hooper, *Slim,* 192.

48. Bledsoe, "The politics of AIDS," 222.

49. Hooper, *Slim,* 358.

50. Ibid., 271.

51. Barnett and Blaikie, *AIDS in Africa,* 44.

52. "A World Apart, Killer Diseases Take Toll," *The Atlanta Journal/The Atlanta Constitution,* 23 May 1995. (I owe this reference to Kearsley Stewart.)

53. Barnett and Blaikie, *AIDS in Africa,* 50.

54. Hooper, *Slim,* 252. He mentioned four actual cases. For alleged parellels outside Africa, see R. Shilts, *And the Band Played On: Politics, People and the AIDS Epidemic* (London and New York, 1987), 165, 196–67, 198, 200, 413.

55. Leclerc-Madlala, "Infect One, Infect All," 363.

56. Ibid., 369. "Pass One Pass All" refers to the insistence, in the apartheid era, that all school pupils must join in a demonstration—that individuals should not gain an advantage by staying in school.

57. Leclerc-Madlala, "Infect One, Infect All," 371.

58. Ibid., 375.

59. Joan Wardrop, "Sleeping with Virgins AIDS Cure," e-mail communication, H-Africa, 10 Dec. 1997.

60. Esteban Montejo, *The Autobiography of a Runaway Slave,* trans. J. Innes (New York, 1968), 42.

61. Hooper, *Slim,* 149.

62. Weiss, *The Haya Lived World,* 156–78.

63. Quoted in Weiss, *The Haya Lived World,* 171.

64. T. Allen, "The Quest for Therapy in Moyo District," in H. B. Hansen and M. Twaddle, *Changing Uganda: The Dilemmas of Structural Adjustment and Revolutionary Change* (London, 1991), 154.

65. Barnett and Blaikie, *AIDS in Africa,* 52.

66. P. Hilts, "Dispelling Myths about AIDS in Africa," *Africa Report* (1988): 30 .

67. Quoted in Mehboob Dada, "Race and the AIDS agenda," in T. Boffin and S. Gupta, *Ecstatic Antibodies: Resisting the AIDS mythology* (London, 1990), 90.

68. Hooper, *Slim,* 207.

69. Barnett and Blaikie, *AIDS in Africa,* 169.

70. Patricia A Turner, *I Heard It Through the Grapevine: Rumor in African American Culture* (Berkeley, 1993), 151ff. Susan Sontag, *AIDS and Its Metaphors* (New York, 1988), 52–3

71. *Weekly Topic,* Jan. 1987, cited in Hooper, *Slim,* 208.

72. *New Vision,* 4 Oct. 1988, quoted in Bledsoe, "The politics of AIDS," 221.

73. Hooper, *Slim* 218.

74. Ibid., 358.

75. Quoted in M. Simpson, "AIDS in Africa," in I. B. Corless and M. Pittman-Lindeman, *AIDS: Principles, Practices and Politics* (New York, 1989), 160.

76. Sontag, *AIDS and Its Metaphors,* 91.

77. *The City Sun,* quoted in Simpson, "AIDS in Africa," 158.

78. Ambrose Evans-Pritchard, "American Pie Made with Rotten Apples," [Auckland, New Zealand] *Sunday Star-Times,* 2 Feb. 1997, reprinted from the London *Sunday Telegraph.*

79. M. Foucault, "Two Lectures: Lecture One: 7 Jan. 1976," in *Power/Knowledge: Selected Interviews and Other Writings,* trans. C. Gordon et al. (New York, 1980), 83.

13

VILLAGE INTELLECTUALS AND THE CHALLENGE OF POVERTY

"Why are blacks poor and whites rich? is one of the hardest questions to answer, and one which is put again and again by the younger generation."

Aylward Shorter on East Africa, in 1985[1]

At this point we turn from the poetics of memory and of rumor and begin to explore symbolic statements of quite a different kind. A study of the Shambaa of northern Tanzania refers to "Peasant Intellectuals,"[2] and the terminology is echoed in this chapter's title. While still expressed chiefly in metaphor, symbol, and myth, the sources to which we now turn embody conscious attempts to interpret experience and make it morally intelligible. Above all, what seemed to need explaining was Africa's poverty vis-à-vis the wealth and power of the West and its representatives. But there are many other dimensions in this search for understanding. One of the most striking is a widespread pattern in which past prophets were remembered, re-interpreted, or, even, invented. They are said to have foretold, in remarkable detail, the nature of the colonial experience. Perhaps, in some instances, these extraordinary intellectuals were historic figures, who understood, with striking insight, the ongoing historical processes affecting their diverse worlds. Alternatively, later traditions may have attributed new prophecies to historic figures. And some prophets may be later inventions—attempts to locate uncontrollable and overwhelming ex-

169

periences within the sphere of African foreknowledge. The tide of colonial conquest could not be halted, but it had been anticipated.

Prophets

Prophets were the intellectuals of their societies, who described, often with extraordinary insight, patterns of political and socio-economic change. [3] Ewenihi is remembered as a nineteenth-century Igbo seer, a member of the Aguinyi clan, who is thought to have anticipated, with striking accuracy, the shape of things to come. "He was said to have foretold the coming of the whiteman, telling the people that he 'saw them white and reflecting in the wilderness,' and that they would usurp the children of the clan." "Those quarrelling over political powers are merely fighting over another's property." He predicted the way in which the sale of land would replace traditional rights of usufruct, and the escalation of land values, saying that those who wanted land would need twenty thousand cowries. He anticipated the decline of traditional religion, when the gods would be left to starve to death, and those that survived would have hot oil put in their eyes. [4]

Of the many East African prophets said to have predicted the colonial experience, perhaps the most notable was the Fipa seer, Kaswa, from southern Tanzania, whose predictions of an age of cannibals and the victory of the cash nexus have already been cited.

> He said: "There are monstrous strangers coming,
> Bringing war, striking you unawares, relentlessly,
> O you people, you're going to be robbed of your country." [5]

He is said to have foretold the way in which the aged would be left alone, as their children departed for the towns.

> And he said: "The grasshoppers are your children,
> And they are flying away, all of them!
> You remain behind, old and dying, and to the very end they are not
>   there! . . ."
> Kaswa said: "A person will clothe his whole body,
> Even his eyes.
> Everything will have its price. . . ." [6]

In Shambaa, in northern Tanzania, a prophet foretold an expanded population, and a pattern of resettlement produced by road construction:

"all places which had forests would become villages and . . . there would be houses along the roads. . . . He had already foretold that there would come white people."[7]

There were similar prophets in Kenya. A Turkana diviner said in c. 1875, "I have seen a great vulture, coming down from the sky, and scooping up the land of Turkana in its talons."[8] A Kamba woman prophet, Syokimau, said people would come with skins like meat, who spoke like birds [that is, unintelligibly] and that there would be a long snake [the railway].[9] A number of Meru prophets, from the 1860s on, also foretold the long snake, in whose service warriors would dig like women.[10]

In the 1930s, when white ascendancy in Kenya seemed immovable, Jomo Kenyatta wrote of a Kikuyu prophet who foretold

> that strangers would come to Gikuyuland from out of the big water, the colour of their body would resemble that of a small light-coloured frog . . . which lives in water, their dress would resemble the wings of butterflies; that these strangers would carry magical sticks which would produce fire. . . . The strangers . . . would later bring an iron snake [which] would spit fires and would stretch from the big water in the east to another big water in the west of the Gikuyu country.[11]

Railways were an important instrument of colonial control, a fact which these metaphors reflect; the snake is deadly, and many workers died in railway (or road) construction. These True Fictions contrast with the rhetoric of empire. In the early twentieth century, Winston Churchill visited East Africa. He called the Uganda railway "one slender thread of scientific civilisation, of order, authority and arrangement, drawn across the primeval chaos of the world."[12]

Prophets had real power to shape events, as colonial officials discovered. A woman prophet, Chanjiri, appeared in Malawi in 1907 and said

> that she had a magic to spread darkness over the land where the white men lived and they would all disappear; therefore, there was no need to pay taxes. The people left their jobs and flocked to the woman. The Government at first did not take the matter seriously until it discovered that the tax returns had shown a shortage. . . .[13]

Legends about Kupe, the magic mountain in Cameroon, published in 1930, froze popular perceptions at a particular moment in time.[14] Local sorcerers were given credit for the advent of the Europeans (in the interests of progress) and vied with them for the symbols of political supremacy.

"Both black and white struggle for the staff of lord Ntoko." The literate were said to possess "the ekong [sorcery] of the European," and a mission station was a halting place for sorcerers on their journey to Kupe. In their astral struggles for supremacy, black and white meet on equal terms. Black sorcerers emulate the feats of white technology and travel on astral trains. Europeans appear all-powerful, but are acting out a scenario determined by Africans. It was a different way of restoring African autonomy to recent history.

The process of locating contemporary events in past predictions continues. AIDS transmission is often attributed to tiny insects. In modern Zambia,

> "There is a word—'tuyebela'—which means small invisible insects," he said. "We were told stories about these by our grandmothers when we were little. They said you would get these and they would make you sick if you had sex before marriage. . . . Now grandma is saying, 'Look! What I told you is true!'"[15]

Prophetic Madness

In Africa, as elsewhere, prophecy is often close to madness—the familiar paradox of Shakespeare's *King Lear.* The insane are alienated from "reality" as others perceive it; standing outside society, they may understands its deficiencies more clearly. Having nothing to lose, they are sometimes empowered to utter a penetrating critique, which no one else has the insight or courage to provide. When Kaswa had completed his prophetic utterances, he disappeared into the earth in a place called Loss of Mind.[16] Ewenihi is remembered as insane, a consequence of the loss of his only son in a local war. The name of Hauka, the Songhai spirit-possession cult described earlier, means craziness.[17] Aylward Shorter writes of a "madman," in a Tanzanian village, in late 1982, who, at a time of economic hardship, criticized government policies when others were afraid to do so.[18]

All this is mirrored in fiction. In Ouloguem's *Le devoir de violence,* the sorcerer Bouremi becomes mad and is able, for the first time, to denounce oppression. "[M]adness is a fine thing, a marvelous alibi, sweet and terrible."[19]

> Those who thought they knew him regarded him as an idealist, illumined for brief moments by some immense idea. . . . [He] had ears only for "his truth."[20]

In Tansi's *L'anté-peuple,* set in West Central Africa, insanity becomes a way of escaping from the intolerable oppression of the state.[21] The hero, once a Training College Principal, now disguised as a naked lunatic, assassinates a politician, but his action leads only to a wholesale massacre of the insane.[22]

A Remembrance of Things Past

While real or invented prophets perceived the shape of things to come, particular visions of moral economy were often formulated in terms of an imagined past. In Africa and elsewhere, the invention of a vanished Golden Age has often been used to critique the present. In the mid eighteenth century it was used to condemn the Atlantic slave trade.[23] Another nineteenth-century Igbo prophet called himself Restorer of the Primitive Style.[24]

The colonial era offered new opportunities and new freedoms. Some individuals became more prosperous, but growing socio-economic disparities led to the sense of tension and division that underlay the extraordinary proliferation of anti-witchcraft movements. Popular inventions of history described the erosion of a sense of community. A group of Nyakusa from southern Tanzania complained in 1937:

> Money destroys the ranks and those who have been chosen and salaried are happy, thus they despise their unfortunate friends of the same rank. In the old days, when there was no money, there was no killing each other [by witchcraft], no jealousy, or falsehoods; while in these present days all these have happened simply because the new customs have upset the old ones, in nothing save in money alone.[25]

There are many narratives of this kind, from contexts widely separated in space and time. What they have in common is the attempt to critique contemporary —and, significantly, local—society by contrasting it with an idealized and selective past.

The golden age has not always been located in the past. In the context of independence struggles, or even of a return to civilian rule in a military state, the future has often become the focus of reasonable and unreasonable hopes.

> Independence will mean that our women and children will be healthy, sickness and death will no longer be as they are now, and our villages will be crowded.[26]

They were soon disappointed. In 1974, the author of a letter to a Nigerian newspaper borrowed the eloquent words of T. E. Lawrence.

> We lived many lives in those swirling campaigns . . . yet when we had achieved, and the new world dawned, the old men came out again and took from us our victory, and remade it in the likeness of the former world they knew. . . . We stammered that we had worked for a new heaven and a new earth, and they thanked us very kindly and made their peace.[27]

In 1979, Nigerians hoped for great things from a return to civilian rule, and queued patiently to vote, on five successive Saturdays. Twenty years later, there was another return to civilian rule, and another election. An Igbo electrician said, "the whole process is irrelevant to me. . . . Politics is a pastime for rich businessmen and corrupt military men." Neo-traditional religion had come to fill the nurturing role once hoped for from the state. The custodian of an Igbo shrine said, "This is where people feel they get real help."[28]

Nothing speaks more eloquently of the disappointments of contemporary Africa than its silences. A Zambian mine worker said in the mid 1980s, "We black people are unable to speak of the future. We can only talk about the past."[29] In the late 1990s, a member of the Nigerian elite told a journalist, "Nigeria is the land of no tomorrow."[30]

The Problem of Poverty

The question perplexing village intellectuals above all others was that of Africa's poverty, vis-à-vis the West. Chapter 4 delineated one symbolic answer—Western goods were made by enslaved African souls for white sorcerers under the sea. Rodney's *How Europe Underdeveloped Africa* (1972) was extremely popular among students in Africa because it attempted to provide an explanation.

Many scattered village intellectuals have struggled with this question. Their narratives are the result of conscious reflection on the shape of history and its injustices. At their heart is a determination to make experience morally intelligible.

Where possible, I have attempted to explore the themes of this book in specific regional settings. But in this instance, scores of similar myths have been recorded, over hundreds of years, in West and West Central Africa.[31] The constant recreation of similar stories is as significant as the details of their content.

These commentaries on Europe's wealth and Africa's poverty are a form of bricolage, assembled from traditions at once indigenous and changing and from various kinds of encounters with strangers. Here I analyze only a small selection from the many instances known to me. They fall into four overlapping categories. The first explains, through stories of a primal choice, why Europeans are rich and Africans poor. The second category ascribes the wealth and power of Europeans to their Trickster qualities. The third consists of retold biblical narratives of apparently arbitrary preference. In the fourth category, the whites are denounced for avarice; in one compelling narrative, a cosmic rebel against God is also the king of the Europeans.

A Cosmic Choice

A black and a white brother—women rarely appear in these texts—take it in turns to select a symbolic object. The consequences of their decisions are momentous, but are concealed from them. The black brother has the first choice, reflecting either his seniority or God's special love for him. The white brother's share is a symbol of literacy.

In the earliest version of the myth, recorded in c.1700, the question which demanded explanation was why Europeans were slave-owners and Africans slaves. By the late nineteenth century, it seemed important to understand how a small minority of Europeans were able to establish and sustain the conquest states we call colonies. In the post-colony, the basic question endures—"Why are blacks poor and whites rich?"

These accounts are abundant, not only because they were so often reinvented, but also because Europeans had a particular interest in recording them. A hidden subtext is that Europeans perceived them as flattering, because of their explicit acknowledgment of white material and technical superiority. The German who recorded a Bakossi (Cameroon) myth in 1893 observed:

> We whites are not only more handsome and intelligent than the blacks. We also possess immense powers of witchcraft. And, most important of all, we need not work with our hands. All these advantages are thought to be an indication that God loves the whites more than the blacks.[32]

But if we look at the details of the myth he narrates, we find that white delusions of supremacy are rejected and Europeans are portrayed as mere middlemen between Africa and superior beings who live on the shore of the other world and are half human, half spirit. Their mental power allows them to make themselves invisible and to obtain whatever they want from God. . . . Now comes the commerce between the three! Actually, it is us, the whites, who have the role of middlemen. We whites rule over the islands and the sea, between this world of the blacks and the other world where the superior beings live. We carry on the trade between them both and make enormous profit from it.[33]

Eurocentric notions of white supremacy are explicitly rejected.

Myths about a momentous choice between symbolic commodities are adaptations of a much wider and probably ancient genre. In the tiny western Igbo polity of Agbor, a little-known story is told to explain its relative weakness vis-à-vis its great neighbor, Benin. Both kings were asked to make a momentous choice between two boxes. The king of Agbor chose one containing axes and cutlasses; the ruler of Benin was left with a box of snail shells filled with sand. He spread the sand to create dry land, and this explains his seniority.[34]

In the earliest account of symbolic choices made by Africans and Europeans, recorded in the Gold Coast in about 1700, Africans chose gold, leaving literacy for Europeans. "God granted their Request, but being incensed at their Avarice, resolved that the Whites should for ever be their Masters, and they obliged to wait on them as their slaves."[35]

A similar myth was recorded at the Asante court, in 1817. The European obtains paper and knowledge and learns how to build ships and embark on international commerce, accurately perceived as the key to white prosperity. African deprivation is due to "the blind avarice of their forefathers."[36] The poor are poor through their own fault. In a missionary version, the Europeans' reward is true religion.[37] In a text collected in Dahomey in the 1880s, Africans again choose gold, leaving literacy to Europeans; God then gives the whites the power to govern the blacks.[38] Now the consequence of black cupidity is colonial encroachment.

In a legend from Ivory Coast published early this century, the African chose a canoe, and the European, a steamer. The former went to a distant country, where his white brother brought him gifts—cloth, tobacco, and manufactured goods. He gave him livestock and chickens in return.

The white replied, "But I have not sold anything to you, I have made you a gift." But the black did not understand, so his brother, in annoyance, said to him, "I wanted to give you a present, you have not accepted it, from now on, although you are my brother, when I bring you something, it will be as trade."[39]

The cash nexus governing the relations of black and white becomes the black's fault, the result of his refusal to accept a gift gracefully.

Books, but not a primal choice, figure in an explanation of colonial conquest recorded in Calabar in 1906. Exceptionally, one of the protagonists is a (white) girl, in a text which begins with a twin tabu.

> The female child having grown up went to live in some other country as she was not loved by her mother. During her lonely journey to that other country she picked up a book which she saw dropped from the sky.

In her new home she mastered the knowledge in the book, married and raised children. Her children "when they were strong . . . drove away the black inhabitants of that country by means of the knowledge of the arts of war they had acquired from the book." Once more, the knowledge obtained from books explains foreign conquest, but the "black ancestor was more loved by their mother, the wife of the god of all the earth."[40]

These West African narratives have many Central African counterparts. A merchant who traded on the Cabinda coast from 1869 to 1873 recorded a version where Mane [king] Pouta [Portugal, Europe] had two sons—Mane Kongo and Zonga.

> Zonga took paper, pens, a telescope, a gun, and powder. Mani Congo preferred copper bracelets, iron swords and bows and arrows.[41]

The brothers parted and Zonga crossed the ocean and became the ancestor of the Europeans.[42]

A story collected in the 1950s, among the Luba, in what was to become eastern Zaire (now the Democratic Republic of Congo), tells how the African, being especially loved by God, was given the first choice and selected a large, heavy box. The white man was left with a small one. The black man's box contained

> hoes and axes, water pots and forked sticks used for carrying loads. And since then the black man has usually had the work of chopping wood, drawing water, and carrying loads. . . . The white man was at first very disappointed that he was left with so small and light a box, and even more so when he opened it and found that it only contained a pencil to put behind his ear and a piece of paper to carry in his pocket. But whereas the wisdom of a black man dies with him because there is nobody to write it down, when the white man learns something new he always puts it onto his paper, . . . And so it is that the pencil and books put the white man in advance of the black.[43]

Stories of symbolic choices are still told in the post-colony. One was collected among the Balanta of Guinea-Bissau, in 1995. Here the choice was between a large bowl of food and a small plate—but a hoe went with the bowl, and a pen with the plate. The African chose the former, and the European the latter.[44] Again, there is the (implicit) condemnation of a fictitious black ancestor's greed, and the assertion of the crucial role of literacy.

A disquieting aspect of many of these stories is the way in which the African is marginalized. He is not merely mistaken, but also greedy and avaricious. Perhaps this is an example of the phenomenon described long ago by Fanon, where the colonized internalize the values of the colonizer. Another disconcerting aspect is the way in which agricultural tools become identified with subordination and suffering. Agriculture was at the heart of these communities' livelihoods and their traditional values. The symbolic importance of iron tools (and weapons) was mirrored in a multitude of rituals found across West and Central Africa. These narratives of symbolic choices reflect the relative deprivation of the peasant farmer, the marginalization and poverty of rural life, and the overpowering attraction of white-collar employment.

The Power of Literacy

The object(s) acquired by the African vary, but the European's share almost always includes a symbol of literacy, which is seen as the key to the progressive accumulation of knowledge and thus to power. Literacy often seemed to have a magical power of its own. Members of a dance society on the East African coast sang:

> To be able to read and speak the language of Europe,
> The gates of Heaven are opened for us.[45]

Alternatively the power and prosperity of the Europeans was ascribed to secret knowledge of a ritual, rather than technical, nature. Missionaries were associated with the superior technology of the whites, and with the military victories of colonial powers. It was at first hoped that they would share the secret ritual knowledge that made this possible. As time went on, and many Christians remained as poor as before, it was often believed that the missionaries were keeping this crucial information secret. The discovery that the Protestant Bible excluded the Apocrypha—and that all Bibles omit Gnostic tests such as the Gospel of Thomas—seemed to confirm this.

In the late 1950s, in Ghana, a society appeared "whose aim was to find out the wonder-working secret magics by means of which Jesus wrought miracles."[46] In the western Niger Delta, there is a tradition of "a lost Bible, far fuller and richer in content than the usual version in use, which was originally given . . . to Isoko Christians, but was then taken away and either lost or destroyed by the missionaries."[47] A tract written in Gabon was called, *La Bible Secrète des noirs selon le Bouity* (The Secret Bible of the Blacks according to Bwiti).[48]

The Colonial Trickster

The archetypal Trickster of African story tellers is physically weak—Anansi the spider, among the Akan, the tortoise among the Igbo—but overcomes more powerful adversaries by his cunning. Often, the Trickster is greedy as well as duplicitous.

The power and wealth of Europeans were often explained by the fact that they had the qualities of Tricksters. The Fang of Gabon initially explained the material resources of the whites by identifying them with the ancestors or ascribing supernatural powers to them, as in the white sorcerers under the sea (pp. 57–8). Later, " there . . . appeared a tendency to assimilate them to the power of evil, and, in various myths, to ascribe their superiority to trickery and duplicity."[49] In chapter 5, we noted the links between Europeans and the Yoruba divinity, Eshu, who has some Trickster qualities ("Esu brought the British to Nigeria").[50] In Swahili, the word for European is *Mzungu.* Its dictionary meanings include, "something wonderful, startling, surprising, ingenuity, cleverness, a feat, a trick, a wonderful device."[51] In Malagasy, Europeans are *vazaha,* a word which also means "crafty," and is, Bloch tells us, "a quality which is typical of Europeans and which is more feared than admired."[52]

A remembered conversation from Zambia, in the 1940s, elaborates the concept of the European Trickster.

> "The hare caused the death of the lion. It need never have happened if the lion had heeded the warning of the bird."
> . . . . "You'd better tell us what it means, Mlongoti."
> "You Europeans are few, but you are very clever, like the hare. . . .You know how to make aeroplanes. But we Africans are many and we are strong, like the lion. We dig ditches and build railway embankments. Can a European dig a ditch? Have you ever seen one? Of course not, they are weak, yet

they always win over us, just like the hare tricked the lion in the legend. The
little bird warned the lion but he would not listen."
  "Who is the bird?"
  "Our forefathers."[53]

Texts that identify colonial Europeans with Tricksters are a form of
subversive discourse. Like stories of white sorcerers who enslave African
souls under the sea, they embody a powerful critique of what they represent.

Biblical Echoes

The Hebrew Bible is full of instances of apparently arbitrary parental or
divine preference, and many of the stories that explain the different fortunes of black and white appear to be influenced by biblical narratives or
explicitly retell them. These narratives are reshaped, in an intricate process of
bricolage, to such an extent that they are sometimes almost unrecognizable.
  Often, the story retold is Genesis 9:20–28, where, after the Flood,
Noah lay drunken and naked in his tent. Ham saw him and told his brothers, who, with their eyes averted, covered their father. When Noah found
out, he cursed Ham's descendants, saying that they would be slaves.
  In the 1880s, Bentley referred to the circulation of the story in the
Kongo kingdom from the time of the earlier Catholic missionaries.[54] An
(unbiblical) gloss to the effect that Africans are the descendants of Ham,
condemned by Noah's curse to servitude, was used to justify slavery in the
New World, and apartheid in South Africa. It may well have figured in
missionary exegesis.
  A bitter and eloquent version collected in Senegal in the late nineteenth century reflects the persistent tendency to marginalize the story's
African protagonist. Noah's eldest son, Toubab, was white; his health was
delicate but he was intelligent, with a particular talent for commerce (Europeans are called Toubab in modern francophone West Africa). The second son, Hassan, was brown and an expert pastoralist. The third, Samba,
was "the colour of the Wolofs," that is, black. He was stronger than his
brothers and an outstanding farmer, whose produce was often sold to Toubab
in exchange for luxuries.
  Noah died and left his wealth to be equally shared among his sons.
While Samba slept in a drunken stupor, Toubab took Noah's valuables,
including his cloth, firearms, and gunpowder, to sea in an ark, and settled

elsewhere. Hassan took Noah's herds to the desert. When Samba awoke, he experienced a moment of despair, but soon consoled himself with brandy and tobacco.

> This is why, for a very long time, the whites have sailed on the sea, with the ark and valuables, and with qualities inherited from Toubab, making a lot of money from trade.
> This is why the Moors have fine herds and willingly disappear into the depths of the desert.
> This is why the blacks, who are the descendants of Samba, are always deceived by the whites and by the Moors, finding consolation for their sad condition only in tobacco and brandy.[55]

European prosperity is due to their ocean-going steamers and their resultant hegemony in international trade. Once more, the African is poor through his own fault.

An elaborate Kitawala (Watchtower) version of the Genesis stories of the Creation and the sons of Noah, collected in Zaire/Congo, was published in 1962. It is too long to paraphrase in its entirety, but an episode is significant.

> Of all the sons of Zendekisa, Amérique was the most gifted and the most intelligent. He invented everything, planes, telephones, radios, guns, rifles, cars. When Ndembo Kanizari learnt of these wonders, he flew into a rage, and carried Amérique away by night, and made him a slave. All that was left to the children of Zendekisa was the spear and bow and arrow, and the poison which they had invented to kill wild animals.[56]

In an extended and complex narrative, the black son is punished for unfilial behavior. But it is a black man who invents all the technological wonders of the western world. The white man enslaves him, and steals his secrets, part of a popular Kongo history of colonialism, in which Europeans used mission teaching and the violence of the colonial state to destroy both metal-working skills and indigenous medicine—so that the sick needed to consult foreign doctors, who sometimes enslaved their souls (echoes of the zombie motif). "Stories are told of local geniuses who were prevented by the Belgians from making trucks or airplanes."[57] In the second issue of the Kongo newspaper, *Kongo Dieto,* in 1959, it was said,

> Our elders knew how to make iron tools, guns and many other things, but when [the Europeans] came to steal our freedom, the old [skills] disappeared.[58]

Genesis 27, where Jacob obtains the blessing due to his elder brother, Esau, by means of deception has also been retold repeatedly. An Ejagham ("Ekoi") version was recorded on the Nigeria-Cameroon borderland early this century.[59] A story recorded among the Limba of Sierra Leone in the early 1960s tells of a white brother, preferred by the mother, and a black one, favored by the father.

> [T]heir father . . . made a book. He wrote everything, how to make a ship, aeroplane, money, how to make everything. He wrote it in the book to help the one he loved. He too, took and made a hoe, he made a cutlass, he looked for millet, he made groundnuts, he made pepper, he made a garden, oranges, everything. . . .

He asked each son to hunt and bring game back. The white son killed a domestic sheep, and was given the book by his mother on the instructions of his (shortsighted) father.

> The unfairness of our birth makes us remain in suffering. . . . If you see the Europeans, everything they are doing they have to put a black man there. He is a clerk; he sits in the store, he does everything. . . .We are brothers of the same parents.[60]

This and other comparable examples of bricolage reflect the way in which the village intellectual draws on all the sources of information available to make sense of a changing world. Changes effected in biblical narratives reflect both the incorporation of motifs from local cultures and the oral and haphazard way in which they were encountered by those unable to read—in sermons, often at second or third hand.

The West Condemned

In many of these narratives, poverty, understandably enough, is seen as a punishment, and wealth and power as signs of divine favor. In some sources, however, the wealth of the whites is attributed to a Faustian pact, or a primal rebellion from God.

An officer who took part in a West African military expedition in 1891–92 recorded a conversation with his Wolof servant, Moussa N'Diaye, who asked, why, if France was so beautiful, were the French invading Africa?

> The devil knows that the whites have beautiful women; every year he comes to the edge of the hole, say the ignorant,[61] to the shore, say the well in-

formed, like Moussa, and there he demands the most beautiful of our companions in return for wonderful inventions. And this is why we are in the Sudan. Having given our women to the devil, we are obliged to look for them elsewhere. The new whites who disembark each year are those who have just traded their wives for some new application of steam or electricity. . . . We are a colony of voluntary widowers, a colony of the victims of the love of progress.[62]

Here, a Faustian pact is made, not by a witch, but by Europeans. The technical achievements of the whites are paid for by the sacrifice of their wives, a choice of wealth in things rather than wealth in people.

A myth collected among the Bete of Ivory Coast, in 1958, during a study of the Deima church, features a mysterious protagonist, Abidise, whose name may be a slight rearrangement of the first four letters of the alphabet, ABCD (most members of the Deima church speak French and their records are in French). Abidise is both "the king of the white race," and the eldest but rejected son of God.

Abidise discovers white, red, and black clay. God sends Jesus to ask for some of it, and when Abidise refuses, Jesus steals some. With the clay, God makes white, black, and red men, adding blood and breath. When Abidise complains, God replies, "When my people die, you take back your clay and I shall take back my breath."

> Abidise said again, "Water and fire belong to God but the earth belongs to me. Men, who are made of earth, will pay me to all eternity." The descendants of Abidise, the whites, have power over the earth. That is why they have imposed a tax on the earth. The blacks do not understand, for they remain strangers on the earth.[63]

The European, Abidise, has overtones of the rebellion of Lucifer. His descendants rule the kingdoms of this world, where Africans are strangers and pilgrims. In its condemnation of European materialism, this subversive text has many parallels. In Tanganyika, a Nyakusa song, recorded in the 1930s, contrasted Western avarice with the core values of the traditionalist and of the Christian.

> The chiefs, the chiefs to whom do they pray!
> To the shades! To the shades! . . .
> The Europeans, the Europeans to whom do they pray?
> To money! To money! . . .
> The baptized, the baptized to whom do they pray?
> To Jesus! to Jesus![64]

A popular Kongo song, published in 1963, ran:

> The White left Europe
> To get money.
> The White came to Africa
> In search of money.[65]

This is echoed in contemporary central African fiction. "Whites worshipped no other God but money."[66] A Yoruba invocation to Aje, god of wealth, is very similar:

> The white man who sailed across the sea to set up a tent
> Is driven by the desire to make money
> Like a deadly insect that bites people in the forest.[67]

In some texts, white prosperity is explained, and in others, it is condemned.

Conclusion

Legends which ascribe African poverty or colonial rule to the folly or greed of an African ancestor make uncomfortable reading, not least because they were welcomed by Europeans in the heyday of colonialism. The felt need to explain the unequal global distribution of resources was not peculiar to Africa. The story of the sons of Noah was also retold in the Pacific, where the descendants of Ham were banished to New Guinea or, alternatively, goods meant for Melanesians were stolen by white Tricksters. "Why are blacks poor and whites rich?" is as much a burning question in the Pacific as it is in East Africa. And if these various explanations seem unsatisfactory, this perhaps reflects both the inadequacy of other explanatory models, and the fact that the experts who analyze global injustice have not, as yet, provided solutions for it.

Notes

1. Aylward Shorter, *Jesus and the Witch Doctor* (London, 1985), 72.
2. S. Feierman, *Peasant Intellectuals: Anthropology and History in Tanzania* (London, 1990).
3. For a discussion of African prophets, see "Introduction" in D. M. Anderson and D. H. Johnson (eds.), *Revealing Prophets* (London and Nairobi, 1995), 1–27.

4. Oral histories collected in Aguinyi by J. I. Ejiofor in 1972; extract in E. Isichei, *Igbo Worlds* (Basingstoke and Philadelphia, 1978), 198.

5. R. Willis, "Kaswa: Oral Traditions of a Fipa Prophet," *Africa* (1970): 253. The word translated as "monstrous strangers" has overtones of cannibalism.

6. Ibid., 253.

7. Quoted in T. Ranger, *The African Churches of Tanzania* (Historical Assoc. of Tanzania, Paper 5, n.d.), 7–8.

8. J . Lamphear, *The Scattering Time: Turkana Responses to Colonial Rule* (Oxford, 1992), 48.

9. J. Forbes Munro, *Colonial Rule and the Kamba* (London, 1975), 27 n.3.

10. J. Fadiman, *When We Began, There Were Witchmen* (Berkeley, 1993), 101–102.

11. J. Kenyatta, *Facing Mount Kenya: The Tribal Life of the Gikuyu* (1938, London, 1953), 42; he names the seer as Mogo wa Kebiro, Muriuki as Cege wa Kibiru. G. Muriuki, *A History of the Kikuyu 1500–1900* (Nairobi and London, 1974), 137.

12. Winston Churchill, *My African Journey,* quoted in J. C. Gruesser, *White on Black* (Urbana and Chicago, 1992), 5.

13. Quoted in G. Shepperson, *Myth and Reality in Malawi* (Evanston 1966), 22.

14. J. Ittmann, *"Der Kupe in Aberglauben der Kameruner,"* Der Evangelische Heidenbote (Basel, 1930), 77–80, 94–95, 111–13.

15. P. Hilts, "Dispelling Myths about AIDS in Africa," *Africa Report* (1988): 31.

16. Willis, "Kaswa: Oral Traditions of a Fipa Prophet," 253–54.

17. P. Stoller, *Fusion of the Worlds: An Ethnography of Possession among the Songhay of Niger* (Chicago, 1989), 148.

18. A. Shorter, *Jesus and the Witchdoctor: An Approach to Healing and Wholeness* (London, 1985), 73. See also J. L. and J. Comaroff, "The Madman and the Migrant: Work and Labor in the Historical Consciousness of a South African People," *American Ethnologist* (1987): 191–209.

19. Y. Ouologuem, *Bound to Violence,* trans. R. Manheim (Oxford, 1971), 82.

20. Ibid.

21. Sony Labou Tansi, *The Antipeople,* trans. J. A. Underwood (London and New York, 1988), 155.

22. Ibid., 163–70.

23. W. Smith, *A New Voyage to Guinea* (London, 1744), 266, citing Charles Wheeler on the Gold Coast.

24. Church Misionary Society Archives (Consulted in London, now in Birmingham, Eng.) CA/3/037/86A, J. C. Taylor, journal entry, 23 Nov. 1864.

25. A letter in the Tanzanian National Archives, quoted in J. Iliffe, *A Modern History of Tanganyika* (Cambridge, 1979), 298.

26. *Kongo Dieto* (Kinshasa) 25 Oct. 1959, quoted in W. MacGaffey, "The West in Congolese Experience," in P. D. Curtin (ed.), *Africa and the West* (Wisconsin, WI, 1972), 59.

27. Quoted in a letter to the editor, *The [Enugu, Nigeria] Renaissance,* 22 Jan. 1974.

28. A. Duval Smith, "Nigeria Votes out the Tricky and the Greedy," *The Independent on Sunday* (London), 28 Feb. 1999.

29. J. Ferguson, "The Country and the City on the Copperbelt," *Cultural Anthropology* (1992): 86.

30. K. Maier, *The House Has Fallen: Midnight in Nigeria* (New York, 2000), xviii.

31. There are numerous examples in V. Görög-Karady, *Noirs et blancs: leur image dans la littérature orale africaine; étude, anthologie* (Paris, 1976) and V. Görög, *"L'origine de l'inégalité des races: Étude de trente-sept contes africains,"* in *Cahiers d'Études africaines* (1968): 290–309.

32. F. Autenrieth, *Inner-Hochland von Kamerun* (Stuttgart-Basel, 1900), 44–6, quoted in H. Balz, *Where the Faith Has to Live: Studies in Bakossi Society and Religion* (Basel, 1984), 112. Balz's translation.

33. Ibid.

34. Chief Nwokoro Obuseh of Agbor, 30 Sept. 1979 (recorded by Peter Obue); similar versions were collected from a number of other informants.

35. W. Bosman, *A New and Accurate Description of the Coast of Guinea* (1705), 2nd ed. (London, 1967), 147.

36. T. E. Bowdich, *Mission from Cape Coast Castle to Ashante,* 3rd ed. (London, 1966), 261–62. See also A. B. Ellis, *The Tshi Speaking Peoples of the Gold Coast of West Africa* (London, 1887), 339.

37. A. J. N. Tremeane (compiler), J. Martin, diary extracts, *Man* (1912): 141.

38. E. Foà, *Le Dahomey* (Paris, 1885), 214.

39. G. Thomann, *Essai de manuel de la langue néoulé* (Paris, 1905), 129–32. I omit the first part of the story, which concerns European and African dining customs, to the detriment of the latter.

40. J. C. Cotton, "Calabar Stories," *Journal of the African Society* (1905–6): 193–94.

41. C. Jeannest, *Quatre Années au Congo* (Paris, 1883), 97–8.

42. Ibid., 98–9.

43. W. F. P. Burton, *The Magic Drum* (London, 1961), 85.

44. I owe this source to email from Walter Hawthorne on 13 Nov. 1996.

45. H. Lambert, "The Beni Dance Songs," *Swahili, Journal of the East African Swahili Committee* 33 (Dar es Salaam, 1962–3): 21, quoted in G. Shepperson, *Myth and Reality in Malawi* (Evanston, IL, 1966), 20.

46. M. Field, *Search for Security: An Ethno-Psychiatric Study of Rural Ghana* (London, 1960), 267–68.

47. S. Barrington-Ward, "'The Centre Cannot Hold': Spirit Possession as Redefinition," in E. Fasholé-Luke et al. (eds.), *Christianity in Independent Africa* (London, 1978), 463–64.

48. J. Fernandez, "Fang Representations Under Acculturation," in P. Curtin(ed.), *Africa and the West* (Madison, WI, 1972), 27 n.52.

49. Ibid., 26.

50. Cited in B. Belasco, *The Entrepreneur as Cultural Hero: Pre-Adaptations in Nigerian Economic Development* (New York, 1980), ix.

51. *Standard Swahili-English Dictionary* (London, 1955) cited in T. Beidelman, "A Kaguru Version of the Sons of Noah: A Study in the Inculcation of the Idea of Racial Superiority," *Cahiers d'Études africaines* (1963): 477 n.14.

52. M. Bloch, *Placing the Dead* (London and New York, 1971), 31.

53. P. Fraenkel, *Wayaleshi* (London, 1959), 14–15.

54. W. H. Bentley, *Pioneering on the Congo* (London, 1900), I: 251.

55. J. B. Berenger-Feraud, *Recueil de contes populaires de la Senegambie* (Paris, 1885; reprint, Nendeln, 1970), 77.

56. J. Labrique, "Interpretation Kitawalienne de la Genèse," appendix, in J. P. Paulus, "Le kitawala au Congo belge," *Revue de l'Institut de Sociologie Solvay* (1956): 267–70.

57. MacGaffey, "The West in Congolese Experience," 59.

58. *Kongo Dieto* (Kinshasa) 25 Oct. 1959, quoted in MacGaffey, "The West in Congolese Experience," 59.

59. Ojong of Oban, in P. A. Talbot, *In the Shadow of the Bush* (London, 1912), 387–89.

60. Suriba Konteh, 28 Feb. 1961, in R. Finnegan, *Limba Stories and Story-Telling* (Oxford, 1967), 261–63. The preceding story emphasises the equality of Africans, Indians and Europeans under God.

61. Some believed that France was located in a huge hole in the sea.

62. A. Baratier, *A travers l'Afrique* (Paris, 1912), 138–39

63. D. Paulme, "Une religion syncrétique en Côte d 'Ivoire: le culte *deima,*" *Cahiers d'Études africaines* (1963), 40–45.

64. M. Wilson, *Communal Rituals of the Nyakusa* (London, 1959), epigraph.

65. G. Balandier, "Les mythes politiques de colonisation et de décolonisation en Afrique," *Cahiers internationaux de Sociologie* (1963): 90.

66. Tansi, *The Antipeople,* 26

67. Belasco, *The Entrepreneur as Cultural Hero,* 143; the last noun is "jungle," in Belasco's text.

14

MAMI WATA:
ICON OF AMBIGUITY

Mamy water go bury me
If I die tomorrow

Ken Saro-Wiwa, *Sozaboy*[1]

In Ronan Bennett's novel *The Catastrophist,* set in the Belgian Congo at the time of independence, water hyacinth, a foreign introduction, is a recurrent symbol. Despite its beauty, it is deadly, choking waterways and making canoe traffic impossible.[2] Its paradoxical nature recalls Mami Wata, a siren who may bring death or sterility to those who approach her too closely. She is often depicted as a European, and her shrines are adorned with icons of Western consumerism, but it is an oversimplification to regard her simply as an Invention of the West. Although she is often dangerous and capricious, she embodies the enduring and compelling attractions of wealth from the sea, and her ambiguities and contradictions are closer to lived experience than the absolute evil of witch or cannibal. In this chapter, I explore the symbolic meaning of an imagined water spirit that is surrounded by Western consumer goods. In the next, I turn to the accretions of symbolic meaning which have developed around these commodities, the ideological construction of a world of things. This is followed, in chapter 16, by an alternative construction of the world beneath the sea.

Clearly, each aspect of Mami Wata has its own history—the name, the visual image(s), the stories of a wife (destined to disappear) from the sea. In Central Africa, she is a dominant motif in popular urban art. In West Africa, she is the focus of many local cults of affliction, and while relatively few people join them, her name and identity are well known, and anecdotes about her abound. In the words of a (hostile) Christian pamphlet published in Nigeria in 1988, "The term 'mammy water' is so widely spread in Nigeria that it becomes difficult to convince people that she doesn't even exist."[3] Mami Wata is now a generalized form of a multitude of local water divinities that vary significantly from each other. "Mami Wata" can be a synonym for such spirits, or a way of referring to one of them outside the local community. She has New World counterparts, who are not necessarily called Mami Wata.

Here, I endeavor to deconstruct a simplistic and unitary notion of "Mami Wata" and explore some of the contradictions and ambiguities implicit in her varied manifestations.

Visual Images

The iconography of Mami Wata —much studied by art historians—is less immediately relevant to the themes of this book than the way she is interpreted in popular culture. But the pluriform images equated with her name are an essential dimension of her elusive and changing identity.

In the popular art of the Democratic Republic of Congo, and in some other contexts,[4] Mami Wata is depicted as a woman with flowing hair, a fish tail, a mirror and a comb. The single-tailed mermaid was first seen on the prows of European sailing ships in the era of the slave trade. The earliest known representation in African art is to be found in an African-Portuguese ivory carved in Sierra Leone before 1743, and probably before 1520 (fig. 1). It is juxtaposed with a crocodile climbing a cross,[5] a sinister image that recalls the sculpture of an executioner, which was roughly contemporary (p. 31). An older icon, a human being with two fish or snake legs, curving outward, has also been linked with Western prototypes, but lies beyond the scope of the present study.

A different and distinctive image in West Africa and beyond shows Mami Wata not as a mermaid but as a woman wreathed in snakes (fig. 3).[6] In the late nineteenth century, a District Officer in southeastern Nigeria commissioned a local carver to copy a chromolith of a snake charmer (fig. 2), and it became popular. It is now found far from the sea, and has been

Fig. 1. The first African image of the single-tailed mermaid. An African-Portuguese ivory carving, collected before 1743, and probably made in Sierra Leone before 1520. Now in the National Museum, Copenhagen. After Fraser, 1972. Drawn by Peter Scott.

documented, for instance, in Mali (fig. 6).[7] Indian copies are very common in West Africa, as are local versions in painting and sculpture. The attraction of the image lies in its foreign origins, which are thought to demonstrate Mami Wata's ontological reality.

These are the dominant images, but there are others. Mami Wata is sometimes shown as a fair-skinned woman rather than as a mermaid.[8] Contemporary devotees sometimes make use of images of Hindu provenance, and in coastal Togo, a three-headed image is venerated as Papa Densu, her husband.[9] In murals copied from the walls of village houses in eastern Liberia, in 1949, she appears in various exotic forms. In one that is explicitly identified as Mami Wata, she has human legs, high-heeled shoes, a complete fish body and two fish tails; she wears earrings, and has a distinctive projecting hair arrangement or headdress (fig. 9).[10] This freedom of artistic expression may reflect a lack of familiarity with foreign prototypes.

Fig. 2. An Indian chromolith of a snake charmer, Bombay 1955. These chromoliths have been widely distributed in West Africa over a long period, and are clearly the prototype of the image of Mami Wata as a woman wreathed in snakes. Drewal believes that the original was produced in Europe c. 1855. After H. J. Drewal, 1988b. Drawn by Peter Scott.

In Portugal, in the 1930s, folk religion figured beautiful women with snakes instead of legs and treasure in their possession. They were called Mouras Encantadas, Enchanted Moors.[11] In an extraordinary mirror image, Portuguese spirits similar to Mami Wata were conceptualized as North African.

Fig. 3. Painted woodcarving of Mami Wata by Akpan Akpan Chukwu, c. 1972. Now in Oron Museum, Nigeria. Its derivation from the chromolith redrawn in figure 2 is apparent. After Salmons, 1972. Drawn by Peter Scott.

Naming Mami Wata

Language leaves fossil imprints, which suggests patterns in the history of ideas. The name Mami Wata is English pidgin. Like "juju" or " chop," it became common currency at the interface between West African coastal societies and European visitors, and may well have been initially dissemi-nated by Kru seamen from Liberia, who were recruited by European vessels

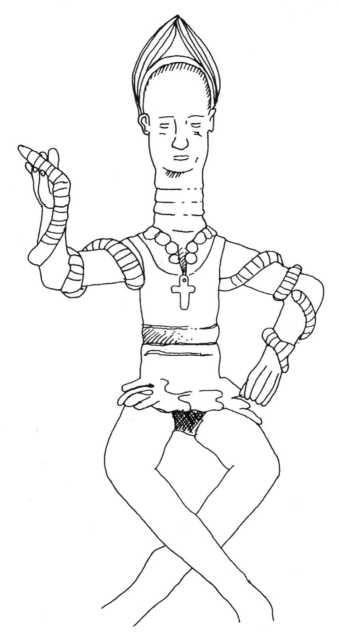

Fig. 4. A clay sculpture of Mami Wata by Nnaji, in an mbari house, Egbelu Obube (near Owerri) c. 1966. This combines the snake-wreathed motif with elements of an older iconography. Note the cross around her neck. After Cole, 1969. Drawn by Peter Scott.

Fig. 5. Mami Wata and Christ. Moral at the shrine of Abidjan Mami Wata, eastern Ghana, 1994. After Opuku and Wicker, 1994. Drawn by Peter Scott.

for service along the West African coast.[12] Pidgin and Creole languages, like Mami Wata, are manifestations of interculture.

The first known reference to Mami Wata (in the form "Watra Mama") comes from the New World—a 1783 dictionary of Surinam Creole that defined her as "*[ein] fabelhaftes, abentheuerliches Ungeheuer im Wasser.*"[13] In the late nineteenth century, a Surinam Maroon author wrote, "Various creatures live in rivers. . . . The people that saw *watramama* say her upper body is human and her lower body a fish; she lacks gills."[14]

It would be simplistic to see these references and her many African manifestations as part of a unitary history, but no student of Mami Wata

Fig. 6. Mami Wata by Sinaba, Mali sign writer. Note the reproduction of the diamond-shaped insert of the child snake charmer from figure 2. This image reflects the dissemination of the Mami Wata icon far from the sea. After Powell, 1994. Drawn by Peter Scott.

Fig. 7. Mami Wata with fish tail and mirror. Redrawn from the frontispiece of Eto's book, which interprets Mami Wata as a demon. After Eto, 1983. Drawn by Peter Scott.

Fig. 8. Mami Wata in the popular urban art of Zaire/Democratic Republic of Congo. Unattributed painting, before 1976. After Szombati-Fabian and Fabian, 1976. Drawn by Peter Scott.

Fig. 9. A village mural of Mami Wata from Bas Cavally, Ivory Coast, 1949. After Dekeyser and Holas, 1952. Drawn by Peter Scott.

can ignore her New World counterparts. Paxson has sought to explain these similarities by suggesting that returning former slaves brought the cult of Mami Wata to West Africa, but this has not won general acceptance.[15]

To my knowledge, the earliest reference to "Mami Wata" in Africa dates from 1914, and occurs in an account of a western Igbo water goddess.

> Nkepetime is commonly regarded as a woman; she is said to live in a shallow pool. . . . [She] answers to the ordinary description of a mermaid and appears to be known in Lagos as "mammy water."[16]

In francophone Africa, the first reference seems to be in a story collected in Popo (now Aného) and published in 1927. It tells of a being in mermaid form called Mami Ouata (thus in English, not French, pidgin).[17]

Both the name and images of a mermaid or of a woman wreathed with snakes spread rapidly in the colonial period. In the 1930s, Igbo mbari houses included sculptures of "A woman in a white shift with a blue headdress and with snakes in her hands and climbing over her . . . equated by my Ibo informant with the European mermaid."[18]

The name and the image have clearly spread still more widely in the decades since independence. In Senegal, where she is a motif in glass painting, she is called Abidjani Mami Wata, or the Djin de Côte d'Ivoire.[19] An Ewe Mami Wata priest in the Volta River region, in eastern Ghana, adopted the name Abidjan Mami Wata, on the advice of a mallam (fig. 5).[20] The significance of "Abidjan" in this context remains obscure. In the Democratic Republic of Congo, she is said to have been introduced by "Hausa" traders from Nigeria in the 1960s.

"Mami Wata" has become a synonym for a large number of quite different water divinities, which are often, apparently, unmodified. An example from Nigeria illustrates the complexities of these relationships. In 1979, Paula Ben-Amos found the lithograph of the woman wreathed with snakes at a Benin shrine to the sea god, Olokun. When she asked whom it represented, "one person answered that it was Mammy Water, but this was quickly amended by others who said it represented one of the traditional wives of Olokun."[21] Local and "traditional" spirits are named as Mami Wata in the course of interactions with the wider society, and it would be a mistake to reify and essentialize these manifestations.[22]

Significantly, Mami Wata is a recurrent motif in the popular music called highlife; like pidgin, it is a form of what has been called interculture. This chapter began with a literary example, and there are many historical ones. The Nigerian musician, Sir Victor Uwaifo, who is said to have attributed his success to Mami Wata, sang in 1960:

If you see Mami Wata O!
Never never run away.

In 1975, the Bembeya Jazz Band from Guinea recorded a Mami Wata song that is played on the Wendl and Weise video, *Die Weisse Frau*.[23] Thiery Yezo (d. 1995), the leader of the Central African Republic band Musiki, also recorded a Mami Wata song.

Indigenous Roots: "Traditional" Water Spirits

The rivers of West Africa and their divinities form a parallel universe to the world of the living. "[M]ost of the rivers and streams within Nigeria take their names from the goddesses and gods of the rivers or the streams."[24] These water divinities were often very different from each other and from the stereotypes of Mami Wata. Among the Ijo of the Niger Delta, water spirits were thought of as either male or female, and as potential sexual partners of the living. They were richly dressed and beautiful, and lived in fine towns under the sea. At the turn of the century, those they possessed were typically women, who acquired spirit husbands.[25]

In Douala, further east, water spirits tended to have their feet reversed—upside down and back to front[26]—a symbol of their ambiguity and unpredictability—and their original iconography was more reminiscent of a hobbit than of a mermaid!

An ancient representation shows a little black creature with a great amount of hair, very large protruding eyes, and turned-up toes. The modern representation is of a white woman with long hair (the *mamy wata)*.[27]

There are also significant differences between the Mami Wata of contemporary popular culture and "traditional" Igbo water spirits, which are still very much alive in the sensibility of local communities.[28] Some of these spirits, such as Njaba, were perceived as male. In the Okigwe area, Imo, Lolo, and Ihuku, goddesses of the streams that bear their names, are harsh and demanding. Lolo abhors alcohol, and kills anyone who dips, for instance, an empty gin bottle into her waters.[29]

Perhaps because of these differences, there has been a strong tendency, in Igboland, to locate Mami Wata worship in a different ritual context, that of the *ogbanje,* the Returner, a child born to die (the equivalent of the Yoruba *abiku*).[30] "Ogbanjes are the evil spirits of Mammy water. . . . They are demonised fishes."[31]

A study of the Mende of Sierra Leone, based on fieldwork in 1945–46, reflects a different pattern—a mermaid who seems to be Mami Wata under a different name, rather than a precursor.

> The *Tingoi* appears as a beautiful siren-like woman with a soft white skin. She lives in the deep water of a river and is seen, sometimes, perched on the brow of a rock combing out her hair with a shining golden comb.

Great riches can be won from her by withholding the comb.[32]

Water spirits are the most obvious prototypes, but there are also close links with myths of rainbow or aquatic serpents with which her cult is closely associated in modern Togo.[33] The diamond serpent was first described among the Temne of Sierra Leone in 1861, a hundred years before the discovery of diamonds there.[34]

By 1912:

> The Krifis [spirits] . . . are lighter in complexion than the negroes, being like white men or brown men they incarnate in a snake called "yaro," variously known as the magic, devil, or diamond snake, and they also visit people in the form of another person.[35]

An-yaron is now a water spirit, in the form of a fair woman, who is called Mami Wata.[36]

Foreign images of mermaids or snake-wreathed women seemed to confirm Mami Wata's ontological reality. A poem in Surinam Creole, called "Kopenhagen," reflects on that city's famous mermaid statue, and the apparently independent confirmation it provides of Watramama's existence.

> Watramama I know you truly
> Your golden comb, where is it?
> . . . Watramama you look at me, still as a mouse
> Ah, I know where this is:
> Surinam![37]

Mami Wata Stories

In a story recorded in coastal Togo in 1927, a poor man sees Mami Wata and seizes her mirror and gold comb; to recover them, she assumes human form, marries him, and gives him a ship full of valuables, requiring only that he conceal her origins (an international mytheme). But when he discloses her true identity, she vanishes; a tidal wave drowns him and carries away his home and treasures.[38]

A narrative recorded in Cabinda, in West Central Africa, in 1961, tells of a woman with magical powers who offered a villager wealth beyond imagining. "Then she sang another song and steamers appeared on the water in great hosts. . . ." But there was a price to pay—he must never again see his father, and the price, in the end, proved one he was unable to pay. "And with such sadness, Mavungu changed back to what he had formerly been, and in sorrow he died."[39] Mami Wata is not mentioned by name, but the parallels are obvious. It is a poignant commentary on wealth obtained at the cost of human relationships. Differently nuanced versions were recorded at the end of the nineteenth century.[40]

Mami Wata is mentioned twice in Chinua Achebe's 1972 collection of short stories, *Girls at War*. In each case, the setting is Onitsha market. In one story he writes of Mami Wata mingling with the crowds there. "You can always tell them, because they are beautiful with a beauty that is too perfect and too cold."[41] In another, he illustrates the way she is thought to bring wealth in things at the cost of wealth in people.

> I knew at once that I had been visited by Mama Wota, the Lady of the River Niger.
> Matthew said again, "It depends on what you want in life. If it is wealth you want you made a great mistake [in fleeing] but if you are a true son of your father then take my hand."
> . . . . [W]here is the man who will choose wealth instead of children? Except a crazy white man . . . .[42]

There is a very similar reflection in Flora Nwapa's novel *Efuru*, set in Oguta. Its eponymous heroine is a successful trader, but her marriages fail, and her only child dies. She sees Uhamiri, the spirit of Oguta Lake, in dreams.

> She was as old as the lake itself. She was happy, she was wealthy. She was beautiful. She gave women beauty and wealth but she had no child. . . . Why then did the women worship her?[43]

In a later story for children, the spirit of Oguta Lake is called Mami Wata.[44]

Although she is called Mami, mother, she is often thought of as hostile to procreation—embodying a choice of wealth in things, rather than of wealth in people. "Instead of children there is a golden tree. Instead of a womb there are golden scallop shells."[45]

"Nne Mmiri" [Mami Wata] . . . could forbid them from marrying. . . . The benefits the devotees enjoy range from riches, beauty, success, extraordinary business acumen, fame. . . . When offended she visits her anger through complex forms of afflictions. . . . No "ogbanje" ever lives a full and natural life cycle.[46]

This source refers to Igboland. Interviews conducted in Liberia, in 1965–66 yielded a similar picture.

They say that Mammy Water sits on top of rocks by the water side. . . . If she has interest to really help you, to give you money, then you will see her in dreams and you and she will have to make a certain compact. If you are a man, you must not marry any woman. If you keep to this promise, she brings money every time she visits you.[47]

These stories are versions of older myths of a Faustian pact. In some accounts, Mami Wata is much like a witch. "Bring me a person's blood, but this person must be only your own brother and sister."[48]

The View from Within

The image of Mami Wata prevailing within bands of initiates is a very different one. They look to her, not only for prosperity, but also for children, healing, and protection. A potential devotee may find Mami Wata "worrying" him or her in dreams or suffer from an affliction such as poor health, mental illness, or infertility and be advised by a diviner or by a Mami Wata priest or medium to seek her aid. These crises often afflict school pupils, and young women, perhaps unconsciously, sometimes escape in this way from an undesired marriage.

Not all the afflicted choose initiation. There are alternatives in Christian exorcism or other protective rituals, and in flight. De Rosny tells of a Duala schoolboy who became apathetic. His fellow students explained, "It's the *jengu,* the water spirit. The *jengu* does not wish Bona to remain at the school." His parents took him north, away from the sea.[49]

The life stories of devotees tend to reflect a history of poverty, and often of mental or physical illness or childlessness. At Lomé, in Togo:

Mamisi Adjoko . . . conducts the initiation of Kanyi, a male factory worker. . . . [T]hree of his children have died and his money "seems to slip through his fingers." Dressed in a woman's white wrapper . . . he enacts his own ritual death. . . .[50]

An Oguta Mami Wata priest tells of a time when she put salt in the fire and wood in the soup (images of insanity) and when she lost many children in infancy. Later "I married [another wife] for my husband and they gave me children."[51]

Spirit-possession cults, like "subjugated knowledges" in general, challenge conventional ways of seeing in a striking way. We have already noted (p. 94) how Mami Wata devotees blur and cross gender boundaries. She is perceived as a siren and seductress, but most of her devotees are women. This creates ambiguities in cultures where overt sexual expression is overwhelmingly if not exclusively heterosexual.[52] These ambiguities are often explicit, and gender ambiguity is equally apparent in similar cults in Haiti.[53]

Some women acquire a water-spirit husband. "Usually when I have a dream I jump into the sea. I go down to the very very bottom and lie down, down there, and he comes."[54] More commonly, woman devotees *become* Mami Wata, in a ritual setting. They lighten their skin with cosmetics, wear elaborate hairstyles, jewelry, and fine clothes, and embody her spirit, like those possessed by Ezili in Haiti.

To her initiates, Mami Wata is a source of mental and physical health, of prosperity, and of children. But in some contexts, she calls her worshippers to their deaths. At Anèho—the same Anèho where cowries were thought to feed on human flesh—an annual festival is held when perhaps a hundred women Mamisi hurl themselves into the dangerous surf; some are rescued unconscious, and some do not survive.[55]

Mami Wata in Central Africa

In Central Africa, Mami Wata is one of the core themes of a popular urban art dating from about 1960.[56] Male artists depict her as the quintessential sex object, a courtesan, another version of the commodified body. She is shown as a siren, an image of temptation, often in explicit opposition to the Bible. In a 1984 painting, *La Seduction* by Cheri Samba, he turns from her and reads the Bible, open at Luke 6:24, "Woe unto the rich."[57]

She is often called *mamba muntu,* crocodile person. In the words of a study of popular culture in Shaba:

> *Mamba muntu* is . . . a generic being which is said to live in many lakes and rivers of the country. . . . Sometimes *mamba muntu* comes to shore to rest and to comb her hair. The one who is lucky enough to obtain a lock, her comb, or any object associated with her, may expect to see her soon in a dream. He may then use these objects as a pawn and in addition he may have

to promise absolute fidelity . . . to the exclusion of other partners and silence about his encounter in which case he will suddenly become very rich.[58]

In Shaba she is also called *la sirène* or *madame poisson*; in the Kasai she is Mami Wata.[59] (Both regions are far inland.)

There also seems to be a growing devotion to female water spirits explicitly linked with Mami Wata, but they tend to go under different names. Mukisi is a Teke water goddess of Kongo origins. Initiates, who are women, "dream of waterfalls and rapids, of journeys in the air and under the ground, of children at play, the wealth of the Whites, of white men and women, of the dead from the European world, the Tsayi dead, of lightning, of large meals, songs, dances and gifts, parrots, pythons and tortoises." The cult promises wealth, but it proves an illusion—a valuable parrot is found, but escapes before it can be captured.[60]

Water Divinities in the New World

Mami Wata has counterparts in black religions in the New World—*santerìa* in Cuba, *candomblé* in Brazil, and *voudoun* in Haiti. The Yoruba Great Witch, Yemanja, has become a dangerous seductive mermaid in Brazil. In Jorge Amado's novel *Sea of Death,* set on the docks of Bahia in the 1930s, "Iemanja is the mother of the waters . . . she never shows herself to men unless they die in the sea. . . . In order to see the mother of waters many had already jumped into the sea, smiling, never to reappear. . . . In ancient times she lived on the coasts of Africa."[61]

The Ezili spirits of Haitian vodoun (Ezili-Fréda and her dangerous Petwo counterpart, Ezili Danto) have no African namesakes. The former is fair, richly dressed and speaks French; she loves perfume, sweet drinks, and gourmet food, and smokes Virginia slims—but in another manifestation, she becomes Ezili-gé-rouge—a cannibal. La Sirène is a mermaid, often equated with the different forms of Ezili, and closely associated with the whale. As with Yemanja, sexuality and death are interwoven—the hat falls into the water, and the wearer follows it and drowns.

> The mermaid, the whale,
> My hat falls into the sea.
> I caress the mermaid,
> My hat falls into the sea.
> I lie down with the mermaid,
> My hat falls into the sea.[62]

The image of the woman wreathed with snakes has reached Haiti in recent years; significantly, she is identified, not with La Sirène or Ezili, but with Danbala, the rainbow serpent; a mural was labeled, *Reine Travaux Dambala,* Danbala's Queen of Works.[63]

Interpreting Mami Wata

Mami Wata's notorious caprice and unpredictability mirror both the perils of the sea and life in the post-colony, where most struggle to survive. "A child goes fishing with his father; the father fishes, the child sits behind on the edge of the canoe. There is suddenly a cry and a splash in the water. The child has vanished; a jengu [water spirit] has taken him. Next morning, the corpse lies on the shore."[64] The uncertainties and injustices of life in contemporary West Africa are also mirrored in diamond mining, where some become rich and others toil but find nothing. In Kono, where diamonds have been mined since the late 1950s, diggers believe that contracts can be made with diamond spirits, sometimes explicitly identified with Mami Wata. "It has the diamond-luck and it has the diamond so it gives the diamond away. In return, it takes its payment. The earth may break and fall on people; so it takes its payment."[65]

Mami Wata was readily associated with European ascendancy in colonial governments and with the continuing wealth and power of the West when colonialism came to an end. A Mamisi in Togo "kept a wooden carving of 'Abolo' or the white man on horseback, an image of colonial inspiration associated with Mami Wata."[66] Her shrines are adorned with consumer goods, often foreign imports—"calico, chalk, pow[d]er tins, white images, cowries, coconuts, . . . fanta and coke bottles."[67] Salmons found a Mami Wata telephone in Ibibioland.[68]

Devotees are often drawn to Mami Wata in dreams and they embody her presence in a state of possession. Whatever aspirations her cults fulfills is formulated in the unconscious mind. To the poor, wealth seems unattainable by any means available in daily life—hence the explanatory role of the extraordinary. There is also an evident element of escapism, of make believe. Luxuries adorn her shrines, but her devotees live in a world where basic necessities are lacking. The medium who acts out the role of Mami Wata or Ezili-Fréda escapes for a moment into a world of beauty and elegance. Voudoun has been described as a religion of indigence—"The loa will live as long as hunger, misery, and affliction endure."[69] These spirits offer a transitory escape from a poverty they have not caused and will not remedy.

Those who depict these spirits in art, or act out their roles in a ritual context of possession, subject the West to the control and critique implicit in representation. Mami Wata and her New World counterparts encapsulate a profoundly ambiguous attitude to modernity and the consumer goods of the Western world. Wealth is attained at the cost of human lives and of family relationships. "Instead of a heart of flesh you find a lump of gold."[70] Riches remain attractive, but the price they exact is recognized and rejected. No single generalization is universally true; in many accounts, Mami Wata offers wealth at the price of life, or of children, but initiates join her cult hoping for offspring, or to preserve the health of children they already have. In some versions, she is much like a witch, but Douala water spirits aid diviners in their struggles with sorcery. In some interpretations she is a Christian, and in others a demon.

In many academic analyses, Africans are eternal recipients, absorbing certain elements from global culture and rejecting others. But this is a flawed model, and it is more accurate to think of the world as a network of Creole cultures.[71] Mami Wata has spread through much of Africa and crosses and recrosses the Black Atlantic. She is a significant component in a global culture, and if she is not recognized as such outside the world of academic specialists, it is because she belongs, for the most part, to the cognitive world of the unlettered and poor.

Notes

1. K. Saro-Wiwa, *Sozaboy: A Novel in Rotten English* (Harlow, 1994), 15.

2. R. Bennett, *The Catastrophist* (London, 1998), 1, 150.

3. L. M. Odinkemelu, *The Problem of Mammy Water,* vol. 2, *Mammy Water in the Society* (privately published, Orlu, Nigeria, 1988), 26.

4. For the former, see the illustrations in B. Jewsiewicki, "Painting in Zaire: From the Invention of the West to the Representation of Social Self," in S. Vogel (ed.), *Africa Explores 20th Century African Art* (New York and Munich, 1991), 18, 170; this is also the image on the frontispiece of Victoria Eto, *Exposition on Water Spirits* (1989; reprint, Warri, 1983).

5. D. Fraser, "The Fish-Legged Figure in Benin and Yoruba Art," in D. Fraser and H. Cole (eds.), *African Art and Leadership* (Madison, Milwaukee, and London, 1972), 277, figs. 14, 10.

6. J. Salmons, "Mammy Wata," *African Arts* (April, 1977): 8–15; H. J. Drewal, "Performing the Other: Mami Wata Worship in Africa," *The Drama Review* (1988): 160–85; and "Mermaids, Mirrors and Snake Charmers: Igbo Mami Wata Shrines," *African Arts* (1988): 38–45.

7. S. Sinaba, "Mami Watta," reproduced in I. Powell, "Africa Colonises the World," *Ventilator* (1994): 64.

8. Salmons, "Mammy Wata," 12. See also the line drawings by Obiora Udechukwu in Flora Nwapa, *Mammywater* (Enugu, 1979).

9. G. Chesi, *Voodoo Africa's Secret Power* (Worgl, Austria, 1980), 148, 253 (a photographic essay, mainly on the "traditional" religion of Togo).

10. P. L. Dekeyser and B. Holas, *Mission dans l'Est Libérien* (Dakar, 1952), 426ff, figs. 181–189. Fig. 184 is identified as Mami Wata.

11. G. Brooks, "The Observance of All Souls' Day in the Guinea Bissau, Region," *History in Africa* (1984): 9.

12. T. Wendl, *Mami Wata oder ein Kult zwischen den Kulturen* (Münster, 1991), 113–16.

13. Kramp, cited in Wendl, *Mami Wata,* 110.

14. "Trefossa" (pseud. H. de Ziel), *Trotji Met een stilistische studie over het gedicht Kopenhagen* (Amsterdam, 1957), 44 n.1. I owe this reference to David Dorward; Elli Mulder assisted me in translating it.

15. B. Paxson, "Mammy Water: New World Origins?" *Baessler-Archiv,* N. S. 31 (1983): 418ff; and see Wendl, *Mami Wata,* 112–13. One of the difficulties is that the motif seems to date only from the 1960s in Freetown.

16. N. W. Thomas, *Law and Custom of the Igbo of the Asaba District* (London, 1914), 14.

17. R. Trautmann, *La Littérature populaire à la Côte des Esclaves* (Paris, 1927), 41–2.

18. G. I. Jones, "Mbari Houses," *Nigerian Field* (1937): 78. Mbari houses, found in the Owerri area, were made in honor of the earth goddess, Ala. When completed, they were allowed to decay.

19. P. Langley, "On Mamy Wata," *African Arts* (May 1979): 11.

20. K. O. Opoku and K. O. Wicker, "Abidjan Mami Water Festival 1994," American Academy of Religion *Religious Studies News* (Nov. 1994): 17–18.

21. Paxson, "Mammy Water," 424.

22. C. Gore and J. Nevadomsky, "Practice and agency in Mammy Wata Worship in Southern Nigeria," *African Arts* (Spring 1997): 60–69.

23. T. Wendl and D. Weise, *Der Geist der Weissen Frau* (video, Institut für den wissenschaftlichen Film, Göttingen, 1988). See Langley, "On Mamy Wata," 11.

24. Odinkemelu, *The Problem of Mammy Water,* 25. The author is a Catholic priest, a charismatic who regards Mami Wata as daemonic.

25. A. G. Leonard, *The Lower Niger and its Tribes* (London, 1906), 228, 230.

26. J. Ittmann, "*Der kultische Geheimbund djengu an der Kameruner Küste,*" *Anthropos* (1957): 141; this is confirmed by E. Ardener, *Coastal Bantu of the Cameroons* (London, 1956), 93, citing T. Monod, *L'industrie des pêches au Cameroun*(Paris, 1928), 133–36.

27. Eric de Rosny, *Healers in the Night,* trans. R. R. Barr (Maryknoll, NY, 1985), 263. Also see R. Austen, "Tradition, Invention and History: The Case of the Ngondo (Cameroon)," *Cahiers d'Études africaines* (1992): 304.

28. I explore this in "Mami Wata and Indigenous Cultures: Two Case Studies—Igboland and the Cameroon Coast," forthcoming in a book on Mami Wata edited by Henry Drewal (Los Angeles: University of California/Fowler Museum).

29. C. N. Ubah, "The Supreme Being, Divinities and Ancestors in Igbo Traditional Religion: Evidence from Otanchara and Otanzu," *Africa* (1982): 96–98.

30. Chinwe Achebe *The World of the Ogbanje* (Enugu, 1986), 15, 22.

31. Eto, *Exposition on Water Spirits,* 3.

32. K. Little, *The Mende of Sierra Leone* (London, 1951), 222–23. See also W. T. Harris and H. Sawyerr, *The Springs of Mende Belief and Conduct* (Freetown, 1968), 39–41.

33. Wendl and Weise, *Der Geist der Weissen Frau* (video)

34. C. F. Schlenker, *A Collection of Temne Traditional Fables and Proverbs* (London, 1861), xi.

35. R. G. Berry, "The Sierra Leone Cannibals," *Proceedings of the Royal Irish Academy* (1912): 59.

36. R. Shaw, "Mami Wata and the Sierra Leone Diamonds" (African Studies Assoc., Orlando, Florida, 1995).

37. Text in Surinam Creole in "Trefossa," *Trotji,* 32 and inside back cover (with Dutch translation).

38. Trautmann, *La Littérature populaire,* 41–42.

39. John Janzen, *Lemba 1650–1930: A Drum of Affliction in Africa and the New World* (New York and London, 1982) 223–28, also xiii. *Mavungu* is a generic name, found in many stories.

40. R. E. Dennett. *Notes on the Folklore of the Fjort (French Congo)* (c. 1898; reprint, Nendeln, 1967), 39–45.

41. Chinua Achebe, "The Sacrifical Egg," in *Girls at War and Other Stories* (London, 1972), 43.

42. Chinua Achebe, "Uncle Ben's Choice," in *Girls at War* (London, 1972), 88–9. He goes on to cite a historic white trader, who wrote his own account of life at Onitsha.

43. Flora Nwapa, *Efuru* (1966; reprint, Oxford, 1978), 221; similar themes are found in her later books.

44. Flora Nwapa, *Mammywater* (Enugu, Nigeria, 1979).

45. Eto, *Exposition on Water Spirits,* 40.

46. Achebe, *The World of the Ogbanje,* 24–5.

47. A Gissi informant, quoted in R. Wintrob, "Mammy Water: Folk Beliefs and Psychotic Elaborations in Liberia," *Canadian Psychiatric Association Journal* (1970): 145.

48. Wintrob, "Mammy Water," 147.

49. de Rosny, *Healers in the Night,* 11.

50. S. L. Kasfir, *African Arts* (1994): 81, summarizing an episode in Wendl and Weise, *Der Geist der Weissen Frau* (video).

51. Sabine Jell-Bahlsen, "*Eze mmiri di egwu*: The Water Monarch is Awesome: Reconsidering the Mammy Water Myths," *Annals of the New York Academy of Sciences* (1997): 126, and her "Mammy Water: In Search of the Water Spirits of Nigeria (video, Univ. of Cal. Extension Center, 1989).

52. This is a complex question needing further research. In southern Nigeria, the institutionalization of transvestitism (seen in Igbo maiden masks, and in many Yoruba ritual contexts, including Gelede) contrasts with the universality of marriage (at least as desired and the norm), and the invisibility of gay relations.

53. Salmons, "Mammy Wata," 11; E. Bourguignon, "Dreams and Dream Interpretation in Haiti, " *American Anthropologist* (1954): 265.

54. de Rosny, *Healers in the Night,* 273 (quoting a woman from coastal Cameroon).

55. Chesi, *Voodoo,* 148, 157.

56. Jewsiewicki, "Painting in Zaire," 146.

57. Ibid., 170.

58. I. Szombati-Fabian and J. Fabian, "Art History and Society: Popular Painting in Shaba, Zaire," *Studies in the Anthopology of Visual Communication* (1976): 17; on the links between *mamba muntu* and *Mami Wata,* see 20 n.24.

59. Szombati-Fabian and Fabian, "Popular Painting in Shaba," 19 n 12.

60. M. C. Dupré, "Comment être femme, un aspect du rituel Mukisi chez les Téké," *Archives de Science Sociale des Religions* (1978): 63–5.

61. Jorge Amado, *Sea of Death,* trans. G. Rabasso (New York, 1984), 15.

62. K. M. Brown, *Mama Lola A Vodou Priestess in Brooklyn* (Berkeley, 1991), 223.

63. M. Houlberg, "Sirens and Snakes: Water Spirits in the Arts of Haitian Vodou," *African Arts* (1996): 34.

64. Quoted in Ittmann, "Der kultische Geheimbund djengu," 142.

65. Quoted in R. Shaw, "Mami Wata and the Sierra Leone Diamonds," paper presented to African Studies Association meeting, Orlando, Florida, 1995.

66. J. Rosenthal, "Foreign Tongues and Domestic Bodies: Gendered Cultural Regions and Regionalized Sacred Flows," in M. Grosz-Ngate and O. H. Kokole (eds.), *Gendered Encounters: Challenging Cultural Boundaries and Social Hierarchies in Africa* (New York, 1997), 197.

67. Eto, *Exposition on Water Spirits,* 26.

68. Salmons, "Mammy Wata", 11.

69. J. Dayan, "Carribean Cannibals and Whores," *Raritan* (1989), 62. The quotation cites Jacques Stéphen Alexis, *Les arbres musiciens* (1957).

70. Eto, *Exposition on Water Spirits,* 40.

71. See K. Barber and C. Waterman, "Traversing the Global and the Local: Fuji Music and Praise Poetry in the Production of Contemporary Yoruba Popular Culture," in D. Miller (ed.), *Worlds Apart* (London and New York, 1995), 240–41.

15

SYMBOLIC APPROPRIATIONS OF MODERNITY

"By his car shall ye know him."
William Boyd, *A Good Man in Africa*[1]

Instead of fading away, as Western technology advanced, "traditional" religion has often appropriated its forms. We have already noted examples of this pattern—the association of vampires with Western medical apparatus and motor transport, the medium who speaks with Mami Wata by telephone. In 1930, myths current in Cameroon suggested that ekong sorcerers had a train (a *masin* or machine) on the magic mountain, Kupe. Sometimes they traveled so far from home that they could not find the way back, and died. Its engine was powered by a captive soul.[2] Like Central African stories of a black ancestor who invented planes (p. 181), myths of this kind place technical innovation within the sphere of African knowledge and control. The technical experts, however, are not engineers but sorcerers. Among the Tiv of Central Nigeria in the 1930s, it was said that

> since the white men came, and the *mbatsav* [sorcerers] have seen the bicycle, they have made bicycles for themselves to ride by night, and motor bicycles too, and cars—nothing is beyond the power of the *mbatsav*.[3]

This chapter explores the ongoing incorporation of Western consumer goods into the changing symbolic universe of popular culture; it deals mainly, but not exclusively, with transport and attire. Cars are a symbol of danger and of social polarization but are also coveted for their convenience and the status they confer; they provide a nuanced index of class relations. Clothing, similarly, mirrors gradations of wealth, but also makes symbolic statements of a different kind

The appropriation of modern technology into neo-traditional world views is an ongoing process. In 1966, a Zaire villager was sentenced to thirty days in jail; he had "confessed to having killed six of his neighbors by witchcraft and sending their souls to Kinshasa in aircraft made of leaves."[4] The much older motif of the captive soul is articulated in a new way. In the early 1990s, an old woman from southwest Cameroon told an inquirer,

> "I have been driving all night. I drive a plane. We use the plane to transport food, rain and such from places of plenty to the Buea area . . . ." She went on to explain to me that she has never seen an airplane, but she knows how a plane can be built. All planes are in the world of witchcraft, and when the white man gets it from the black man, he then interprets it into real life. As it is with planes, so with televisions, radios, telephones etc.[5]

In Sierra Leone, people speak of witch guns, and in northern Ghana, in the 1990s, witches were said to have tanks and missiles.[6] Marshall, writing of Nigerian Pentecostals, describes the recurrent motif of a "spiritual world under the sea," where luxury cars are made and "the devil makes people 'dance to his tune' by controlling them through his computer."[7]

Some of these images, like the links between cars and vampires, intensify the power—and hence the terror—of imagined predators. In the same way, electricity, has been linked with vampires. In Buhaya, it was said that

> [t]here are houses in Mwanza where they steal people's blood. They use electricity, and your body, it dries up. They steal your blood and just toss your corpse into a big hole in the back. I have been in these houses! The front door is made of wood, and they have written, "Danger, Electricity" . . . on it.[8]

The symbolic meanings of electricity are complex and far reaching. It is mysterious, useful, and potentially lethal, a powerful metaphor for modernity that has also been applied to AIDS. "AIDS is racing like electricity," say the Haya. Access to electricity is one of the variables that differentiate rich and poor—the former have electricity and use generators during power cuts. An article on energy sources in Africa is subtitled, "Power to *some* people."[9] " [S]uch institutions concretely embody a structure of privileged appropriation that has forcefully reconfigured the rural moral landscape."[10]

Way of Death[11]

Roads and railways played a crucial role in the creation and preservation of colonial states, so that it is not surprising that they loomed large in the visions of African prophets. In Africa, as in Australia, road-makers often disturbed important sacred sites. In 1917, in the Ekiti (Yoruba) town of Efon, a man became the Alaye (king), called *Omo Oyinbo,* son of the European, because he encouraged modernization in general and road construction in particular. Many years later, his widow told a researcher

> the story of how there was a gentle oracular spirit who lived in the forest by Efon (the wife of a long deceased Alaye) where she looked after the wild creatures and answered peoples' queries; in 1927 she told Aladejare, the Alaye, that "her pot of indigo dye had been broken by the new road, and that she was leaving Efon to return no more."[12]

This is an eloquent symbolic history of the apparent victories of modernity. There is a striking and not dissimilar symbolism in the fact that Joseph Babalola, the Christian prophet who led a great revival in Ekiti, and inspired bonfires of traditional religious objects, was originally the driver of a road grader.

In the 1920s, a number of popular women's movements sprang up in southeastern Nigeria. The women were hostile to the new roads, which they linked with death, partly because of the danger of accidents, but also because they believed—accurately enough—that they were the way through which infections reached the village. During the influenza pandemic of 1918–19, it was suggested that "the Motors were breeding the sickness."[13] In 1925, those involved in an Igbo women's protest movement demanded that the old footpaths be reopened and the roads created by the colonial government be destroyed.[14]

Modern highways bring both opportunity and danger. In the mid 1950s, Field met Ghanaian lorry drivers at a shrine, "bringing their new lorries and themselves for protection from accidents, enemies and financial ruin. 'There is death and life in lorry work.'"[15] Highways facilitate the journeys of long distance traders and of labor migrants, but high accident rates are linked with excessive speed, inadequate maintenance, both of vehicles and road surfaces, and, in recent years, a chronic shortage of spare parts. A study of Yoruba taxi drivers in the 1980s found that 80% of Muslims and 60% of Christians had protective charms in their vehicles, "a resort to symbolic action in the face of uncertainties. In Nigeria armed robbers may attack and steal the vehicle. The roadside mechanic may have mistakenly connected two wires that can ignite and burn the vehicle. . . . The treads on the tyres have become unrecognisable because of wear. . . ."[16] The Yoruba call the road the "long coffin which holds 1400 corpses."[17] There is a comparable Igbo proverb that to go on a road journey is like taking an oath (which will kill one if one swears falsely).

In the early years of independence, it was assumed that improvements in transport, an expanded educational system, and industrialization would lead to "development." The mirage of development receded and the infrastructure decayed. In some parts of Nigeria, villagers levy unofficial road tolls in return for filling potholes.

To the risk of road accidents is added a new association with AIDS, giving a further dimension to the concept, Way of Death. "No group in Africa is more heavily infected with infection than the truckers, prostitutes, and soldiers who ride the highways and visit the truck stops."[18]

Kane Kwei is a Ghanaian who makes coffins that are both elaborate and original and are to be found in major museum collections. One takes the form of a Mercedes and another of a Boeing 727. To the Western observer, they are a bizarre memento mori, a commentary on the vanity of a life devoted to wealth and luxury. This is not their intention. They are intended as a celebration of the life of the deceased (one, intended for onion farmers, is in the form of an onion) but the coffin car reminds us of how often in Africa—and indeed elsewhere—cars become coffins.[19]

Death and the road are recurrent themes in Wole Soyinka's poetry. He wrote elegiacally of an accident victim:

> For him who was
> Lifted on tar sprays
> And gravel rains
> In metallic timbres
> Harder than milestone heart[20]

But it is his play, *The Road*, which explores the theme most fully. Sergeant Burma survived five years of war and then drove an oil tanker. "But of course his brakes failed going down a hill."[21]

> Come then, I have a new wonder to show you . . . a madness where a motor-car throws itself against a tree—Gbram! And showers of crystal flying on broken souls . . .[22]

Where sacred sites were disturbed by road construction in southern Niger in the late 1980s, their spirits did not depart peacefully like their Efon counterpart, but were thought to range along the highways, wreaking havoc. They often took the form of beautiful women, betrayed only by their hoofed feet.[23] The ritual equipment of a Niger diviner included an advertising sign for Dunlop tires, a female figure not unlike Mami Wata, except for the fact that her lower body was not a fish tail, but a tire. She was thought to be an evil spirit, who caused accidents on a major highway by turning into a car and crashing into oncoming vehicles. A Frenchman was said to have photographed her in the moment of transformation.[24]

A Nigerian woman Pentecostal, in a curiously similar image, described "how evil spirits enter vehicles, transforming themselves into roaring lions 'in the spiritual realm' in order to cause accidents to get blood for their 'international blood banks.'"[25] In modern Africa, the poor sell their blood to the rich for money. In Iyayi's novel *Violence,* set in Nigeria, the protagonist sells his blood to a man in a blue Mercedes for fifteen Naira a pint. "And this he had done not once nor twice but many times."[26]

It was not only in Efon that "traditional" spirits departed, when a road was built. In Jamba's novel *Patriots,* set in Angola, a new bridge is built across the Cuando river, and the resident rainbow serpent disappears.[27]

Other sources suggest that "tradition" is ultimately victorious. In the late 1970s, in Calabar, the Nigerian Ports Authority is said to have offered sacrifices to a local sea goddess to end accidents that had plagued construction work.[28] In Igboland, a German engineer set out to build a bridge across the Njaba river, but its eponymous divinity made the bridge collapse. The engineer gave Njaba's priest money for substantial sacrifices. The bridge was built but the engineer died—an outcome Njaba had foretold.[29]

In Cameroon, a bridge across the Wouri river links Douala with the hinterland.

> Dreamers call it a symbolic link between the modern world and tradition. In reality, this seemingly inoffensive bridge favours modernism and hastens the death of customs. The residents understood this very well when they demanded that the Batignolles Company cast certain offers to the bottom of the deep, to appease the *niengu* before pouring the last arch. The engineers guffawed, then complied, understanding nothing.[30]

Symbolic Cars

Like vampire cowries, cars sometimes take on a sinister life of their own. Kaswa's vision of the future included a nightmare vision of animate mechanized transport.

> The strangers come in flying machines with popping eyes,
> Purging fire from their arses.
> They bring the millipede and the tortoise.

There are many Fipa stories about "flying machines," which include cars, and modern informants identify the protruding eyes with headlights, the excreted fire with car exhausts, the train with the millipede and the car with the tortoise. "In this alarmingly transformed world, the products of man's social labor take on a frightening life of their own."[31]

We have noted the predilection of colonial vampires for fire engines, or other forms of motor transport. "In Nyasaland [in the 1950s] the rumor had it that the vampires used a gray Land Rover with a shiny metal back which looked a little like a bully-beef tin blown up, to transport away their human cargo."[32] There are parallels in Haitian voudoun. "At Port-au-Prince, the populace stood in great panic of a 'tiger-car' which kidnapped children to eat them."[33]

In Sierra Leone, in the 1950s, Alligator Men were thought to travel in a submarine that looked like a car. "What I saw looked like a box with a glass front. . . . The glass was like the glass windows of a car."[34]

At much the same time, in Cameroon, a young Bakweri man claimed to have been attacked by zombies who were driving an astral lorry.[35] Mayer, writing of Ghana in the 1990s, suggests that "many an owner of a minibus used for public transport is said to give the Devil a bloody human sacrifice in exchange for the financial success of his enterprise every year."[36] In a sense, this is a True Fiction; many people die each year in these vehicles, because of their poor maintenance and excessive speed.

In a different symbolic structure, motor vehicles have become universal and powerful symbols of class differentiation. There are of course, other status symbols, but the car is immediately visible and provides a precise index of its owner's means and a measurable goal to which one may aspire. Cars and money are often symbolically equated. In contemporary Tanzania, the five shilling coin is called a Scania, after the bus of this name, while the 500 shilling note introduced in 1989 is a Pajero (an expensive four-wheel drive).[37]

When I lived in Nyerere's Tanzania in 1969–71, waBenzi was a term of strong disapproval. Echoes survive in the Uganda story of the predatory AIDS sufferer in the White Mercedes (p. 161). In Buganda, a neologism of recent vintage refers to the prosperous in derogatory tones as maayikka, "my car."[38] Luxury cars symbolize the corruption and greed of the powerful.

In 1980, Fela Anikulapo-Kuti sang, in "Authority Stealing,"

> Instead of workers, we have officials
> Instead of buses, dem dey ride motor car
> Instead of motor cycles, na helicopter . . .
> If gun steal eighty thousand naira, pen go steal two billion naira.[39]

In Africa, the poor walk; someone slightly more prosperous owns a bicycle and aspires to a motorcycle, "a machine," in significant Nigerian pidgin. The gradations move upwards—through old cars to chauffeur-driven luxury models. In the words of one of Achebe's characters:

> No condition is permnent. . . . Even common bicycle I no get. But my mind strong that one day I go jump bicycle, jump machine and land inside motor car! And somebody go come open door for me and say *yes sir!*[40]

At the bottom of the motor-vehicle prestige pyramid was the Volkswagen Beetle (which I drove for many years!). "If you gonna be killed by a car, you don't wanna be killed by a Volkswagen. You wanra Limousine, a Ponriac or something like that."[41] The titles of two Nigerian novels include the brand name of an expensive car. In Ekwensi's 1961 *Jagua Nana*, "They called her Jagua because of her good looks and stunning fashions. They said she was Ja-gwa, after the famous British prestige car."[42] After experiencing successive tragedies, Jagwa resolves to become a trader. "I wan' to become proper merchant princess. I goin' to buy me own shop, and lorry, and employ me own driver."[43]

Nkem Nwankwo's novel *My Mercedes is Bigger Than Yours* was published fourteen years later.[44] Its protagonist, Onuma, buys a Jaguar with borrowed money and, for a time, enjoys the adulation of his village. But again, Things Fall Apart; the car runs off the road and is stripped before he can recover it. He tries unsuccessfully to recoup his finances in politics and finally commits murder, driving away in his victim's Mercedes. Like novels about money magic, Nwankwo's is a moral fable, teaching that an excessive materialism leads only to disaster. Cars also loom large in Boyd's 1981 comic novel *A Good Man in Africa*.

Mercedes Benzes came at the top of the list; you hadn't arrived until you did in a Mercedes. They were for heads of state, important government officials, high-ranking soldiers, very successful businessmen and chiefs. Next came the Peugeot for the professional man. . . . It spelt respectability. Citroens, grade three, were for young men on the make. . . .[45]

Ironically, the Nigerian financial crisis which began about that time made the acquisition of new vehicles impossible, except for the extremely rich. Spare parts became scarce and prohibitively expensive. The former elite, with the exception of the very rich, drove aging and poorly maintained vehicles, if any.[46] In the 1990s and later, Nigerians spoke of traveling by leggedes-Benz (on foot).[47]

Cars are important symbols in late-1980s' novels about money magic (discussed in chapter 11). In Babarinsa's *Anything for Money,* Kadara decides to practice money magic when a man who owns both a Rolls Royce and an airplane wins his girlfriend. When he acquires wealth, his first action is to change his third-hand Volkswagen for a "Mercedes Benz Automatic 450SL."[48] (The specificity is striking.)

My Mercedes is Bigger Than Yours opens and closes with passages comparing Onuma's car with a mistress.[49] But while vehicles are humanized— echoes of commodity fetishism—people are treated like things. "The things that made him a personality . . . had atrophied for lack of use. In his pursuit of ephemera he had discounted . . . human beings."[50] And meanwhile, Onuma himself has become a commodity to others. "[He] had been nothing but a pawn all these months, a tool for all kinds of combatants to use."[51]

These varied sources embody a complex view of moral economy. The car is a status symbol, both coveted and resented. But the dangers of road transport are acknowledged, and cars are often linked with human or supernatural predators.

Clothes

Change in society expressed in terms of the microcosm of the human body has been a recurrent theme in this book. The multivalent symbolic meanings of the body's coverings are one dimension of this process. Sahlins wrote of America, in words which are at least equally true of Africa, that "the system of . . . clothing amounts to a very complex scheme of cultural categories and the relations between them, a veritable map—it does not exag-

gerate to say—of the cultural universe."[52] Clothing is a visible mirror of
social differentiation that lends itself to many subtleties of expression. It
has provided a map of class relations in Africa for centuries. Fernandes,
writing at the beginning of the sixteenth century, described the connection
between elite attire and foreign trade among the Wolof of Senegal:

> The great lords of Gyloffa [Jolof] are well dressed in cloths of *marlotas.* These
> cloths are brought there by Christians by sea and also overland by the Moors.
> Common people wear cotton shirts which reach their knees. . . .[53]

In a historical novel set on the fringes of the Niger Delta in 1918,
Amadi described the same linkages between status, resplendent dress and
foreign trade:

> Massive rings of gold graced the Eze's ten fingers. His heavy flowing shirt
> with an inner lining of purple was made of that costly stuff known as Opukapa.
> It was a very rare material found only in the treasure chests of those who had
> traded with the white man from across the roaring Abaji now known as the
> Atlantic.[54]

The symbolic meanings of cars and of clothes sometimes merge, and
the wealthy women who dominate the textile trade of Lomé are called
Nana Benz.[55] In Waterman's account of a Muslim Yoruba funeral celebration, in 1979, he describes a man who arrives in a Mercedes, wearing an
expensive lace gown decorated with the Mercedes logo.[56]

The wealthy have often opted for neo-traditional dress, which lends
itself to ostentation, because of the large quantity of frequently very expensive cloth required. This mirrors the cultural values of societies that place
great importance on clothing. A Yoruba proverb compares it with children—"children are the clothes of men."[57] It also reflects the way in which
the beneficiaries of the post-colony have often resorted to ethnic or cultural
patriotism to gloss over socio-economic differences. Fabric is also used for
propaganda, and politicians have often spent large sums on cloth to give
away, decorated with their own portraits.

In 1982, a high quality damask outfit cost $67 in Senegal, more than
a month's income for many households; if it was machine-embroidered it
cost much more. Poorer women wear machine-printed cotton called legos
(after Lagos, Nigeria), but its patterns often copy expensive cloth. A het-
erodox branch of the Mourides, the Baye Fal, use scraps of legos to make
bright patchwork clothes, which, like their dreadlocks and their alcohol
and cannabis consumption, demarcate their distinctive subculture. The

complexities of the language of cloth do not end here, for the state textile industry produces a print that copies Baye Fal patchwork.[58]

Materialism Rejected

While cars and clothes become part of the fabric of popular imagination, there is also a strand of thought that condemns Western style consumerism. Articulate traditions, which are often, but not always, rooted in Islam, sometimes reject materialism. In 1930, a Hausa poet warned against Western dress, Western clothes, the learning of English and hurricane lamps:

> Whatever article of their clothing, if you wear it . . .
> If you pray a thousand times you will not be vindicated—
> And the same applies to the maker of hurricane lamp globes. . . .
> Towel and washing-blue, and powder, whoever uses them,
> Certainly on the Last Day the Fire is his dwelling.[59]

He warned his hearers against washing blue, rather than cars, because the former was within their means, the latter unimaginably beyond them.

The Cameroon mallam popularly known as Maitatsine died a violent death in Kano, Nigeria, in 1980, during a revolt of the disinherited in which some four thousand died. [60] He had a similar message, "preaching that anyone wearing a watch, or riding a bicycle, or driving a car, or sending his child to the normal State schools was an infidel."[61]

Conclusion

These symbolic narratives are often most eloquent in their mutual inconsistencies. Car ownership confers great prestige but motor vehicles are also associated with dangerous predation. Werecrocodiles have submarines that look like cars. The Man in a White Mercedes deliberately infects others with AIDS. The Man in a Blue Mercedes buys blood for a pittance. Road or bridge construction is an apparent triumph of modernity, but ancient spirits—and those of recent vintage—exact their own revenge.

While the products of modern technology are integrated with older cognitive worlds, contemporary African nations suffer from inflation, shortages, unemployment, and a dearth of commodities seen in its most extreme form in recurrent famines. Societies that were once self-sufficient have, through a complex historical process I explore elsewhere, come to depend on imports, including imported food. This deprivation is peculiarly painful because the consumerism so characteristic of the Western world is mirrored, even exceeded, in the conspicuous consumption so characteristic of a tiny minority, Africa's rich and powerful. Foreign television programs reflect a receding and unattainable world of things. We have noted a Togo cloth design called Dallas, after the American TV series about millionaire oil barons.[62]

Consumption, in the sense of eating, is a central theme in this study. But the word, of course, has different meanings, evident in expressions such as "consumer goods," or "conspicuous consumption." One scholar, writing of the West, finds it significant that "consumption" formerly meant tuberculosis—like Lemba sickness, a form of wasting disease.[63]

In recent years, many studies of the cultural meaning of consumer goods have appeared; most of them focus on choices and behavior in the Western world. McCracken, writing of the interaction between culture and consumption, observes:

> By "culture" I mean the ideas and activities with which we construe and construct our world. . . . Culture and consumption have an unprecedented relationship in the modern world. No other time or place has seen these elements enter into a relationship of such intense mutuality. Never has the relationship between them been so deeply complicated.[64]

Possessions and their absence have acquired multiple layers of symbolic meaning. Cars, in particular, both reflect an elaborate socio-economic calculus, and embody a subversive critique of economic inequalities.

Notes

1. William Boyd, *A Good Man in Africa* (Harmondsworth, 1981), 29.

2. J. Ittmann, *"Der Kupe in Aberglauben der Kameruner,"* *Der Evangelische Heidenbote* (Basel, 1930), 111.

3. R. East, trans. and ed., *Akiga's Story* (Oxford, 1939), 248. "Akiga" was Akighirga Sai.

4. W. MacGaffey, "The West in Congolese Experience," in P. D. Curtin (ed.), *Africa and the West* (Madison, WI, 1972), 61.

5. Quoted in P. Geschiere, *The Modernity of Witchcraft* (Charlottesville, 1997), 3.

6. D. Rosen, "Dangerous Women: 'Ideology', 'Knowledge' and Ritual Among the Kono of Eastern Sierra Leone," *Dialectical Anthropology* (1981): 159; S. Drucker-Brown, "Mamprusi witchcraft, Subversion and Changing Gender Relations, " *Africa,* (1993): 534.

7. R. Marshall, "'God is not a Democrat': Pentecostalism and Democratisation," in P. Gifford (ed.), *The Christian Churches and the Democratisation of Africa* (Leiden, 1995), 251.

8. Brad Weiss, *The Making and Unmaking of the Haya Lived World* (Durham, NC, and London, 1996), 203, 211.

9. P. O'Keefe and J. Soussan, "Energy: Power to Some People," *Review of African Political Economy* (1991): 107–114. My italics.

10. Weiss, *The Haya Lived World*, 211.

11. See J. Miller, *Way of Death: Merchant Capitalism and the Angolan Slave Trade* (London, 1988).

12. J. D. Y. Peel, *Aladura: A Religious Movement Among the Yoruba* (London, 1968), 94.

13. Quoted in S. Martin, *Palm Oil and Protest: An Economic History of the Ngwa Region, South-Eastern Nigeria, 1800–1980* (Cambridge, 1988), 71.

14. District Officer Awgu to Resident, Onitsha Province, 12 Mar. 1926, and other documents, in Nigerian National Archives, Enugu. Onitsha Province 391/1925. For more detail on this movement, see E. Isichei, *A History of the Igbo people* (London and Basingstoke, 1976), 151–52.

15. M. Field, *Search for Security: An Ethno-Psychiatric Study of Rural Ghana* (London, 1960), 123.

16. O. B. Lawuyi, "The World of the Yoruba Taxi Driver: An Interpretive Approach to Vehicle Slogans," *Africa* (1988): 4–5.

17. B. Belasco, *The Entrepreneur as Culture Hero: Preadaptations in Nigerian Economic Development* (New York, 1980), 26.

18. P. Hilts, "Dispelling Myths about AIDS in Africa," *Africa Report* (1988): 27.

19. S. Vogel, ed., *Africa Explores 20th Century African Art* (New York and Munich, 1991), 110; see also V. Burns, "Travel to Heaven: Fantasy Coffins," *African Arts* (1974): 24–5.

20. Wole Soyinka, "In Memory of Segun Awolowo," in *Idanre and Other Poems* (London, 1967), 14.

21. Wole Soyinka, *The Road* (London, 1965), 83.

22. Ibid., 11.

23. A. Masquelier, "Encounter with a Road Siren: Machines, Bodies and Commodities in the Imagination of a Mawri Healer," *Visual Anthropology Review* (1992): 56, 66.

24. Ibid., 57 and 58, fig. 1.

25. R. Marshall, "'God is not a Democrat'," 250.

26. Festus Iyayi, *Violence* (Harlow, 1979), 154–55. This reflects the fact that the relatives of a patient who needs, for instance, two pints of blood, are required to find two pints for the blood bank.

27. S. Jamba, *Patriots* (London, 1990), 18.

28. R. Hackett, *Religion in Calabar: The Religious Life and History of a Nigerian Town* (Berlin and New York, 1989), 181.

29. Narrated by Ohanenye in Sabine Jell-Bahlsen, "Mammy Water: In Search of the Water Spirits in Nigeria" (Ogbuide Films, Berkeley, 1989), reviewed by S. L. Kasfir, *African Arts* (1994): 80.

30. Eric de Rosny, *Healers in the Night,* trans. R. R. Barr (Maryknoll, NY, 1985), 259.

31. R. Willis, "Kaswa: Oral Traditions of a Fipa Prophet," *Africa* (1970): 252–53.

32. P. Fraenkel, *Wayaleshi* (London, 1959), 201. The symbolic role of cars is studied in L. White, "Cars Out of Place: Vampires, Technology and Labour in East and Central Africa," *Representations* (1993): 27–50.

33. A. Métraux, Haiti Black Peasants and Their Religion, trans. P. Lengyel (London, 1960), 97.

34. Milan Kalous, *Cannibals and Tongo Players* (privately printed, Auckland, New Zealand, 1974), 82.

35. E. Ardener, "Witchcraft Economics and the Continuity of Belief," in M. Douglas, *Witchcraft Confessions and Accusations* (London, 1970), 151.

36. B. Meyer, "'Delivered From the Powers of Darkness': Confessions of Satanic Riches in Christian Ghana," *Africa* (1995): 238.

37. Weiss, *The Haya Lived World,* 182.

38. H. N. Mugambi, "From Story to Song: Gender, Nationhood and the Migratory Text," in M. Grosz-Ngaté and O. H. Kokole, *Gendered Encounters: Challenging Cultural Boundaries and Social Hierarchies in Africa* (New York and London, 1997), 220.

39. C. Waterman, *Juju: A Social History and Ethnography of an African Popular Music* (Chicago, 1990), 226.

40. Braimoh in Chinua Achebe, *Anthills of the Savannah* (London, 1988), 193.

41. Say Tokyo Kid in Soyinka, *The Road,* 27.

42. Cyprian Ekwensi, *Jagua Nana* (London, 1961), 5.

43. Ibid., 192.

44. Nkem Nwankwo, *My Mercedes is Bigger Than Yours* (London, 1981).

45. William Boyd, *A Good Man in Africa* (Harmondsworth, 1981), 29.

46. This theme is explored in J. P. Daloz, "Voitures et prestige au Nigeria," *Politique Africaine* (1990): 148–53.

47. R. Marshall, "Power in the Name of Jesus," *Review of African Political Economy* (1991): 31.

48. Akinbolu Babanrinsa, *Anything for Money* (London and Basingstoke, 1985), 80–2.

49. Nwankwo, *My Mercedes,* 5, 127.

50. Ibid., 126.

51. Ibid., 124.

52. M. Sahlins, *Culture and Practical Reason* (Chicago, 1976), 179.

53. V. Fernandes, *Description de la Côte Occidentale d'Afrique* (1506–10), ed. and trans. T. Monod, A. Texeira da Mota, and R. Mauny (Bissau, 1951), 13.

54. Elechi Amadi, *The Great Ponds* (London, 1975), 83.

55. E. Ayina, "Pagnes et Politiques," *Politique africain* (1987): 48.

56. Waterman, *Juju,* 209–10.

57. Quoted in H. J. Drewal, "Pageantry and Power in Yoruba Costuming," in J. Cordwell and R. Schwartz (eds.), *The Fabric of Culture: The Anthropology of Clothing and Adornment* (Paris, 1975), 217.

58. This account is based on D. Heath, "Fashion, Anti-fashion and Heteroglossia in Urban Senegal," *American Ethnologist* (1992): 19–33. For more on the Baye Faal, and their links with Rastarianism (and the *tyeddo* tradition) see N. Savishinsky, "The Baye Faal of Senegambia: Muslim Rastas in the Promised Land," *Africa* (1994): 211ff.

59. Quoted in M. Hiskett, *The Sword of Truth* (New York, 1973), 163–65.

60. E. Isichei, "The Maitatsine Risings in Nigeria 1980–1985: A Revolt of the Disinherited," *Journal of Religion in Africa* (1987): 194ff; this paper was first presented to a conference in Dunedin, New Zealand in August 1985. Much has been written on the subject since.

61. A. N. Aniagolu (Chairman), "Report of Tribunal of Inquiry on Kano Disturbances," (1981), para. 141.

62. Ayina, "Pagnes et Politiques 47–54.

63. R. Porter, "Consumption: Disease of the Consumer Society?" in J. Brewer and R. Porter, *Consumption and the World of Goods* (London, 1993), 70.

64. G. McCracken, *Culture and Consumption* (Bloomington and Indianapolis, 1990), xi.

16

CONVERGING WORLDS, POLARIZED WORLDS:

THE REALM BENEATH THE SEA REVISITED

> This year the Lord told me: "The greatest problem in Nigeria today is how to curb the activities of water spirits in her midst."
> Victoria Eto, founder of Shallom Christian Mission, Nigeria, in 1983[1]

> For many Haitians, everything he sees, the trees, the rocks, are merely the pale reflection of a real world which is alive beneath us, under the sea.
> Jeanne Philippe, Haitian artist, in 1994[2]

The first of these two epigraphs was written by a Nigerian woman graduate who founded an independent church and believed that Mami Wata was a demon who had been her father's "spirit wife."[3] The second comes from within the Haitian voudoun tradition. These believers, apparently so different, have one thing in common—they are agreed on the ontological reality of water spirits, though not, clearly, on their nature and the appropriate response to them. In the previous chapter, we saw how both a Niger diviner and a Nigerian Christian described evil spirits that cause road accidents.

Some West African Christians believe there is a Satanic sphere beneath the sea, where luxury goods are manufactured and souls are controlled through a computer. This chapter explores these apparently para-doxical convergences, and the way in which the image of Satanic agency proliferates in the post-colony.

Nineteenth-century missionaries who looked on indigenous spirits as demons had one important point in common with African communi-ties—they accepted the reality of their existence. On the other hand, be-cause they did not believe in witchcraft, colonial officials punished the accuser or the witchcraft-eradicator rather than the supposed witch, and, as we have seen, caused much anxiety and resentment.

As time went on, both expatriate missionaries and indigenous Chris-tian theologians and church leaders were increasingly likely to regard both witchcraft and traditional spirits as figments of the imagination. In a reac-tion against the way in which many of their predecessors condemned Afri-can cultures as Satanic, they reinvented the religions of the past as a par-ticular people's Old Testament. This was possible because they assumed that these spirits had no ontological reality, which is, of course, also the assumption of the ethnographer.

This approach has been energetically criticized from a variety of view-points. The Nigerian evangelical, Byang Kato, attacked both Mbiti and Idowu on the grounds that Christianity's claims to truth are exclusive, and that there is no other way to salvation.[4] Archbishop Ngada and his fellow South African independent church leaders, who together authored the pam-phlet, *Speaking for Ourselves,* suggested a critique of a different kind. "An-thropologists, sociologists and theologians from foreign Churches have been studying us for many years and they have published a whole library of books and articles about us. . . .[We] do not recognise ourselves in their writings."[5] What they deplored, however, was not an inadequate under-standing of African cultures, but a failure to give central importance to the work of the Holy Spirit.

Emmanuel Milingo, the former Catholic archbishop of Lusaka, was also a critic of foreign ethnographers and missionaries. The conflict that developed between the institutional church and Milingo is a striking ex-ample of two opposing Christian views of neo-traditional religions in gen-eral and spirit possession in particular. Milingo became archbishop in 1969; in 1973, he embarked on a healing ministry that became enormously popu-lar. He accepted the reality of neo-traditional spirits, which he identified with demons and exorcised, to the disquiet of his fellow bishops and clergy.

> Some years back I told a group of priests that I was able to speak with the
> dead and the evil spirits. They almost uttered the word "*Anatemasit,*" mean-

ing "May he be accursed." . . . I have never come across any Western missionary who has accepted what I have written about the spirit world. . . .[6]

In 1982 he was summoned to Rome; the following year he resigned his see and was given a minor post in the Vatican, continuing his healing ministry, which he was instructed to give up in 1996.

Like so many African Christians, Protestant and Catholic, he was deeply convinced of the reality of witchcraft, and denounced foreign ethnographers for their skepticism.

> I have read of many episodes of witchcraft, and am certain that most of the writers have never met a witch. They quote so many essays from research scholars who have never actually dealt with a witch. Dealing with the devil may be the same. . . .I have talked with the witches and I have dealt with the dead."[7]

East African Spirits and Their Interpreters

Earlier in this book, I described spirit possession cults as a form of mimesis, embodying a social critique. To some missionaries, however, possessing spirits were real demons. There is interesting material on this from East Africa. Here as elsewhere, there has been a striking spread of spirit possession cults in areas where they were previously unknown. Often, they spread inland from the coast, where they were called, in Swahili, *shetani*. Since this was the word missionaries used for Satan, it is easy to see how they were readily perceived as demonic. Shorter pointed this out with reference to *migawo*, nature spirits, introduced this century among the Kimbu.

> The hostility of missionaries to the *migawo* is based partly on a misunderstanding of their nature. Speaking Swahili, they refer to the *migawo* as *shetani* (plur. *mashetani*). In Christian contexts this word is used for Satan."[8]

A recent study of spirit possession among the Madi states that the spirits which possess are called *satani*.[9] But it describes a medium for whom possession is an integral part of her Catholicism.

The spread of spirit possession, *orpeko*, among the Maasai from the 1960s on is of great interest[10]; their sole "traditional" divinity was enkAi, and they lacked potentially possessing divinities or an ancestor cult. "The Maasai conceptual system does not include any categories of extra-human spirits, except the Supreme Being. . . .Possession, then, would seem an anomaly."[11]

It is Maasai women who are possessed, and in some areas as many as 50% are affected in this way. Unlike zar or bori, where the possessed become members of a cult group, orpeko is regarded as an illness and as the cause of a number of different physical symptoms—what is sought is a cure from it.

The possessing spirits fall into three categories. Nature spirits include the lion, snake, and leopard. Human spirits include representatives of other ethnic groups, such as the Gogo or Swahili, as well as Masaai and Mzungu (the European, who demands books, Western clothes, or soap). The third category includes shetani (again, the Swahili word for possessing spirits, and the missionary word for Satan), mumiani, jini (djinns), and other spirit beings from the coast.[12]

To Hurskainen and Hodgson, the movement reflects the marginalization and powerlessness of Maasai women, strengthens women's bonding, and enables them to become Christians (which was, in other circumstances, discouraged).[13]

A different account of orpeko vividly illustrates the gulf between the ethnographer and those who see these spirits as ontological realities and demons. Benson, an expatriate missionary, became persuaded of the reality of these spirits by several factors—the physical strength of the possessed, their ability to speak apparently unknown languages fluently, and the fact to which other sources attest, that baptism is the generally accepted cure. Like many African Christians, he became more aware of New Testament references to demons and exorcism: "[M]y theological and biblical stance has altered."[14] These varying interpretations provide an interesting parallel to the disagreements between Milingo and his fellow bishops.

Is Mami Wata a Demon?

The changing, complex, and inconsistent relationship between Mami Wata and Christianity reflects the difficulty of making valid generalizations. A Mami Wata sculpture in an Igbo Mbari house, photographed in 1966–67, shows her with a cross around her neck (fig. 4),[15] and some devotees say explicitly that she is a Christian—part of the image of the foreign Other.[16] Duala (often male) water people, on the other hand, are hostile to the Bible. "The Duala mer-people hate European objects. . . . [T]hey particularly detest paper (conceived of as the Bible)."[17] Among the Bakweri, "The secluded mermaids hate European goods, which have increased male power."[18]

The Edo leader of a small independent Christian church sometimes consults Mami Wata by night, at the Ikpoba River, with offerings of "white plates, biscuits, Fanta soda, mirrors."[19] In one Ghanian Mami Wata shrine, there is a mural where a mermaid and Jesus are depicted side by side (fig. 5).[20]

Unlike the foreign art historians and ethnographers who find her shrines fascinating, some African Christians—especially charismatics, Pentecostals, and members of independent churches—believe that Mami Wata has an ontological reality, which is evil. In 1988, a Nigerian member of the Assemblies of God published a booklet called *Delivered from the Powers of Darkness*. He tells how he was encouraged by a rich girlfriend to join an "Occult Society in India." He signs a contract with a beautiful woman, "the queen of the coast." She takes him under the sea, where Satan lives, and shows him "laboratories" where commodities such as cars, cloth, and perfume are manufactured, with the intention of distracting humanity from God.[21]

An Igbo Catholic priest linked with the Charismatic movement wrote a pamphlet entitled *The Problem of Mammy Water*. It is a study of demons and exorcism. Chapter 2 is entitled, "Do Spirits live under Rivers?" and comes to an affirmative conclusion.[22] "All pythons, snakes and boas are possessed by demons. . . . Pour holy water on any of them."[23] The late Victoria Eto considered water spirits were demons, but paradoxically, her *Exposition on Water Spirits* depicts its subject in memorable and beautiful detail. Aquatic demons travel in crystal submarines[24] and mirror the hierarchies of the secular world; their cowries and gems echo older images of wealth beneath the sea. "Lake Marines . . . bear the titles of Princes and Princesses. They wear all types of precious stones on their bodies. They deposit stars, diamonds and crystals in their victims."[25] She writes of a girl for whom a water spirit "had built crystal houses . . . and had given her boatloads of golden articles . . . .The demon taught her a song. . . .Sung in mixed Ibo, the song called upon her as a property of the sea and says she must return to the sea."[26]

To the devotee, possessing spirits are "real"; he looks to them for healing in affliction and help in difficulties. To the ethnographer (who assumes they are not "real"), they are a creative form of mimesis that represents and critiques a changing world. To many missionaries and African Christians, possessing spirits are "real"—but evil—entities,

The Demonization of "Tradition"

The tendency to equate the powers of "traditional religion" with demons, and to equate a particular divinity with Satan, as we have seen, has nineteenth-century roots. Early Catholic and Evangelical missionaries to Africa had a good deal to say about Hell and the Devil. In a very real sense, they and their successors reinvented the "traditional" religion of those among whom they worked.

The first Catholic missionary to eastern Igboland wrote, in words with innumerable parallels: "All those who go to Africa as missionaries must be thoroughly penetrated with the thought that the Dark Continent is a cursed land, almost entirely in the power of the Devil."[27]

Particular spirit beings were radically transformed in Christian exegesis. Nineteenth- and early twentieth-century missionaries would select a particular divinity to equate with Satan—Ekwensu among the Igbo, Eshu among the Yoruba. In 1922, a Catholic missionary in western Igboland described Ekwensu as one "whose one purpose is to frustrate the goodness of God and to disseminate evil."[28] Ekwensu is now equated with the Devil in ordinary Igbo usage. He was originally a violent and boisterous spirit, linked with war, and driven away in time of peace,[29] one of a number of turbulent and unpredictable spiritual beings which, in an overwhelmingly Christian Igboland, are still forces to be reckoned with. Achebe quotes a new proverb to the effect that "baptism . . . is no antidote against possession by Agwu, the capricious god of diviners and artists."[30]

The Ogbanje, the spirit child born to die, now often associated with Mami Wata, is sometimes identified with Satanic forces. In the words of an Asaba writer:

> "It is a devilish society.
> Before an ogbanje comes to the world,
> he must meet the Devil with whom he or she makes a pact. . . ."
> "Nevertheless," as Nwanmo had hinted:
> "repudiation of Mr Devil could turn
> the tide for good. So did Esogbuzia
> the twin, an ogbanje, who renounced
> Satan and is still alive."[31]

Not all the manifestations of traditional religion have been demonized. Igbo Christians of all ideological persuasions call their children by names which incorporate various forms of Chukwu (the "traditional" Supreme God) and take it for granted they refer to the God of Christianity.

The Yoruba divinity, Eshu, discussed at some length earlier in this book, has undergone comparable transformations. Clarke, a pioneer Baptist missionary in the 1850s, considered that "Esu is the worship of the devil. . . ."[32] Bishop Crowther's Yoruba dictionary, published in 1870, defined Eshu as "Satan, the god of mischief."[33]

Frobenius, who visited Ife in 1910, recognized the complexities and positive attributes of this divinity.

> Edju! The Devil—as the black and white missionaries . . . have taught them to believe. Wherever a missionary has set his foot, the folks today talk of the Devil, Edju. Yet go into the compounds . . . and they will tell you, "Ah, yes! Edju played many tricks. . . .But Edju is not evil. . . .he gave us the Ifa oracle. . . . But for Edju, the fields would be barren."[34]

"Satan" is translated "Eshu" in the Yoruba Bible,[35] and this has passed into general usage. "Now [in the 1970s] even Eshu worshippers who speak a little English, as well as Yoruba Christians and Muslims, will refer to Eshu as 'the devil.'"[36] Meyer has documented a similar process in Ghana among Ewe Presbyterians.[37] Nor is the demonization of tradition peculiar to Africa: in the Pacific, the old religion of Fiji is now called *na lotuvakatevoro,* the devil's religion.[38]

Paradoxically, charismatics and Pentecostals affirm the reality of "traditional" spirit beings, but radically transform them in the process.

The Devil and the Power of Europe

We have seen how Eshu was identified with the Devil, the market, and Europeans. In the late nineteenth century, at Medina, high on the Senegal, Monteil recorded an account that also reflects, in a different way, an association of Western commerce with diabolical forces in popular consciousness.

> [In the time of Faidherbe] says Silman [Suleman], we thought that all the remarkable objects the Europeans brought were made by the Devil. Why did Europeans come to look for peanuts? Simply because it is the Devil's favourite food. . . . They were people who got their merchandise from the devil and could only live on water. Because of this, we called them toads.[39]

The significance of peanuts here is their role in the Senegambian export economy. Other West African and African American sources, perhaps fortuitously, also associate peanuts with bad luck or witchcraft.

Satanic Imagery in the Post-Colony

In *Anthills of the Savannah* (1987), Chinua Achebe, an outspoken critic of the shortcomings of postcolonial Nigeria, wrote of the appropriateness of Hell as an image for the sufferings of the poor:

Free people may be alike everywhere in their freedom but the oppressed inhabit each their own peculiar hell. The present orthodoxies of deliverance are futile to the extent that they fail to recognise this.[40]

Ngugi's 1982 novel *Devil on the Cross* describes independent Kenya as Satanic. "The Devil's Feast! Come and See for yourself—a Devil-Sponsored Competition to Choose Seven Experts in Theft and Robbery. Plenty of Prizes![41] He contrasts the profiteering of the elite with the self-sacrifice and generosity of the Mau Mau guerillas. This is profoundly ironical, for Mau Mau was often demonized by Europeans.[42]

But while creative writers denounce oppressive regimes as demonic, the imagery of the Born Again becomes a tool in political conflicts. Twelve years after *Devil on the Cross,* the government of Daniel arap Moi appointed a commission to look into "devil worship." To his political opponents, it was a ploy to divert attention from Kenya's real problems and to condemn his critics.

The commission says devil worshippers have brought a plague of human sacrifice, cannibalism, "incantations in unintelligible language" and rape of children—and gives hints on how to spot Lucifer's agents at work. Citizens should look out for the "magic horns of witchcraft," the numbers 666, images of witchcraft on broomsticks, nudity and snakes. Other giveaways are "obsession with sex, especially lesbianism/homosexuality."[43]

An archbishop headed the commission, and a Pentecostal minister was among its members. The latter was reported as saying that

it found devil worship at every level in society but mostly among the elite. "The elites entice people into it with money," Mr Adoyo said. "Materialism and affluence do not answer spiritual longings. . . .they want mysterious powers to control people." He named no names but said those who have "joined the bandwagon of economic and political freedoms" played into the hands of devil worshippers.[44]

Moi's opponents used the discourse of Satanism differently. "Some Kenyans suspect the president is trying to dispel rumors of his own liaisons with Lucifer, especially after it became widely known that if you held a 50–shilling note to the light, the water-mark showed a snake round the president's neck."[45]

Frederick Chiluba, who won the Zambian elections of 1991, made much of his own Born Again credentials. His supporters used this kind of accusation as a political tool, "with accusations that President Kaunda was involved in witchcraft, idolatry and transcendental meditation. . . .President Chiluba refused to move into his official home . . . until its buildings had been cleansed from witchcraft and demonic influence by a team of pastors."[46] He subsequently declared Zambia a Christian nation. Accusations of corruption proliferated, and the standard of living continued to decline.[47]

Interpretations

Scholars differ in their evaluation of Pentecostal/charismatic/Born Again churches in Africa. To Marshall

> [P]entecostalism provide[s] . . . an alternate vision in its reconceptualisation of a morally chaotic world. . . .[P]entecostalism speaks a language which renders understandable the absurd and anarchic realities of contemporary urban life, enabling action and mastery.[48]

To Gifford, the world view of the Born Again, whether expounded by African Christians or by American evangelists, is a form of false consciousness. The widespread belief that the world will soon end does not encourage endeavors to improve it. Evils such as war, epidemics, or famine are attributed to demons, rather than seen as human problems to be tackled by human action. When food was scarce, in Doe's Liberia, "a speaker at a prayer breakfast explained that . . . Liberia's particular evil spirit was 'a demon of shortages.' He went on to urge his listeners to pray for the exorcism of this demon so that rice could become plentiful again."[49] This is not unlike the view that the worst of the multifarious problems faced by Nigerians in the 1980s was the proliferation of water spirits (p. 226).

Marshall emphasizes the way in which Born Again church leaders denounce the materialism of the wider society. But, like Gifford, she also documents the way in which at least some of them have absorbed its values.

Marshall is unusual among academic analysts of religion in Africa in her sympathy for the Born Again world view. Most deprecate the rejection of "traditional" African culture, and find its polarization of experience misleading, its magical remedies for poverty useless or harmful. These last two criticisms could be well be made of colonial vampires and Mami Wata, respectively, which ethnographers tends to portray with sympathy. We return to these complexities in the last chapter of this book.

Notes

1. Victoria Eto, "Preface," *Exposition on Water Spirits* (Warri, 1989).

2. Jeanne Philippe, interview in *The New York Times,* 24 June 1994, quoted in R. F. Thompson, "From the Isle beneath the Sea: Haiti's Africanizing Vodou Art," in D. Cosentino (ed.), *Sacred Arts of Haitian Vodou* (Los Angeles, 1995), 91.

3. Eto, "Preface," *Exposition on Water Spirits.*

4. Byang Kato, *Theological Pitfalls in Africa* (Kisumu, Kenya, 1975), 180.

5. N. H. Ngada, "Preface," *Speaking for Ourselves* (Institute for Contextual Theology, Braemfontein, 1985).

6. E. Milingo, *The World in Between* (London, 1984), 119.

7. Ibid., 36.

8. A. Shorter, "The Migawo, Peripheral Spirit Possession and Christian Prejudice," *Anthropos* (1970): 124.

9. T. Allen, "The Quest for Therapy in Moyo District," in H. B. Hansen and M. Twaddle, *Changing Uganda: The Dilemmas of Structural Adjustment and Revolutionary Change* (London, 1991), 156.

10. A few Maasai were affected in this way during the cattle pandemic of the late nineteenth century.

11. A. Hurskainen, "The Epidemiological Aspect of Spirit Possession Among the Maasai of Tanzania," in A. Jacobson-Widding and D. Westerlund, *Culture, Experience and Pluralism: Essays on African Ideas of Illness and Healing* (Uppsala, 1989), 139.

12. Ibid., 144–45. For mumiani, see pp. 113.

13. Ibid., and D. Hodgson, "Embodying the Contradictions of Modernity: Gender and Spirit Possession Among Maasai in Tanzania," in M. Grosz-Ngaté and O. Kokole (eds.), *Gendered Encounters: Challenging Cultural Boundaries and Social Hierarchies in Africa* (London, 1997), 111ff; there are, of course, differences in content and style between these analyses.

14. S. Benson, "The Conquering Sacrament: Baptism and Demon Possession Among the Maasai of Tanzania," *Africa Theological Journal* (Tanzania, 1980), 58.

15. H. M. Cole, "Mbari is Life," *African Arts* (Spring 1969): 12 (sculpture by Nnaji at Egbelu Obube).

16. H. J. Drewal, "Mermaids, Mirrors and Snake Charmers: Igbo Mami Wata Shrines," *African Arts* (1988): 44.

17. E. Ardener, "Belief and the Problem of Women," in S. Ardener, *Perceiving Women* (London, 1975), 16 n.7; on the hatred of paper, see J. Ittmann, "Der kultische Geheimbund djengu an der Kameruner Küste," *Anthropos* (1957): 143.

18. Ittmann, "Der kultische Geheimbund djengu," 147.

19. C. Gore and J. Nevadomsky, "Practice and Agency in Mammy Wata Worship in Southern Nigeria," *African Arts* (1997): 65.

20. K. O. Opoku and K. O. Wicker, "Abidjan Mami Water Festival 1994," *Religious Studies News* (1994).

21. Birgit Meyer, "Delivered from the Powers of Darkness," Confessions of Satanic Riches in Christian Ghana," *Africa* (1995): 242, 251 n.16.

22. L. M Odinkemelu, *The Problem of Mammy Water: Mammy Water in the Society* (Nigeria, 1988), 19.

23. Ibid., 32.

24. Eto, *Exposition on Water Spirits,* 23.

25. Ibid., 11.

26. Ibid., 13.

27. Holy Ghost Fathers Archives, Paris. 191/A/5, MS. biography of Fr. Lutz by Fr. Ebenrecht, f. 35

28. P. J. Correia, "L'animisme Igbo et les divinités de la Nigeria," *Anthropos* (1922): 365.

29. See E. I. Metuh, *God and Man in African Religion: A Case Study of the Igbo of Nigeria* (London, 1982), 76.

30. Chinua Achebe, *Anthills of the Savannah* (London, 1988), 105.

31. Fred Okonicha Konwea, "Ibiakwa," in *A Voice of Verse: 101 Poems* (privately printed, Benin, 1975), 73–4. The first three lines are spoken by an ogbanje. On 105 he explains that this poem narrates a family history of generations of ogbanje.

32. W. H. Clarke, *Travels and Explorations in Yorubaland (1854–1858)* (Ibadan, 1972), 282–83.

33. S. A. Crowther, *Grammar and Vocabulary of the Yoruba Language* (London, 1870), quoted in S. Farrow, *Faith, Fancies and Fetich or Yoruba Paganism 1929* (New York, 1969 reprint), 86.

34. L. Frobenius, *The Voice of Africa,* (1913; reprint, New York, 1968), I: 229.

35. E. B. Idowu, *Oludumare, God in Yoruba Belief* (New York, 1963), 80 n.1.

36. J. Pemberton, "Eshu-Elegba: The Yoruba Trickster God," *African Arts* (1975): 26.

37. B. Meyer, "'If You Are a Devil, You Are a Witch and if You Are a Witch, You Are a Devil': The Integration of "Pagan" Ideas into the Conceptual Universe of Ewe Christians in Southeastern Ghana," *Journal of Religion in Africa* (1992): 112.

38. N. Thomas, "The Inversion of Tradition," *American Ethnologist* (1992): 221, 229.

39. C. Monteil, "Fin de siècle à Médine," *Bulletin de l'IFAN,* sér. B (1966): 149. Monteil was in Medina from 1897 to 1899; Silman (Souleyman Goundiamou) was his interpreter. (Faidherbe left Senegal in 1865.)

40. Achebe, *Anthills of the Savannah,* 99.

41. Ngugi wa Thiong'o, *Devil on the Cross* (London, 1982), 28.

42. Ibid., 39.

43. Chris MacGreal (in Nairobi), "Moi Raises the Devil to Keep Kenya in Line," *Guardian Weekly,* 13 Oct. 1996. The actual text of the report was not released.

44. B. Adoyo, in MacGreal, "Moi Raises the Devil to Keep Kenya in Line."

45. Chris MacGreal, "Guerilla's Tribal Violence and the Devil," *Otago Daily Times,* Dunedin, New Zealand, 10 Oct. 1996 (a differently edited version of the same article).

46. J. Clifton, "Zambian Leader a Crowd Puller," [Auckland, New Zealand] *Sunday Star Times,* 24 Sept. 1995.

47. P. Gifford, "Chiluba's Christian Nation: Christianity as a Factor in Zambian Politics 1991–1996," *Journal of Contemporary Religion* (1998): 363–81.

48. Marshall, "'God is not a Democrat'," 248, 250; also her "Power in the Name of Jesus", *Review of African Political Economy* (1991): 21–37. Marshall writes of Pentecostals, but Pentecostalism is distinguished by speaking in tongues. What these churches all have in common is a belief in the necessity of a conversion experience, an absolute dichotomy between saved and unsaved.

49. Paul Gifford, "Christian Fundamentalism and Development in Africa," *Review of African Political Econom* (1991): 15; and see his *Christianity and Politics in Doe's Liberia* (Cambridge, 1993).

17

EATING THE STATE:

RIDICULE AND THE CRISIS OF THE QUOTIDIAN

Le pouvoir se mange entier.
(Power is eaten whole.)

Maxim current in Shaba, Zaire, in 1985[1]

Distorted consumption has been a core metaphor in this study—the sinister predation of white cannibals, bloodsucking cowries, or colonial vampires. But not all images of depraved consumption are of this kind. The one-legged cannibal of southern African folklore clearly belongs to the world of once-upon-a-time, comparable with the giant with similar propensities who lived at the top of Jack's beanstalk. Metaphors of "eating the state," of chopping bribes, are often employed by those who do just that. In popular discourse they may express disgust, resignation, or humor. The lexicon of derision often reflects a resigned jocularity, which is very different from the collective nightmares of the poetics of rumor. Humor is one of the most important ways of dealing with the crisis of the quotidian.

In this chapter. I explore the metaphor of "eating the state," *la politique du ventre,* and two closely related themes—the politics of the gut, and commentaries on the sexual voracity of Big Men, often articulated in idioms of consumption. I then go on to examine a subversive discourse found in parody and in diverse form of wordplay, among them the reinterpretation of initials and acronyms.

235

Eating the State

The colony or post-colony and its agents were, as we have seen, sometimes described in idioms of cannibalism or witchcraft. This is a True Fiction—the state (more precisely, the ruling elite) eats its subjects by consuming the resources without which they cannot survive. "Witchcraft persists as a practical discourse of hidden agency because economic development in the larger sense has failed."[2]

In contemporary Africa, consumption is a powerful metaphor for the gluttonous avarice of corrupt governments. The image of eating the state and its resources is rooted in a much older and strikingly widespread political discourse. In the early nineteenth century, a visitor to Northern Nigeria, using this metaphor, warned of the danger of European encroachment. "By God," said the Marroquin, "they eat the whole country—they are no friends: these are the words of truth."[3]

In a book based on fieldwork in Uganda, in 1950–52, Fallers wrote:

> Throughout much of Bantu Africa, the word for "eating" is used to express a wide range of meanings associated with power and property. In traditional Busoga, a ruler who conquered a neighbouring territory was said to "eat it." Today a man who secures for himself an appointment to chieftainship "eats" the office and an embezzler "eats" the money he misappropriates.[4]

Among the Luba of eastern Zaire, the elephant is a symbol of chieftaincy, not only because of its size and strength, but "because it eats more than other animals."[5] In East Africa, a political faction is called *kula,* eating, and corruption is *chai,* tea. In Uganda, the smuggling and black market networks that developed when the official economy collapsed in the Amin years were called *magendo,* the pilgrimage of the greedy. Those involved in it were called *mafutamingi,* the fat ones.[6] Hutu refugees in Tanzania say bitterly of local officials, "They eat our sweat."[7] In Zaire, a politician began a speech, "*Depuis que j'ai mangé mon pouvoir.*"[8]

Kenyans speak of the fruits of Uhuru, Nigerians of chopping bribes and dividing the national cake. "Chop," in pidgin, is both a noun (food) and a verb (to eat). It has, of course, multiple meanings, (one chops down a tree.)

Chinua Achebe's 1966 novel *A Man of the People* condemned both the corruption of the First Republic and the apathy of "the People" who permitted it. It is permeated with images of consumption that directly mirror popular political discourse.

The people themselves, as we have seen, had become even more cynical than their leaders and were apathetic into the bargain. "Let them eat," was the people's opinion, "after all when white men used to do all the eating did we commit suicide? Of course not. And where is the all-powerful white man today? He came, he ate and he went. But we are still around."[9] . . .

[T]he fat-dripping, gummy, eat-and-let-eat regime just ended—a regime which inspired the common saying that a man could only be sure of what he had put away safely in his gut or in language ever more suited to the times: "You chop, me self I chop, palaver finish."[10]

The First Republic fell in the same year (1966), and newspaper head-lines proclaimed, with what proved to be a sadly premature elation, "Bribe? E Done Die. Chop-Chop—E No Dey."[11]

Cyprian Ekwensi's *Survive the Peace* is set in Igboland just after the Nigerian civil war. A village elder, Pa Ukoha, explained this catastrophe as the nemesis of uncontrolled consumption:

When some black men begin to rule they become too greedy. They eat and fill their stomachs and the stomachs of their brothers. That is not enough for them. They continue till their throats are filled. And that too is not enough. They have food in their stomachs and in their throats and they go on till their mouths are full and then proceed to fill their bags. But no one else outside their families or their tribe must partake of this food. . . . This is what brings the trouble in Africa.[12]

Nigeria's draft constitution of 1976 defined political power as "the opportunity to acquire wealth and prestige, to be able to distribute benefits in the form of jobs, contracts, scholarships, and gifts of money and so on to one's relatives and political allies."[13] Among the parties proposed to contest the 1979 elections was one called "I Chop, You Chop."[14]

None of this, of course, was peculiar to Nigeria. Kourouma's *The Suns of Independence,* which appeared in 1968, was set in a thinly disguised Ivory Coast and Mali. The protagonist fails to obtain a share in the rewards of Independence.

What then did Independence bring Fama? Only the national identity card and the party membership card. These are the poor man's share, dry and hard as bull's meat. Let him tear at them with the fangs of a starving mastiff, he'll get nothing out of them; nothing to chew, nothing to suck, just pure gristle.[15]

Armah, wrote of the last days of Nkrumah's Ghana:

The policeman who had spoken raised his right hand and in a slow gesture pointed to his teeth. The driver understood.[16]

Cameroonians speak of *la politique du ventre,* the politics of the belly. Bayart appropriated the phrase as the subtitle of his book, *The State in Africa.*[17] In Douala, an innocent victim is called *nyama boso beta,* the meat inside the pantry door.[18]

In 1989, Doe, then the brutal military ruler of Liberia, told a school audience there,

> All we want are your votes, and finish with you; that's all we do. We play with the people's brains, convince them and confuse them. After we've finished talking politics, you know what we look for? We want to eat.[19]

While the powerful eat the state, ordinary people suffer from hunger. In the 1970s, when Nigeria's oil boom was at its height, a Yoruba bride sang:

> He said, "When the locusts have no farm and no river,
> What do you expect the locusts to eat?"[20]

A poem to much the same effect appeared in an Ivory Coast newspaper in 1980. "Our Father who art in heaven/Give us this day/Rice/Yams/Bananas/For/We are dying/All of Hunger/And my God/We haven't even/The right/ To say/That we are dying/Of hunger."[21]

The Politics of the Gut

The imagery of defecation is inextricably linked with that of consumption, the politics of the belly with the politics of the gut. Cheney-Coker describes the decline of Sierra Leone in images of rubbish and dog droppings.

> Now the postal stamps and monetary bills, the ones with the head of the president, the ones that no one wanted to buy, were infested with the stench of the garbage that the country had become. Everywhere you looked, you could see the dogshit and dead dogs where once there had been beds of violets and fountains with clear alabaster statues.[22]

Images of garbage and excrement thread their way through contemporary West African fiction and becomes part of a complex of metaphors representing the misery of the urban poor, the gluttony of the rich. Armah's powerful novel *The Beautyful Ones are not yet Born* contrasts the lifestyle of a poor but honest man with that of one who has gained immense wealth through corruption. Images of food and defecation dominate the book. The poor suffer from bad food and filthy latrines; when the government falls, the corrupt minister escapes, head first, through such a latrine.[23]

A song by Fela Anikulapo-Kuti contrasts Africa's natural abundance with the poverty of the night-soil collector.

> Land boku [plenty] from north to south
> Food boku from top to down
> Gold dey underground like water
> Diamond dey underground like sand
> Oil dey flow underground like river. . . .
> Na for here man still dey carry shit for head.[24]

A night-soil collector, bucket on head, threads his way through Oyegoke's *Cowrie Tears*.[25] The Venezuelan founder of OPEC, Juan Pablo Alfonzo, employed the imagery of defecation in a passionate denunciation.

> I call petroleum the devil's excrement. It brings trouble. . . . [L]ook at this *locura*—waste, corruption, consumption, our services falling apart . . . and debt we shall have for years. . . . We are drowning in the devil's excrement.[26]

The Nuer of the southern Sudan consider that money obtained by work as night-soil collectors should not be used for cattle purchases. Some Nuer women who sold beer in townships kept it separate—"It's going straight to the government."[27]

Sexual Voracity

Male sexuality, predation, and consumption are often symbolically linked. In a Bemba (Zambia) marriage ceremony, described in the early 1930s, the bridegroom appears with his bow, as a hunter. "I have tracked my game through the forest and now I am killing the meat."[28] In Tanzania, at Haya weddings, the bride's relatives sing, "Sweet banana, sweet banana is ripe/It is ripe and I plucked it."[29]

Sexual voracity, like gluttonous consumption, is popularly attributed to Big Men, and most of the double-entendres Toulabor explores in Togo refer to the phallus.[30] In Zaire, the praise name "Mobutu the great warrior who triumphs over all" became "The cock, who can't see a hen go by."[31] When Sani Abacha, Nigeria's hated dictator, died suddenly and mysteriously in 1998, urban legends sprang up that are obliquely reflected in a popular song.

> Abacha, Sani Abacha!
> A-butcher of Abuja!
> Alive you were a kleptocrat.
> Dead you've turned a lootocrat!
> No wonder Kama Sutra,
> Snuffed out your stinking aura.[32]

Word Games

Subversive discourse often takes the form of word games—parody, neologisms, the reinterpretation of acronyms, the transformation of meaning by modifying the tonal structure of a word or phrase. In the 1980s and 1990s, such discourse tends to reflect constraints on freedom of speech, but the same ebullient wordplay was evident in political cut and thrust in the early years of Nigeria's independence. The second volume of Wole Soyinka's autobiography is somewhat enigmatically entitled *Ibadan, the Penkelemes Years.* The neologism Penkelemes was invented by the radical politician Adelabu— it is a form of "peculiar mess."[33] Akintola, the Western Region Premier, destined to die in the coup that overthrew the First Republic in 1966, called the radical S. G. Ikoku *Ikoko,* hyena.[34] His own initials, S. L. A., became *Ese-Ole,* Feet of a Robber.[35]

In Cameroon, the initials of the *Rassemblement Democratique du Peuple Camerounais,* RDPC, became *redépécer,* cut it up and dole it out.[36] In Togo, the initials of the *Rassemblement du Peuple Togolais* were variously interpreted as *Rassemblement des profiteurs togolais,* or *Rongeurs du peuple togolais.*[37] During Nigeria's Second Republic, the corrupt National Party of Nigeria was called the Naira Party of Nigeria. When ECOMOG[38] forces intervened in Sierra Leone's civil war, the acronym was glossed, Every Car Or Moving Object Gone. In Nigeria, in the mid 1990s, there was a bizarre organization called Youths Earnestly Ask for Abacha. Soyinka renamed it, Youths Expire in the Abyss of Abasement.[39] In the Zambian elections of 1991, the Movement for Multi-Party Democracy (MMD), headed by Chiluba, defeated Kaunda's UNIP. As the shortcomings of the new regime became apparent, the acronym was glossed, "Mass Movement for Drug Dealers," or, "Make Money and Depart."[40]

In Togo, stone-throwing youths who demonstrated for democracy in 1991 were called Ekpemog, an analogy with ECOMOG. Ekpe means "stone" in Ewe; the implication was that they were a legitimate army.[41] In Zambia, during the Copperbelt riots of 1986, T-shirts were printed with the words "Looters Association of Zambia."[42] The meaning was much the same.

In 1974, when Togolese were compelled to replace Christian names with "traditional" ones, many rebuked the government through their choices—Dansomo, the snake is across the path, Kusomo, Death bars the way. So unequivocal was their meaning that those who did this were punished.[43]

Political mockery flourished in Zaire in Mobutu's last years, when the move to multi-party democracy made dissent somewhat safer.[44] In a quest for security, he spent much of his time on a yacht on the Zaire estuary. Radio trottoir called him Noah. Towards the end of his regime, a popular song ran, "There's a big lorry blocking the road and the little cars can't get past."[45] After Mobutu fled into exile, in 1997, students in Nairobi chanted, with reference to President Daniel arap Moi, "Moi-butu out."[46]

A study of the politics of derision in Sankara's Burkina Faso is particularly interesting in the light of the admiration with which he is regarded—and his words quoted—in the West, not least because of his premature death.[47] Dubuch describes the widespread mimicry of his political speeches.[48] Sankara denounced his enemies as corrupt or rotten and described the revolution as a car from which some would fall to their deaths.

> At work, at home, among friends, one would be threatened with "falling out of a car".... The accused would reply that he was firmly seated. One hears people condemning, in jest, "rotten colleagues," "rotten parents," "rotten uncles," and "rotten children."

The new national name, Burkina Faso, became Burkina-façon or Burkina-facho; its people, the Burkinabé, were called Burkina-bêtes (animals) or Burkina-boeufs (cattle). The government newspaper, *Sidwaya* (Truth has arrived), was called *Zirwaya* (Lies have arrived). Slogans such as "Le colonialisme a bas!" became "Le colonialisme.... Awa." Awa means "is coming," or "has arrived." All this, as Dubuch points out, is a telling commentary on the discrepancy between revolutionary rhetoric and daily lived experience.

In some circumstances, humor and euphemism have become a technique for surviving tragedy. In East Africa, AIDS is ironically called Slim.

In the Western world, people aspire to be slim. In Uganda, dying Africans are, involuntarily, slim. In Kenya, AIDS is known as *misada,* economic aid. The gunfire of the murderous years Ugandans remember as Obote II was called popcorn.[49]

Werbner's moving *Tears of the Dead* documents a tragic example of semantic shift. 1979 was the year of majority rule in Zimbabwe; Mugabe called it the Year of the People's Storm, *Gukurahundi*—a reference to spring rain after the storm of a war of liberation. But from 1983 to 1988, there was a phase of violent repression in Matabeleland, associated with the notorious Fifth Brigade. To the victims of this violence, Gukurahundi took on a new meaning. "For people of Bango, it was a *Shona* name that meant, 'the sweeping away of rubbish' and the 'rubbish' the Shona soldiers intended to sweep away were the people of Matabeleland themselves."[50]

Subversive Pidgin

Pidgin is a form of interculture, often used in subversive discourse, in part because of its universality, which makes it intelligible to the speakers of different African languages. In western Nigeria, the juju musicians who work within the framework of client-patron relations tend to sing in Yoruba. Fela Anikulapo-Kuti, who died in 1997, always sang in pidgin. He declared his nightclub an independent republic and was imprisoned by every regime for ten years. A member of an elite family, he sang of class distinctions and socio-economic injustice. Pidgin spoke to all Nigerians, regardless of their ethno-linguistic identity or socio-economic status. Like others, he developed the metaphor of eating the state.

> Monkey dey work, baboon dey chop
> Baboon dey hold dem key of store
> Monkey dey cry, baboon dey laugh
> One day monkey eye come open now.[51]

Pidgin grows at the interface between Africa and the West, as does the political opportunism and corruption it critiques. There is a sense that it mocks or ridicules its object because it is felt to be, in Saro-Wiwa's terminology, "rotten"[52] or inferior—reflecting, at multiple removes, the marginalization of pidgin and Creole languages by English or French native speakers.

Ambiguities

As Toulabor points out, with much insight, there are many ambiguities in the discourse of derision. The phallic double-entendre can be understood as a celebration of male sexuality and power. Even the images of defecation, so readily understood as expressions of disgust, can be seen as affirmations of a common humanity. An Ewe proverb points out that those who urinate and defecate cannot hide their nakedness from the earth.[53]

Popular discourse has often been ambiguous, tinged with a grudging respect for the Big Men's courage and luck. Western Igbo still speak with a good-humored mixture of cynicism and admiration of the politician of the First Republic who built a major highway that stopped at his mother's door. Like teasing among friends, the lexicon of derision may actually endear those in power to the governed.[54] The reinterpreted acronyms sometimes reflect, not indignation, but humorous resignation. When electricity fails in Nigeria, the sudden darkness is hailed with a cheerful gloss on the initials of NEPA, the Nigerian Electrical Power Authority—Never Expect Power Always.

But despite these ambivalences, in unfree states parody and wordplay carve out a space for criticism and independent thought. They embody a "paradoxical pre-vision" that reminds the hearer that official panegyrics are a lie.

Much the same pattern has been observed in a large number of African states, whether their rulers are soldiers or civilians—the adulation on which the powerful feed and which makes critical debate dangerous or impossible, the large framed photographs of the head of state, obligatory in government offices, the public executions of criminals, attended by enthusiastic crowds, the elaborate and enormously expensive funerals, and the full page In Memoriams. Official sources in Malawi referred to Banda as "His Excellency the Life President (Paramount Chief) Dr Hastings Kamuzu Banda, the Ngwazi [conqueror]."[55] The lexicon of derision is a salutary corrective.

Totalitarian regimes are challenged by laughter, as well as by the poetics of rumor, and the safest form of dissent often lies in oblique idioms of mockery. They constitute an element in what Toulabor, whose studies in Togo pioneered this theme, calls *"une résistance multiforme."*[56] Oppressive regimes, past and present, have been undermined both by the poetics of rumor and by jokes. The latter, perhaps, are the more effective.

Notes

1. Also the title of a play written and performed near Lumbumbashi, in 1986. See J. Fabian, "Jamaa, a Charismatic Movement Revisited," in T. D. Blakeley et al., *Religion in Africa: Experience and Expression* (London, 1994), 271, 274 n.23.

2. A. Apter, "Atinga Revisited: Yoruba Witchcraft and the Cocoa Economy," in J. and J. L. Comaroff (eds.), *Modernity and Its Malcontents: Ritual and Power in Postcolonial Africa* (Chicago and London, 1993), 124.

3. E. W. Bovill, *Mission to the Niger* (Hakluyt, 1966), Denham's narrative, II: 478.

4. Lloyd Fallers, *Law Without Precedent: Legal Ideas in Action in the Courts of Colonial Busoga* (Chicago, 1969), 83 n.5.

5. Fabian, "Jamaa," 271.

6. T. Barnett and P. Blaikie, *AIDS in Africa: Its Present and Future Impact* (London, 1992), 72.

7. J. Ferguson, "De-Moralizing Economies: African Socialism, Scientific Capitalism and the Moral Politics of 'Structural Adjustment,'" in S. F. Moore (ed.), *Moralizing States and the Ethnography of the Present* (American Anthropological Association, Arlington, Va., 1993), 88.

8. Fabian, "Jamaa," 274 n.23.

9. C. Achebe, *A Man of the People* (London, 1966), 162.

10. Ibid., 167.

11. *The Morning Post,* cited in W. Schwarz, *Nigeria* (London, 1968), 199.

12. Cyprian Ekwensi, *Survive the Peace* (London, 1976), 77.

13. Quoted in G. Williams and T. Turner, "Nigeria," in J. Dunn (ed.), *West African States: Failure and Promise* (Cambridge, 1978), 133.

14. R. Joseph, *Democracy and Prebendal Politics in Nigeria* (Cambridge, 1987), 150.

15. Ahmadu Kourouma, *The Suns of Independence,* trans. A. Adams (London, 1981), 14.

16. Ayi Kwei Armah, *The Beautyful Ones Are Not Yet Born* (London, 1971), 214.

17. J. F. Bayart, *The State in Africa: The Politics of the Belly,* trans. M. Harper, C. and E. Harrison (Harlow, 1993), xvii.

18. Eric de Rosny, *Healers in the Night,* trans. R. R. Barr (Maryknoll, NY, 1985), 255.

19. "Matchet" (pseud.), "Doe on God and power," *West Africa* (10–16 July, 1989): 1123.

20. K. Barber, *I Could Speak Until Tomorrow* (London, 1991), 91.

21. L. Sahiri, "Prière à dieu," *Fraternité Matin* (Abidjan, 16 Sept. 1980), 9, quoted in M. Schatzberg, "Power, Legitimacy and 'Democratisation' in Africa," *Africa* (1993): 447.

22. Syl Cheney-Coker, *The Last Harmattan of Alusine Dunbar* (Oxford, 1990), x.

23. Armah, *The Beautyful Ones Are Not Yet Born,* 195–99.

24. Fela Anikulapo-Kuti, "No Bread" (1975), in C. Waterman, *Juju: A Social History and Ethnography of an African Popular Music* (Chicago, 1990), 225

25. Lekan Oyegoke, *Cowrie Tears* (Harlow, 1982) 23–24, 58, 144, 146–47, 157.

26. Quoted in M. Watts, "The Shock of Modernity: Petroleum, Protest and Fast Capitalism in an Industrialising Society," in A. Pred and M. Watts(eds.), *Reworking Modernity: Capitalisms and Symbolic Discontent* (New Brunswick, 1992), 21.

27. S. Hutchinson, "The Cattle of Money and the Cattle of Girls Among the Nuer, 1930–83" *American Ethnologist* (1992): 300–306.

28. A. Richards, *Bemba Marriage and Present Economic Conditions* (Livingstone, 1940), 93.

29. B. Weiss, *The Making and Unmaking of the Haya Lived World* (Durham, NC, and London, 1996), 138.

30. C. Toulabor, *"Jeu de mots, jeu de vilains, Lexique de la dérision politique au Togo,"* *Politique Africaine* (1981): 61–63.

31. *Africa Confidential,* 29 Aug. 1997.

32. C. Duodu, "Nigeria Beggared by Lootocracy," *International Guardian Weekly,* 29 Nov. 1998, 5 (reprinted from the [London] *Observer*).

33. Wole Soyinka, *Ibadan, the Penkelemes Years: A Memoir, 1946–65* (London, 1995), 326.

34. Ibid., 201.

35. Ibid., 323.

36. A. Mbembe, "Provisional Notes on the Postcolony," *Africa* (1992): 6.

37. Toulabor, "Jeu de mots," 67.

38. ECOMOG is a "peacekeeping force" of the Economic Community of West African States, dominated by Nigeria. The acronym stands for Economic Community of West African States Monitoring Group.

39. K. Maier, *The House Has Fallen: Midnight in Nigeria* (New York, 2000), 274.

40. P. Gifford, "Chiluba's Christian Nation: Christianity as a Factor in Zambian Politics 1991–1996," *Journal of Contemporary Religion* (1998): 372.

41. S. Ellis, "Rumour and Power in Togo," *Africa* (1993): 473.

42. Ferguson, "De-Moralizing Economies," 88.

43. Toulabor, *"Jeu de mots,"* 67.

44. J. P. Diamani, *"L'humour politique au Phare du Zaire,"* *Politique Africaine* (1995): 151–57; his main theme is a political cartoon series.

45. *Africa Confidential,* 29 Aug. 1997.

46. Ibid., 1 Aug. 1997.

47. See for instance, B. Davidson, *Black Man's Burden: Africa and the Curse of the National State* (London, 1992), 241, and *Thomas Sankara Speaks: The Burkina Faso Revolution 1983–87* (New York, 1988).

48. The account that follows is based on C. Dubuch, *"Langage du pouvoir, pouvoir du langage,"* *Politique Africaine* (1985): 44–53. The word I translate as rotten is *pourri,* which can mean either corrupt or rotten.

49. Ed. Hooper, *Slim: A Reporter's Own Story of AIDS in East Africa* (London, 1990), 4, 17, 130, 186.

50. R. Werbner, *Tears of the Dead* (Edinburgh, 1991), 162.

51. Text in Waterman, *Juju,* 225.

52. Ken Saro-Wiwa, *Sozaboy: A Novel in Rotten English* (Harlow, 1994).

53. Toulabor, *"Jeu de mots,"* 71, and *Le Togo sous Éyadéma,* 308.

54. Toulabor, *Le Togo sous Éyadéma,* 294, 309.

55. R. Dowden, "Dr Hastings Banda," *The Independent* [London], 27 Nov. 1997.

56. C. Toulabor, *Le Togo sous Éyadéma,* (Paris, 1986) 294, 309.

18

CONCLUSION

"Life has no experts."

Line from an Anaguta song, 1984

In this book I have used the particular—histories and ethnographies, oral testimonies and archival materials, novels, songs, and plays—as sources from which to reconstruct "a whole set of knowledges that have been disqualified as inadequate to their task or insufficiently elaborated: naive knowledges, located down on the hierarchy, beneath the required level of cognition or scientificity."[1]

The many and varied expressions of these sources embody particular views of moral economy that have a striking mutual consistency and are rooted, very often, in an understanding of life as a zero-sum game: the idea that there is a limited amount of wealth in society, and therefore that prosperity is won at the cost of the impoverishment of others.

The sacrifice of wealth in people to wealth in things is condemned, and exploitation is identified with depraved and gluttonous consumption. In a closely knit complex of images, money or things acquire the properties of living things, while people are commodified. Slaves—commodified bodies—turn into statues, or become industrial raw material. Wombs are changed to plastic bags. Vampire cowries feed on human bait, and human "spare parts" are used to create magical money. In a different mythical complex, slavery endures in the mind long after both the export of slaves and domestic slavery have ended, and the witch is conceptualized as an owner of zombies.

Strangers, of course, brought wealth as well as death from the sea, and some sources reflect the attractions, as well as dangers, of "things." Where poverty seems a life sentence, magical paths to wealth become important—for instance, the capture of a mermaid's comb. But Mami Wata is dangerous and unpredictable and the wealth she offers comes often at a human cost. "Instead of a womb there are golden scallop shells."[2]

Strangely, petroleum has also been described in much the same way.

> Oil creates the illusion of a completely changed life. . . . The concept of oil expresses perfectly the eternal human dream of wealth achieved through lucky accident. . . . In this sense oil is a fairy tale and like every fairy tale a bit of a lie.[3]

In a sense, the dark images that thread their way through the poetics of rumor seem more immediately appropriate to the Atlantic slave trade then to the colonial or postcolonial experience. Twentieth-century changes, of course, affected different regions and individuals differently—there were both victims and beneficiaries, many both at once, in different ways. Historians of Africa have written much on the violence with which colonialism was imposed, and the catastrophes which (sometimes fortuitously) accompanied it. To many, the colonial era—and still more, the postcolonial—opened the way to new opportunities. But most of the images analyzed in this study emanate from the disinherited.

There are real as well as imagined horrors in contemporary Africa—we need look no further than civil war (with its frequent deployment of child soldiers), famine, and AIDS. Part, though not all, of Africa's crisis is generated in the West—in the export of sophisticated weapons of destruction (including, until recently, landmines) or in the dumping of toxic waste. A chilling leaked document by the chief economist of the World Bank, endorses this latter practice.

> I think the economic logic behind dumping a load of toxic waste in the lowest-wage country is impeccable and we should face up to that. . . .I've always thought that under-populated countries in Africa are vastly *under*-polluted.[4]

Many Africans have died as a result of fake medicines. Some of the latter are innocuous (except for the fact that they do not protect or cure) and some are lethal. In 1990, 109 Nigerian children died when given a syrup which turned out to be antifreeze. In 1996, 2500 to 3000 children died in Niger, after being injected with fake anti-meningitis vaccine.[5]

Rigid and ill-conceived economic policies, imposed from abroad, exact their own child sacrifices. In the words of a Zambian mine worker:

> There is a gloom in the nation because of the lack of medicines in hospitals and children are dying like nobody's business and scarcity of essentials since the IMF programs.[6]

The "illegitimate knowledges" which form the theme of this book are perhaps most insightful, least open to cavil, when they denounce oppression and injustice. Do they suggest an alternative?

Often, as we have seen, the popular imagination idealizes the past. Sometimes a phrase captures academic imaginations and takes on a life of its own. This is true of Hyden's much debated formula, the economy of affection. By this, he meant community links between kin, neighbors, or co-religionists, which provide "a safety net" for the poor.[7] His model has been criticized as static, even as a return to Merrie Africa. It overlooks the very considerable socio-economic stratification of rural life, and the tensions this engenders.[8] It was said of an Akwapim cocoa farmer in 1958, "He says everyone hates him and wants to kill him because they envy him his big farms."[9] The economy of affection was probably never realized in rural Africa, past or present. What it does represent is a powerful ideal, and one which threads its way, explicitly or by implication, through many expressions of popular sensibility.

The economy of affection, in theory, created a trickle-down effect. This is still a dominant theme in popular discourse. The praises sung by juju musicians at elite Yoruba parties reflect the continuing importance of patron-client relations. It is a distorting mirror, since they derive their livelihood from the largesse of the rich. The economy of affection worked erratically, for it presupposed the existence of a prosperous person in the family or neighborhood. In the 1980s, as the salaried became less able and less willing to help, and the kleptocracy of rulers seemed to be the cause of the nation's ruin, confidence in the redemptive power of the economy of affection eroded, and magical paths to riches became compellingly attractive.

Very often, the economy of affection has become part of official ideology. It was at the heart of Nyerere's—transparently sincere—ideal of Ujamaa, yet his program of compulsory villagization disrupted many rural communities. In a poem published in 1973, a Tanzanian pointed out, with profound insight, that Ujamaa could be just as magical as the miraculous water of Maji Maji.

> Now again we believe
> And again believe
> That it is enough to believe.
> Now we believe in Azimio [ideology],
> Believe again that it is weapon enough,
> That it is
> God and alchemy.
> That utterance alone
> Castrates the imperialist
> And his metal is impotence, flourished.
>
> Not so, not so.
> Do not die.
> Do not fail.[10]

Daniel arap Moi of Kenya had his own version of the economy of affection.

> *Nyayoism* is neither foreign nor unfamiliar to traditional Africa, but it is new as a philosophy for the trans-tribal management of a nation. . . . The philosophy and practice of sharing both the fortunes and calamities of the extended family, clan or tribe are guided and fortified by nothing else but love.[11]

Here, it becomes part of an apologia for the status quo.

The vision of an economy of affection in the past underpinned Kaunda's ideal of Humanism in Zambia. In 1966, he wrote:

> I am a firm believer in a co-operative way of life as it was practiced in simple village-life fashion. . . . The general rule was everyone helping their relatives and friends. The infirm were the responsibility of the entire village unit.[12]

This contrasts with the words of a Zambian mine worker, twenty-one years later:

> [A]ll these books have not brought anything [for] a Zambian to enjoy. So personally, how dare we toil over a book which has brought hunger on my body—imagine I got two boys, not knowing what was to come. I am unable to meet their needs, then to hell with humanism or socialism. . . .[13]

The point was not that Kaunda was insincere, but that Humanism did not necessarily lead to economic wellbeing. It is not unlike the cynical grassroots response to Thomas Sankara's revolutionary rhetoric in Burkina Faso, mentioned in the last chapter.

In the colonial era and beyond, it was very widely believed that society would be gradually transformed by Western education. The early Improvers, such Wole Soyinka's father, the headmaster Essay,[14] gave their children an education which made the extraordinary achievements of the next generation possible. Peel has analyzed the concept of development in the Yoruba town of Ilesha. Several words were used to describe it, among them *olaju,* "enlightenment." In 1974, various people explained:

> Olaju through education for our children. . . .
> Olaju has come, electricity, piped water, tarred roads. . . .
> The olaju of the radio . . .

Improvement was an individual goal, but local patriotism, expressed in a multitude of local associations, was inseparable from it. The name of a leading Ilesha traders' association was, "We make the town agreeable."[15]

For decades, in Nigeria as elsewhere, university education was a Golden Fleece that virtually guaranteed a comfortable lifestyle. Education seemed to benefit, not only the individual, but the community and society as a whole. An Ilesha teacher wrote in a local newspaper in 1952, "the modern weapons with which to fight our present enemies like Illiteracy, Ignorance, Bribery, and all sorts of social corruption is Education."[16]

In the 1980s, as the value of the naira fell catastrophically, and unemployment soared, things fell apart. It was no longer self-evident that education was the passport to financial security. The short-lived mirage of universal free education dissolved, and the poor became less able and less willing to make sacrifices for their children's schooling. The way to Improvement was blocked or led nowhere

In 1976, the Ugandan, Taban lo Liyong, wrote :

> With holes to fill and mouths to feed
> With deserts to farm and minds to stuff
> How soon will Swahili save us? . . .
>
> For the wars that are raging again
> Is African goodness good enough?
> When my father was young
> He believed in school education
> How dim can the dawn be?[17]

True Fictions?

Africanist scholars, understandably enough, have had little to say about vampire rumors or blood magic. Recent studies of the poetics of rumor, in its varied manifestations, tend to regard it as a source of true insights into the colonial and postcolonial situation, and in a sense this is the case, and an underlying assumption of this book. But the question is a complex one. In an earlier chapter, I contrasted Marshall's and Gifford's very different interpretations of the resurgence of fundamentalist churches in Africa and the views they express. Marshall considers them a true mirror of "the absurd and anarchic realities of contemporary urban life." Is contemporary Nigeria, for all its shortcomings, really absurd and anarchic? Does the suggestion render invisible the vast numbers who continue to lead productive and positive lives?

The weakness of the Born Again viewpoint lies in its dualism, its rejection of the wider society as irredeemably evil. In the words of an extensively used correspondence course :

> Satan's world system includes commerce politics, religion, education, entertainment, world kingdoms, world organisations and many other things.[18]

This is, in Marxist terms, a form of false consciousness, in that it condemns and rejects society rather than working to change it. Is the academy in danger of replacing the optimism that underpinned Africanist history with a pessimism that sees vampirism, cannibalism, and blood magic as appropriate mirrors of African life? Images of total and irremediable evil—the colonial or postcolonial ruler as witch or vampire—are perhaps as unsatisfactory as Merrie Africa. Scholars have perhaps accepted these stereotypes too readily because of their own tendency to create heroes and villains.

To historians of radical or left-wing sympathies—myself among them—Nyerere could once do no wrong. But even his admirers came to have doubts about enforced re-settlement or one-party democracy. The justice of the struggle against white minority rule in Rhodesia/Zimbabwe seemed self-evident. But in the late 1980s, informants in Matabeleland persistently said that Smith's forces had done them much less harm than those of Mugabe.[19] The world reveres Mandela but South Africa's poor are increasingly disillusioned. Dualistic models simply do not fit the complexities of past or present reality.

Images of colonial or postcolonial vampires, ekoneurs, or practitioners of blood magic are not only literary constructs. They have a life outside the parallel universe of the imagination. They exact two categories of victim. The first consists of those who are persecuted, tortured, or killed because they are thought to be Shapeshifters, witches, or practitioners of blood magic. Their cries of pain and innocence form a recurrent, if subordinate theme in this book.

> "A crowd howl at an old man hiding under a bed. Dismantled sheets of rusty corrugated iron lie in the vicinity."[20]

> "They put medicine in my eyes. . . .My eyes hurt so much that I called peoples names as members of the Society and confessed, but I am innocent and was lying."[21]

Where the moral imagination leads crowds to lynch supposed vampires or those accused of causing impotence by casual contact, it is a form of false consciousness, however real the pain, injustice, and trauma to which it gives expression. According to official sources, cases of alleged witchcraft led to 3, 692 deaths in Tanzania between 1970 and 1984.[22]

If some individuals, believing these symbolic constructions, have come to act out the role of lion or leopard men or to practice blood magic, they are victims too. Jackson called leopard men "victims of their own rituals and of their own convoluted and clandestine strategies."[23]

When writing this book, I tried to understand popular sensibility on its own terms, to listen to multiform and often ambiguous or inconsistent voices, and understand at least some of the patterns into which they fall, the "paradoxical pre-visions" they embody, the moral economies to which they give expression. In a sense the dark images of vampires and blood magic are True Fictions, mirroring the despair, suffering, and trauma of the poor. But in poverty, there is sometimes ground for hope—often in work done by the poor for each other. The work done by AIDS victims for AIDS victims in Uganda is an example.

Between 1983 and 1985 I recorded many songs among the Anaguta of Central Nigeria, and especially from the gifted bard, Ita Tua. In long extempore compositions, he lamented his own lack of Western education and grieved for lost opportunities. But he also celebrated the distinctive strengths of his own culture.

> The Anaguta have beautiful things.
> If your hand does not miss your foot may.
> They should have told the hand.

In 1982, as the Nigerian economy fell apart, the musician, King Sunny Ade, sang

> Poverty does not prevent a fish from swimming in the water. . . .
> Poverty does not prevent a bird from flying in the sky.[24]

The Power of Captives

The Congo novelist Tansi tells of a fugitive who found neither safety nor justice on either side of the Zaire river. He converses with an old woman who told him:

> "Here you can be charged with the way you walk, even. This country's the limit, you know."
>
> "Everywhere's the limit," Dadou told her. "It makes me laugh, all the talk of white minorities when the whole of Africa is teeming with black minorities."
>
> "Don't say things like that, please. People might think we were talking politics. . . .Here we only talk politics at meetings. At any other time it's called rebellion and is severely punished. . . .What we talk about there is the river and fish. Beyond that . . . it's prison."[25]

In the colony and post-colony, the power of captives lay partly in rumor. Colonial officials recorded rumors carefully, because they knew they could lead to riots or other forms of civil disobedience. The Women's War in southeastern Nigeria in 1929, which led to a major official inquiry and changes in local government, began with a rumor that women were to be taxed. A Nigerian politician who held office both in the Second Republic and in Abacha's military government lamented:

> Rumors have done incalculable harm in many African countries. When rumors start to fly in any African society, tension and crisis must be expected.[26]

Where dissent takes the form of ridicule or parody in unfree states—forms of expression that require considerable courage—the effect is to reduce the autocrat's arbitrary powers and make his overthrow more likely.

Those who critique oppression and injustice do not, very often, expect to change anything. Perhaps it is sufficient simply to be heard. In a book published in 1987, Achebe retold an Igbo story about a leopard who was about to kill a tortoise on a lonely road. The latter asked for a respite, and spent the time thus gained in scratching up the road.

> "Why are you doing that?" asked the puzzled leopard.
> The tortoise replied: "Because even after I am dead I would want anyone passing by this spot to say, yes, a fellow and his match struggled here."[27]

The interpretation of myths and symbols is much like literary or art criticism. Each generation reads the text or painting differently. I have offered readings of the multifarious fragments from which I have constructed this book. It is the recurrence of certain motifs, in different sources and contexts, that I believe validates particular interpretations. In any history, both the act of interpretation and the selection of "relevant" passages from a great mass of documentation involves complex and often imperfectly perceived subjectivities.

> This, Sancho, that I clearly perceive to be Mambrino's helmet, seems to you to be a barber's basin, and to another it will appear as something else.[28]

Notes

1. M. Foucault, "Two Lectures: Lecture One: 7 Jan. 1976," in *Power/Knowledge: Selected Interviews and Other Writings* (New York, 1980), 82.

2. Victoria Eto, *Exposition on Water Spirits* (Warri, 1989), 40.

3. R. Kapuscinski, *Shah of Shahs* (New York, 1982), quoted in M. Watts, "Oil as Money: the Devil's Excrement and the Spectacle of Black Gold," in S. Corbridge, N. Thrift, and R. Martin, *Money, Power and Space* (Oxford, 1994), 408.

4. Lawrence Summers, memo, 12 Dec. 1991, quoted in extenso in J. B. Foster, "'Let them eat Pollution': Capitalism and the World Environment," *Monthly Review* (1993): 10–11 (from *The Economist,* 8 Feb. 1992). It was later said that this was intended to "provoke debate."

5. Tim Judah, "Drug Companies Unite to Combat Flood of Fakes," [Auckland, New Zealand] *Sunday Star-Times,* reprinted from [London] *Sunday Times,* 24 Nov. 1996.

6. Quoted in J. Ferguson, "De-Moralizing Economies: African Socialism, Scientific Capitalism and the Moral Politics of "Structural Adjustment," in S. F. Moore (ed.), *Moralizing States and the Ethnography of the Present* (Arlington, Va., 1993), 87.

7. G. Hyden, *No Shortcuts to Progress: African Development in Management Perspective* (Los Angeles, 1983), 8–17.

8. See for instance R. Lemarchand, "African Peasantries, Reciprocity and the Market," *Cahiers d'Études Africaines* (1989): 33ff.

9. M. Field, *Search for Security: An Ethno-Psychiatric Study of Rural Ghana* (London, 1960), 307. The speaker was a supplicant at an anti-witchcraft shrine, who possibly suffered from mental health problems. These cases reflect, in extreme form, the tensions prevalent in the wider society.

10. Pheroze Nowroejee, "Maji Maji 1973," quoted in M. Wright, "Maji Maji Prophecy and Historiography," in D. M. Anderson and D. H. Johnson (eds.), *Revealing Prophets* (London and Nairobi, 1995), 140 n.6.

11. Quoted in Lemarchand, "African Peasantries," 35.

12. Kenneth Kaunda, *Zambia Independence and Beyond,* 32, quoted in J. Ferguson, "The Country and the City on the Copperbelt," *Cultural Anthropology* (1992): 83.

13. Quoted in Ferguson, "De-Moralizing Economies," 85.

14. Wole Soyinka, *Ake: The Years of Childhood* (London, 1981); the nickname was a wordplay on his initials.

15. J. Peel, "*Olaju*: A Yoruba Concept of Development," *Journal of Development Studies* (1978), 141–42, 153.

16. Quoted in Peel, "Olaju", 163 n.39.

17. Taban lo Liyong, *Ballads of Underdevelopment* (Kampala, Nairobi, Dar es Salaam, 1976), 45.

18. Paul Gifford, "Christian Fundamentalism and Development in Africa," *Review of African Political Economy* (1991): 16.

19. R. Werbner, *Tears of the Dead* (Edinburgh, 1991), 161–73.

20. E. Ardener, "Some Outstanding Problems in the Analysis of Events," in E. Schwimmer(ed), *The Yearbook of Symbolic Anthropology* (London, 1978), 110–11. See p. 102.

21. Confidential Minute papers, 163/1917, S[ierra] L[eone] Archives, in Kalous, *Cannibals and Tongo Players of Sierra Leone* (Auckland, 1974), 78. See p. 129.

22. S. Mesaki, "Witch-killing in Sukumaland," in R. Abrahams (ed.), *Witchcraft in Contemporary Tanzania* (Cambridge, 1994), 52.

23. Michael Jackson, *Paths Towards a Clearing: Radical Empiricism and Ethnographic Inquiry* (Bloomington, 1989), 114.

24. C. Waterman, *Juju: A Social History and Ethnography of an African Popular Music* (Chicago, 1990), 146.

25. Sony Labou Tansi, *The Antipeople,* trans. J. A. Underworld (London and New York, 1988), 108–109.

26. Ebenezer Babatope, *The Abacha Regime and the June 12 Crisis: A Struggle for Democracy* (Lagos, 1995), 147.

27. Chinua Achebe, *Anthills of the Savannah* (London, 1988), 128.

28. Cervantes, *Don Quixote,* Part II, ch. 25.

BIBLIOGRAPHY

Some sources cited only once are excluded, as are journal articles and archival and newspaper references, which are given in full on each occasion. Specialist monographs on the slave trade referred to in chapter 2 are not listed here again. In most cases a short title is given for books.

Books

Abraham, A. *Topics in Sierra Leone History: A Counter-Colonial Interpretation* Freetown: Leone Publisher, 1976.

Achebe, Chinua. *A Man of the People.* London: Heinemann, 1966.

———. *Girls at War and other stories.* London: Heinemann, 1972.

———. *Anthills of the Savannah.* London: Heinemann, 1988.

Achebe, Chinwe. *The World of the Ogbanje.* Enugu: Fourth Dimension, 1986.

Adams, E. C. L. *Nigger to Nigger.* New York and London: C. Scribner's Sons, 1928.

Adams, John. *Sketches, Taken During Ten Voyages to Africa, Between the Years 1786 and 1800.* London, n. d.

Alldridge, T. J. *A Transformed Colony: Sierra Leone As It Was.* London, 1910. Reprint, Westport, CN: Negro Universities Press, 1970.

Amadi, Elechi. *The Great Ponds.* London: Heinemann, 1969.

———. *Ethics in Nigerian Culture.* Ibadan: Heinemann, 1982.

Amado, Jorge. *Sea of Death.* Trans. G. Rabassa. New York: Avon, 1984.

Anderson, D. M. and D. H. Johnson, eds. *Revealing Prophets.* London and Nairobi: Ohio University Press, 1995.

Appadurai, A, ed. *The Social Life of Things: Commodities in Cultural Perspective.* Cambridge: Cambridge University Press, 1986.

Ardener, E. *Coastal Bantu of the Cameroons.* London: International African Institute, 1956.

Ardener, S., ed. *Perceiving Women.* London: Malaby Press, 1975.

Arens, W. *The Man-Eating Myth: Anthropology and Anthropopaghy.* New York: Oxford University Press, 1979.

Arens, W. and I. Karp. *Creativity of Power: Cosmology and Actions in African Societies.* Washington: Smithsonian Institution Press, 1989.

Armah, Ayi Kwei, *The Beautyful Ones Are Not Yet Born.* London: Heinemann, 1971.

Atkins, J. *A Voyage to Guinea, Brazil and the West Indies.* 1735. Reprint, London: Cass, 1970.

Babarinsa, A. *Anything for Money.* London and Basingstoke: Macmillan, 1985.

Babatope, Ebenezer. *The Abacha Regime and the June 12 Crisis: A Struggle for Democracy.* Lagos: Ebino Topsy, 1995.

Balz, H. *Where the Faith Has to Live: Studies in Bakossi Society and Religion.* Basel: Basler Mission, 1984.

Bannerman-Richter, Gabriel. *The Practice of Witchcraft in Ghana.* Winona, MN: Apollo Books, 1982.

Baratier, A. *A travers l'Afrique.* Paris, 1912.

Barbot, A. *Description of the Coasts of North and South Guinea.* London, 1746.

Barber, B. *Jihad vs. McWorld.* New York: Ballentine, 1996.

Barber, K. *I Could Speak Until Tomorrow.* Edinburgh: Edinburgh University Press for International African Institute, 1991.

Barnett, T. and P. Blaikie. *AIDS in Africa: Its Present and Future Impact.* London: Bellaven, 1992.

Bates, D. *The Mango and the Palm.* London: Rupert Hart-Davis, 1962.

Bayart, J. F. *The State in Africa: The Politics of the Belly.* Trans. M. Harper, C. and E. Harrison. London and New York: Longman, 1993.

Beatty, K. J. *Human Leopards.* London: Hugh Rees, 1915.

Beidelman, T. O. *Moral Imagination in Kaguru Modes of Thought.* Washington: Smithsonian Institute Press, 1993.

Beier, Ulli. *Yoruba Myths.* Cambridge: Cambridge University Press, 1980.

Belasco, B. *The Entrepreneur as Culture Hero: Pre-adaptations in Nigerian Economic Development.* New York: Bergin, 1980.

Bentley, W. H. *Pioneering on the Congo.* 2 vols. 1900. Reprint, London and New York: Johnson, 1970.

Berenger-Feraud, J. B. *Recueil de contes populaires de la Senegambie.* Paris, 1885. Reprint, Nendeln: Kraus, 1970.

Berman, B. and J. Lonsdale. *Unhappy Valley: Conflict in Kenya and Africa.* London: James Currey, 1991.

Blake, J. W., ed. *Europeans in West Africa, 1450–1560.* Hakluyt Society, 2nd ser. vols. 86–7, 1941. Reprint, Nendeln: Kraus, 1967.

Bloch, M. *Placing the Dead.* New York: Seminar Press, 1971.

Boddy, J. *Wombs and Alien Spirits: Women, Men and the Zar Cult in Northern Sudan.* Madison: University of Wisconsin Press, 1989.

Bosman, W. *A New and Accurate Description of the Coast of Guinea.* 1705. Reprint, London: Cass, 1967.

Bourdieu, P. *Outline of a Theory of Practice.* Trans. R. Nice. Cambridge: Cambridge University Press, 1977.

Bourdieu, P. *Language and Symbolic Power.* Trans. G. Raymond and M. Adamson. Cambridge: Polity, 1991.

Bowdich, T. E. *Mission from Cape Coast Castle to Ashantee.* 1819. 3rd ed. London: Cass, 1966.

Boyd, William, *A Good Man in Africa.* Harmondsworth: Penguin, 1981.

Brewer, J. and R. Porter, eds. *Consumption and the World of Goods.* London: Routledge, 1993.

Brown, J. Tom. *Among the Bantu Nomads.* London, 1926. Reprint, New York: Negro Universities Press, 1969.

Brown, K. M. *Mama Lola: A Vodou Priestess in Brooklyn.* Berkeley: University of California Press, 1991.Bureau, R. *Ethno-sociologie religieuse des Duala et apparenté.* Yaoundé: Recherches et Études Camerounaises 7/8, 1962.

Burton, Richard. *A Mission to Gelele, King of Dahome.* 1894. 2nd ed. London: Routledge, 1966.

———. *First Footsteps in East Africa.* 1886. Reprint, London: Routledge, 1966.

Burton, W. F. P. *The Magic Drum: Tales from Central Africa.* London: Methuen, 1961.

Carver, Richard. *Truth from Below.* Published by Article 19, n.p., 1991.

Chatwin, Bruce. *The Viceroy of Ouidah.* London: Picador, Jonathan Cape, 1980.

Cheney-Coker, Syl. *The Last Harmattan of Alusine Dunbar.* Oxford: Heinemann, 1990.

Chesi, G. *Voodoo Africa's Secret Power.* Trans. E. Klambauer. Worgl: Perlinger, Austria, 1980.

Chinweizu, O. Jemie and I. Madubuike. *Towards the Decolonisation of African Literature.* Enugu, 1980. Reissue, Washington: Howard University Press, 1983.

Claridge, G. C. *Wild Bush Tribes of Tropical Africa.* London: Seeley Service, 1922.

Clarke, W. H. *Travels and Explorations in Yorubaland, 1854–1858.* Ibadan: Ibadan University Press, 1972.

Clifford, J. and G. Marcus. *Writing Culture: The Poetics and Politics of Ethnography.* Berkeley: University of California Press, 1986.

Comaroff, J. and J. H. Comaroff, eds. *Modernity and Its Malcontents: Ritual and Power in Postcolonial Africa.* Chicago and London: University of Chicago Press, 1993.

(de) Compiègne, V. *L'Afrique Équatoriale Okanda Bangouens-Osyéba.* Paris, 1875.

Coplan, D. *In the Time of Cannibals: The Words and Music of South Africa's Basotho Migrants.* Chicago: University of Chicago Press, 1994.

Corless, I. B. and M. Pittman-Lindeman, eds. *AIDS: Principles, Practices and Politics.* New York: Hemisphere, 1989.

Cosentino, D., ed. *Sacred Arts of Haitian Vodou.* Los Angeles: University of California/ Fowler Museum, 1995.

Curtin, P., ed. *Africa Remembered.* Madison: University of Wisconsin Press, 1967.

Dabydeen, David. *Turner: New and Selected Poems.* London: Cape Poetry, 1994.

Dapper, O. *Description d l'Afrique.* Amsterdam, 1686. Reprint, New York and London: Johnson, 1970.

Davidson, Basil. *No Fist is Big Enough to Hide the Sky.* London: Zed, 1981.

———. *The People's Cause: A History of Guerillas in Africa.* Harlow: Longman, 1981.

Davis, Wade. *The Serpent and the Rainbow.* London: Collins, 1986.

Debrunner, H. *Witchcraft in Ghana.* 2nd ed. Accra: Presbyterian Book Depot, 1961.

Dekeyser, P. L. and B. Holas. *Mission dans l'Est Libérien.* Dakar: Mémoires de l'Institut français d'Afrique noir, 1952.

Dennett, R. E. *Notes on the Folklore of the Fjort*[French Congo]. 1897. Reprint, Nendeln: Kraus, 1967.

Donnan, E. *Documents Illustrative of the History of the Slave Trade to America.* 4 vols. Washington: Carnegie Institute, 1930–35.

Donner, Etta, *Hinterland Liberia.* Trans. W. M. Dean. London and Glasgow: Blackie, 1939.

Douglas, M. *Purity and Danger.* New York, 1966.

———, ed. *Witchcraft Confessions and Accusations.* London: Tavistock, 1970.

Dubb A., ed. *Myth in Modern Africa.* Lusaka: Rhodes Livingstone Institute, 1960.

East, R., trans. and ed. *Akiga's Story.* 1939. Reprint, Oxford: Oxford University Press for International African Institute, 1965.

Edwards, P., ed. *The Life of Olaudah Equiano.* Harlow: Longman, 1988.

Ekwensi, Cyprian. *Jagua Nana.* London: Hutchinson, 1961.

———. *Survive the Peace.* London: Heinemann, 1976.

Ellis, A. B. *The Tshi-Speaking Peoples of the Gold Coast of West Africa.* London: Chapman and Hall, 1887.

Emecheta, Buchi. *Naira Power.* London and Basingstoke: Macmillan, 1982.

Eto, Victoria. *Exposition on Water Spirits.* Warri, Nigeria: Shallom Christian Mission, 1989.

Fallers, Lloyd. *Law Without Precedent: Legal Ideas in Action in the Courts of Colonial Busoga.* Chicago: University of Chicago Press, 1969.

Fanon, Frantz, *The Wretched of the Earth.* Harmondsworth: Penguin, 1970.

"Fantouré, Alioum" (pseudonym). *Tropical Circle.* Trans. D. Blair. Harlow: Longman, 1981.

Farrow, S. *Faith, Fancies and Fetich or Yoruba Paganism.* 1926. Reprint, New York: Negro Universities Press, 1969.

Feierman, S. *Peasant Intellectuals, Anthropology and History in Tanzania.* London: University of Wisconsin Press, 1990.

Fernandes, V. *Description de la Côte Occidentale d'Afrique, 1506–10.* Trans. and ed. T. Monod, A. Texeira da Mota, and R. Mauny. Bissau: Centro de Estudes de Guiné Portuguesa, 1951.

Field, M. *Search for Security: An Ethno-Psychiatric Study of Rural Ghana.* London: Faber, 1960.

Finnegan, R. *Limba Stories and Story-Telling.* Oxford: Clarendon, 1967.

Foà, E. *Le Dahomey.* Paris, 1895.

Foucault, M. *The Archaeology of Knowledge.* Trans. A. M. Sheridan Smith. New York: Pantheon, 1972.

———. *Power/Knowledge: Selected Interviews and Other Writings.* Trans. C. Gordon et al. New York: Pantheon, 1980.

Fraenkel, Peter. *Wayaleshi.* London: Weidenfeld and Nicholson, 1959.

Frobenius, L. *The Voice of Africa,* I. 1913. Reprint, New York: Benjamin Blom, 1968.

Georgia Writers' Project, *Drums and Shadows: Survival Studies.* Athens: University of Georgia Press, 1940.

Geschiere, P. *The Modernity of Witchcraft.* Charlottesville and London: Virgina University Press, 1997.

Gifford, Paul, *Christianity and Politics in Doe's Liberia.* Cambridge: Cambridge University Press, 1993.

Gilroy, Paul. *The Black Atlantic: Modernity and Double Consciousness.* London: Verso, 1993.

Gittins, A. J. *Mende Religion: Aspects of Belief and Thought in Sierra Leone.* Nettetal: Steyler Verlag, 1987.

Goody, Jack. *Death, Property and the Ancestors.* London: Tavistock, 1962.

Görög-Karady, V. *Noirs et blancs: leur image dans la littérature orale africaine; étude, anthologie.* Marseilles: Société d'Études linguistiques et anthropologique de France, 1976.

Gray, Martin and Robin Law, eds. *Images of Africa: the Depiction of Precolonial Africa in Creative Literature.* Stirling: Centre of Commonweath Studies, University of Stirling, 1990.

Greene, Sandra. *Ethnicity and Social Change on the Upper Slave Coast.* Portsmouth: Heinemann, 1996.

Grosz-Ngaté, M. and O. H. Kokole. *Gendered Encounters: Challenging Cultural Boundaries and Social Hierarchies in Africa.* New York and London: Routledge, 1997.

Gruesser, J. C. *White on Black.* Urbana and Chicago: University of Illinois Press, 1992.

Hackett, R. *Religion in Calabar: The Religious Life and History of a Nigerian Town.* Berlin and New York: Mouton de Gruyter, 1989.

Harms, R. *River of Wealth, River of Sorrow.* New Haven and London: Yale University Press, 1981.

———. *Games Against Nature: An Eco-Cultural History of the Nunu of Equatorial Africa.* Cambridge: Cambridge University Press, 1987.

Henderson, R. *The King in Every Man.* New Haven and London: Yale University Press, 1972.

Hendrickson, H., ed. *Clothing and Difference.* Durham, NC and London: Duke University Press, 1996.

Herskovits, F., ed. *The New World Negro.* Bloomington: Indiana University Press, 1966.

Herskovits, M. and F. *Rebel Destiny: Among the Bush Negroes of Durch Guiana.* New York: McGraw-Hill, 1934.

Hogendorn, J. and M. Johnson. *The Shell Money of the Slave Trade.* Cambridge Cambridge University Press, 1986.

Hooper, Ed. *Slim: A Reporter's Own Story of AIDS in East Africa.* London: Bodly Head, 1990.

Hurbon, L. *Voodoo: Search for the Spirit.* Trans. L. Frankel. New York and London: Abrams, 1995.

Hurgronje, C. Snouck. *Mekka in the Latter Part of the 19th Century.* Trans. J. H. Monahan. 1931. Reprint, Leyden: Brill, 1970.

Huxley, Elspeth. *The Sorcerer's Apprentice.* London: Chatto and Windus, 1951.

Iliffe, J. *A Modern History of Tanganyika.* Cambridge: Cambridge University Press, 1979.

———. *The African Poor: A History.* Cambridge: Cambridge University Press, 1987.

Isichei, E. *A History of the Igbo People.* Basingstoke: Macmillan, 1976.

———. *A History of Nigeria.* Harlow: Longman, 1983.

———. *A History of African Societies to 1870.* Cambridge: Cambridge University Press, 1997.

Iyayi, Festus. *Violence.* London: Longman, 1979.

Jackson, Michael. *Paths Towards a Clearing: Radical Empiricism and Ethnographic Inquiry.* Bloomington: Indiana University Press, 1989.

Jacobson-Widding, A. *Red-White-Black as a Mode of Thought.* Uppsala: Acta Universitatis Upsaliensis, 1979.

Jamba, S. *Patriots.* London: Viking, Penguin, 1990.

Janzen, John, *Lemba 1650–1930: A Drum of Affliction in Africa and the New World.* New York and London: Garland, 1982.

Jeal, T. *Livingstone.* London: Heinemann, 1973.

Jeannest, C. *Quatre Annees au Congo [1869–73].* Paris, 1883.

Joseph, R. *Democracy and Prebendal Politics in Nigeria.* Cambridge: Cambridge University Press, 1987.

Kalous, Milan. *Cannibals and Tongo Players of Sierra Leone*. Auckland; published by author, 1974.

Kato, Byang. *Theological Pitfalls in Africa*. Kisumu, Kenya: Evangel Publishing House, 1975.

Kenyatta, J. *Facing Mount Kenya: The Tribal Life of the Gikuyu*. London: Secker and Warburg, 1938.

Konwea, Fred Okonicha. *"Ibiakwa": A Voice of Verse, 101 Poems*. Benin: n.p., 1975.

Kourouma, Ahmadu. *The Suns of Independence*. Trans. A. Adams. London: Heinemann, 1981.

Kramer, F. *The Red Fez: Art and Spirit Possession in Africa*. Trans. M. Green. London: Verso, 1993.

Laird, MacGregor and R. A. K. Oldfield. *Narrative of an Expedition into the Interior of Africa*. 2 vols. 1837. Reprint, London: Cass, 1971.

Law, R. *The Slave Coast of West Africa, 1550–1750*. Oxford: Clarendon Press, 1991.

Leonard, A. G. *The Lower Niger and its Tribes*. London: Macmillan, 1906.

Leyshon, A. and N. Thrift. *Money/Space: Geographies of Monetary Transformation*. London and New York: Routledge, 1997.

Lindskog, B. *African Leopard Men*. Trans. E. T. Zetterberg. Uppsala: Studia Ethnographica Upsaliensa, 1954.

Little, K. *The Mende of Sierra Leone*. London: Routledge, 1951.

Livingstone, David, *Livingstone's African Journal 1853–1856*. Ed. I. Schapera. London: Chatto and Windus, 1963.

———. *The Last Journals of David Livingstone*. 2 vols. Ed. H. Waller. London, 1874.

Liyong, Taban lo. *Ballads of Underdevelopment*. Kampala, Nairobi, Dar es Salaam: East African Literature Bureau, 1976.

MacGaffey, W. *Religion and Society in Central Africa: The BaKongo of Lower Zaire*. Chicago and London: University of Chicago Press, 1986.

Martin, S. M. *Palm Oil and Protest: An Economic History of the Ngwa Region*. Cambridge: Cambridge University Press, 1988.

Marwick, M. *Sorcery in its Social Setting: A Study of the Northern Rhodesian Cewa*. Manchester: Manchester University Press, 1965.

Matthews, J. *A Voyage to the River Sierra-Leone*. 1788. Reprint, London: Cass, 1966.

McCaskie, T. C. *State and Society in Precolonial Asante*. Cambridge: Cambridge University Press, 1995.

McCracken, G. *Culture and Consumption*. Bloomington and Indianapolis: Indiana University Press, 1990.

Meebelo, H. *Reaction to Colonialism: A Prelude to the Politics of Independence in Northern Zambia 1893–1939*. Manchester: Manchester University Press for the Institute of African Studies, University of Zambia, 1971.

Métraux A. *Haiti: Black Peasants and their Religion*. Trans. P. Lengyel. London: Harrap, 1960.

Middleton, J. *The Study of the Lugbara*. New York: Holt Rinehart and Winston, 1970.

Milingo, E. *The World in Between*. London: C. Hurst; Maryknoll, NY: Orbis Books, 1984.

Miller, J. *Way of Death: Merchant Capitalism and the Angolan Slave Trade*. Madison: University of Wisconsin Press, 1988.

Milton, K., ed. *Environmentalism: The View from Anthropology*. London: Routledge, 1993.

Mofolo, T. *Chaka: An Historical Romance*. Trans. F. H. Dutton. 1931. Reprint, London: Oxford University Press, 1981.

Montejo, Esteban. *The Autobiography of a Runaway Slave*. Trans. J. Innes. London: Bodly Head, 1968.

Munro, J. Forbes. *Colonial Rule and the Kamba*. Oxford: Clarendon Press, 1975.

Muriuki, G. *A History of the Kikuyu 1500–1900*. Nairobi and London: Oxford University Press, 1974.

Newton, John, *Thoughts upon the African Slave Trade*. London, 1788. In B. Martin and M. Spurrell, eds. *The Journal of a Slave Trader*. London: Epworth, 1962.

Ngada, N. H., et al. *Speaking for Ourselves*. 1560 Springs: Order of Preachers (Southern Africa), 1985.

Ngugi'wa, Thiong'o. *Petals of Blood*. London: Heinemann, 1977.

———. *Devil on the Cross*. London: Heinemann, 1982.

Nwankwo, Nkem, *My Mercedes is Bigger Than Yours*. London: A. Deutsch, 1975.

Nwapa, Flora, *Efuru*. London: Heinemann, 1966.

———. *Mammywater*. Enugu: F. Nwapa and Co., 1979.

Odinkemelu, Luke M. *The Problem of Mammy Water: Mammy Water in the Society*. Nigeria: n.p., 1988.

Okri, Ben. *The Famished Road*. London: Jonathan Cape, 1991.

———. *Songs of Enchantment*. London: Jonathan Cape, 1993.

———. *Infinite Riches*. London: Phoenix House, 1998.

Osei-Poku, Kwame. *Blood for Money*. Accra: Educational Press and Manufacturers, 1989.

Otten, C. *A Lycanthropy Reader: Werewolves in Western Culture*. Syracuse, NY: Syracuse University Press, 1986.

Ouologuem, Y. *Bound to Violence*. Trans. R. Manheim. London: Heinemann, 1971.

Owen, Nicholas. *Journal of a Slave Dealer*. London: Routledge, 1930.

Oyegoke, L. *Cowrie Tears*. Harlow: Macmillan, 1982.

Parrinder, G. *Religion in Africa*. London, Pall Mall: 1969.

Parry, J. and M. Bloch. *Money and the Morality of Exchange*. Cambridge: Cambridge University Press, 1989.

Peel, J. D. Y. *Aladura: A Religious Movement Among the Yoruba*. London: Oxford University Press for the International African Institute, 1968.

Pelton, R. D. *The Trickster in West Africa: A Study of Mythic Irony and Sacred Delight*. Berkeley: University of California Press, 1980.

Pereira, Duarte Pacheco. *Esmeraldo de Situ Orbis*. Trans. and ed. G. H. T. Kimble. Hakluyt, 2nd series, vol. 79, 1937.

Pierson, W. D. *Black Legacy: America's Hidden Heritage*. Amherst: University of Massachusetts Press, 1993.

Puckett, N. N. *Folk Beliefs of the Southern Negro*. 1926. Reprint, Montclair, NJ: Patterson Smith, 1968.

Punter, D. *The Literature of Terror*. London: Longman, 1980.

Rankin, F. H. *The White Man's Grave: A Visit to Sierra Leone in 1834*. 2 vols. London, 1836.

Reade, W. Winwood. *Savage Africa*. London, 1863.

Reeves Sanday, Peggy. *Divine Hunger: Cannibalism as a Cultural System*. Cambridge: Cambridge University Press, 1986.

Richards, A. *Bemba Marriage and Present Economic Conditions*. Livingstone: n.p., 1940.

(de) Rosny, Eric, *Healers in the Night*. Trans. R. R. Barr. Maryknoll, NY: Orbis Books, 1985.

Ruel, M. *Leopards and Leaders*. London: Tavistock, 1969.

Ryder, A. F. C. *Benin and the Europeans.* London: Longman, 1969.

Sahlins, M. *Culture and Practical Reason.* Chicago: University of Chicago Press, 1976.

Sai, Akighirga. *Akiga's Story.* Trans. R. East. 1939. Reprint, London: Oxford University Press for the International African Institute, 1965.

Saro-Wiwa, K. *Sozaboy: a Novel in Rotten English.* Harlow: Longman, 1994.

Schlenker, C. F. *A Collection of Temne Traditional Fables and Proverbs.* London, 1861.

Schön, J. F. and S. Crowther. *Journals* [1841 Niger expedition]. 2nd ed. London: Cass, 1970.

Scott, James, *Weapons of the Weak: Everyday Forms of Peasant Resistance.* New Haven and London: Yale University Press, 1985.

Shepperson, G. *Myth and Reality in Malawi.* Evanston, IL: Northwestern University Press, 1966.

Shilts, R. *And the Band Played On: Politics, People and the AIDS Epidemic.* London: Viking; New York: St. Martin's Press, 1987.

Shipton, P. *Bitter Money: Cultural Economy and Some African Meanings of Forbidden Commodities.* Washington: American Ethnological Society Mongraphs, 1989.

Shorter, A. *Jesus and the Witchdoctor: An Approach to Healing and Wholeness.* London: Geoffrey Chapman; Maryknoll, NY: Orbis Books, 1985.

Smith, W. *A New Voyage to Guinea.* London, 1744.

Snelgrave, W. *A New Account of Some Parts of Guinea, and the Slave trade.* 1734. Reprint, London: Cass, 1971.

Sontag, Susan. *AIDS and its Metaphors.* New York: Farrar Strauss and Giroux, 1989.

Soyinka, Wole. *A Dance of the Forests,* Part Two. *Collected Plays,* I. London: Oxford University Press, 1973.

———. *The Road.* London: Oxford University Press, 1965.

———. *Ake: The Years of Childhood.* London: Random House, 1981.

———. *Ibadan, the Penkelemes Years: A Memoir 1946–65.* London: Minerva, 1995.

Stephenson, E. *Chirupula's Tale.* London: Geoffrey Books, 1937.

Stewart, C. *Demons and the Devil: Moral Imagination in Modern Greek Culture.* Princeton: Princeton University Press, 1991.

Stoller, P. *Fusion of the Worlds: An Ethnography of Possession Among the Songhay of Niger.* Chicago: University of Chicago Press, 1989.

Talbot, P. A. *In the Shadow of the Bush.* London: Heinemann, 1912.

Tansi, Sony Labou. *The Antipeople.* Trans. J. A. Underworld. London and New York: Boyars, 1988.

Taussig, M. T. *The Devil and Commodity Fetishism in South America.* Chapel Hill: University of North Carolina Press, 1980.

Thomann, G. *Essai de manuel de la langue néoulé.* Paris: E. Leroux, 1905.

Thomas. N. W. *Law and Custom of the Ibo of the Asaba District.* London: Harrison and Sons, 1914.

Thompson, R. F. *Black Gods and Kings.* Bloomington: Indiana University Press, 1976.

———. *African Art in Motion.* Los Angeles: University of California Press, 1979.

Toulabor, C. *Le Togo sous Éyadéma.* Paris: Éditions Karthala, 1986.

Trautmann, R. *La Littérature populaire à la C ôte des Esclaves.* Travaux et mémoires de l'Institut d'Ethnologie no. 4. Paris, 1927.

"Trefossa" (pseudonym de H. Ziel). *Trotji met een stilistische studie over het gedicht Kopenhagen.* Amsterdam: Bureau for Linguistic Research in Surinam, University of Amsterdam, 1957.

Turner, Patricia A. *I Heard It Through the Grapevine: Rumor in African-American Culture.* Berkeley: University of California Press, 1993.

Unsworth, Barry. *Sacred Hunger.* New York: Penguin, Doubleday; London: H. Hamilton, 1992.

Vansina, J. *Paths in the Rainforest.* Madison: University of Wisconsin Press, 1990.

Vaughan, Megan. *The Story of an African Famine.* Cambridge: University of Cambridge Press, 1987.

Verdier R. *Le Pays Kabiyè.* Paris: Éditions Karthala, 1982.

Vogel, S., ed. *Africa Explores 20th Century African Art.* New York: Centre for African Art; Munich: Prestel-Verlag, 1991.

von Oppen, A. *Terms of Trade and Terms of Trust.* Münster: Lit Verlag, 1993?

Warner, Marina. *Six Myths of Our Time.* New York: Vintage, 1994.

Waterman, C. *Juju: A Social History and Ethnography of an African Popular Music.* Chicago: University of Chicago Press, 1990.

Watts, M. *Silent Violence: Food Famine and Peasantry in Northern Nigeria.* Berkeley and Los Angeles: University of California Press, 1983.

Weigert, S. *Traditional Religion and Guerilla Warfare in Modern Africa.* London: Macmillan; New York: St. Martin's Press, 1996.

Weiss, B. *The Making and Unmaking of the Haya Lived World.* Durham, NC, and London: Duke University Press, 1996.

Wendl, Tobias. *Mami Wata oder ein Kult zwischen den Kulturen.* Münster: Lit Verlag, 1991.

Werbner, R. and T. Ranger. *Postcolonial Identities in Africa.* London: Zed Books, 1996.

Werbner, R. *Tears of the Dead.* Edinburgh: Edinburgh University for the International African Institute, 1991.

Wilks, I. *Asante in the Nineteenth Century: The Structure and Evolution of a Political Order.* 2nd ed. Cambridge: Cambridge University Press, 1989.

Williams, T. D. *Malawi the Politics of Despair.* Ithaca, NY and London: Cornell University Press, 1978.

Wilson, M. *Communal Rituals of the Nyakusa.* London: Oxford University Press for the International African Institute, 1959.

Winterbottom, T. *An Account of the Native Africans in the Neighborhood of Sierra Leone.* 2nd ed. 2 vols. 1803. Reprint, London: Cass, 1969.

Articles and Chapters in Books

Allen, T. "The Quest for Therapy in Moyo District." In H. B. Hansen, and M. Twaddle, *Changing Uganda, The Dilemmas of Structural Adjustment and Revolutionary Change,* 149–61. London: James Currey, 1991.

Ampofo, A. "Controlling and Punishing Women in Ghana." *Review of African Political Economy* 56 (1993): 102–10.

Apter, A. "Atinga Revisited, Yoruba Witchcraft and the Cocoa Economy." In J. and J. H. Comaroff, eds., *Modernity and its Malcontents Ritual and Power in Postcolonial Africa,* 111–28. Chicago and London: University of Chicago Press, 1993.

Ardener, E. "Witchcraft, Economics and the Continuity of Belief." In M. Douglas, *Witchcraft Confessions and Accusations,* 141–61. London: Tavistock, 1970.160

———. "Belief and the Problem of Women." In S. Ardener, *Perceiving Women,* 1–16. London: Malaby Press, 1975.

———. "Some Outstanding Problems in the Analysis of Events." In E. Schwimmer , ed., *The Yearbook of Symbolic Anthropology* 1 (1978): 103–22.

Austen, R. "The Moral Economy of Witchcraft: An Essay in Comparative History." In Jean and John Comaroff, eds., *Modernity and its Malcontents: Ritual and Power in Postcolonial Africa,* 89–110. Chicago and London: University of Chicago Press, 1993.

Ayina, E. "Pagnes et Politiques." *Politique Africaine* (1987): 47–54.

Balandier, G. "Les mythes politiques de colonisation et de décolonisation en Afrique." *Cahiers internationaux de Sociologie* 33 (1963): 85–96.

Barber, K. "Popular Reactions to the Petro-Naira." *Journal of Modern African Studies* 20 (1982): 431–50.

Barber, K. and C. Waterman. "Traversing the Global and the Local: Fuji Music and Praise Poetry in the Production of Contemporary Yoruba Popular Culture." In D. Miller, ed., *Worlds Apart: Modernity Through the Prism of the Local,* 240–62. London and New York: Routledge, 1995.

Bascom, W. "Social Status, Wealth and Individual Differences Among the Yoruba." *American Anthropologist* 53 (1951): 490–505.

Bassani, E. "Additional Notes on the Afro-Portuguese Ivories." *African Arts* 27 (1994): 34–45.

Beidelman, T. "Witchcraft in Ukaguru." In J. Middleton, and E. H. Winter, *Witchcraft and Sorcery in East Africa,* 57–98. London: Routledge, 1963.

———. "A Kaguru Version of the Sons of Noah: A Study in the Inculcation of the Idea of Racial Superiority." *Cahiers d'Études africaines* 12 (1963): 474–90.

Benson, S. "The Conquering Sacrament: Baptism and Demon Possession among the Maasai of Tanzania." *Africa Theological Journal* 9 (1980): 52–61.

Berry, R. G. "The Sierra Leone Cannibals." *Proceedings of the Royal Irish Academy* 30 (1912): 15–69.

Bledsoe, C. "The Politics of AIDS, Condoms, and Heterosexual Relations in Africa: Recent Evidence from the Local Print Media." In W. P. Handwerker, ed., *Births and Power: Social Changes and the Politics of Reproduction,* 197–223. Boulder, CO: Westview Press, 1990.

Bourguignon, E. "Dreams and Dream Interpretation in Haiti." *American Anthropologist* 56 (1954): 262–68.

Brain, J. "Witchcraft and Development." *African Affairs* 81 (1982): 371–84.

Brooks, G. "The Observance of All Souls' Day in the Guinea Bissau, Region." *History in Africa* 11 (1984): 1–34.

Burns, V. "Travel to Heaven: Fantasy Coffins." *African Arts* 7 (1974): 24–5.

Ceyssens, R. "Mutumbula. Mythe de l'Opprime." *Cultures et Development* 7 (1975): 483–536.

Chamberlin, C. "The Migration of the Fang into Central Gabon During the Nineteenth Century: a New Interpretation." *International Journal of African Historical Studies* 11 (1978): 429–56.

Cole, H. M. "Mbari is Life." *African Arts* (Spring, 1969): 8–17.

Comaroff, J. and J. H. Comaroff . "The Madman and the Migrant: Work and Labor in the Historical Consciousness of a South African People." *American Ethnologist* 19 (1987): 191–209.

————. "Goodly Beasts, Beastly Goods: Cattle and Commodities in a South African Context." *American Ethnologist* 17 (1990): 195–216.

Comaroff, J. "Consuming Passions: Child Abuse, Fetishism, and 'The New World Order'." *Culture* 17 (1997): 7–25.

Cotton, J. C. "Calabar Stories." *Journal of the African Society* 5 (1905–6): 191–96.

Daloz, J. -P. "Voitures et prestige au Nigeria." *Politique Africaine* (1990): 148–53.

Diamani, J. P. "L'humour politique au *Phare* du Zaire." *Politique Africaine* (1995): 151–57.

Drewal, H. J. "Efe: Voiced Power and Pageantry." *African Arts* 7 (1974): 26–29.

————. "Performing the Other: Mami Wata Worship in Africa." *The Drama Review* 32 (1988): 160–85.

————. "Mermaids, Mirrors and Snake Charmers: Igbo Mami Wata Shrines." *African Arts* 21 (1988): 38–45.

Drucker-Brown, S. "Mamprusi Witchcraft, Subversion and Changing Gender Relations." *Africa* 63 (1993): 531–49.

Dubuch, C. "Langage du pouvoir, pouvoir du langage." *Politique Africaine* (1985): 44–53.

Dupré, M. -C. "Comment être femme, un aspect du rituel Mukisi chez les Téké." *Archives de Science sociale des Religions* 46 (1978): 57–83.

Ekpo, D. "Towards a Post-Africanism: Contemporary Africa Thought and Postmodernism." *Textual Practice* 9 (1995): 121–35.

Ellis, S. "Tuning in to Pavement Radio." *African Affairs* 88 (1989): 321–30.

————. "Rumour and Power in Togo." *Africa* 63 (1993): 462–75.

Evans-Pritchard, E. "Cannibalism: A Zande text." *Africa* 26 (1956): 73–74.

Feierman, S. "Therapy as a System-in-Action in Northeastern Tanzania." *Social Science and Medicine* 15B (1981): 353–60.

Ferguson, J. "De-Moralizing Economies: African Socialism, Scientific Capitalism and the Moral Politics of 'Structural Adjustment'." In S. F. Moore, ed., *Moralizing States and the Ethnography of the Present*, 78–92. Arlington, VA.: American Anthropological Association, 1993.

————. "The Country and the City on the Copperbelt." *Cultural Anthropology* 7 (1992): 80–92.

Fernandez, J. "Fang Representations Under Acculturation." In P. Curtin, ed., *Africa and the West*, 3–48. Madison: University of Wisconsin Press, 1972.

Fetter, B. "The Luluabourg Revolt at Elisabethville." *African Historical Studies* 2 (1969): 269–77.

Fisiy C. and P. Geschiere. "Judges and Witches: Or How is the State to Deal with Witchcraft?" *Cahiers d' Études africaines* 118 (1990): 135–56.

————. "Sorcery, Witchcraft and Accumulation: Regional Variations in South and West Cameroon." *Critique of Anthropology* 11 (1991): 251–78.

Foster, George M. "Peasant Society and the Image of Limited Good." *American Anthropologist* 67 (1965): 293–315.

Frank, B. "Permitted and Prohibited Wealth: Commodity Possessing Spirits, Economic Morals and the Goddess Mami Wata in West Africa." *Ethnology* 34 (1995): 331–46.

Fraser, D. "The Fish-Legged Figure in Benin and Yoruba Art." In D. Fraser and H. Cole , eds., *African Art and Leadership*, 261–94. Madison, Milwaukee and London: University of Wisconsin Press, 1972.

Gifford, P. "Christian Fundamentalism and Development in Africa." *Review of African Political Economy* 52 (1991): 9–20.

Ginzberger, A. "Accommodation to Poverty: The Case of the Malagasy Peasant Communities." *Cahiers d'Études africaines* 90 (1983): 419–42.

Gobert, E. G. "Le pudendum magique, le problème des cauris." *Revue Africaine* 95 (1951): 5–62.

Goody, E. "Legitimate and Illegitimate Aggression in a West African State." In M. Douglas, *Witchcraft Confessions and Accusations,* 207–45. London: Tavistock, 1970.

Gore, C. and J. Nevadomsky. "Practice and Agency in Mammy Wata Worship in Southern Nigeria." *African Arts* (Spring 1997): 60–69.

Görög, V. "L'origine de l'inégalité des races, Étude de trente-sept contes africains." In *Cahiers d' Études africaines* 30 (1968): 290–309.

Gottlieb, A. "Witches, Kings and the Sacrifice of Identity. . . " in W. Arens and I. Karp, *Creativity of Power: Cosmology and Actions in African Societies,* 245–72. Washington and London: Smithsonian Institute, 1989.

Grottanelli, V. "Discovery of a Masterpiece: A 16ᵗʰ-Century Ivory Bowl from Sierra Leone." *African Arts* 8 (1975): 14–23.

Heath, D. "Fashion, Anti-fashion and Heteroglossia in Urban Senegal." *American Ethnologist* 19 (1992): 19–33.

Héritier, F. "Des cauris et des hommes: production d'esclaves et accumulation de cauris chez les Samo (Haute-Volta)." In C. Meillassoux, ed., *L'esclavage en Afrique précoloniale,* 477–507. Paris: F. Maspero, 1975.

Herskovits, M. J. and F. S. Herskovits. "Tales in Pidgin English from Nigeria." *Journal of American Folk-Lore* 44 (1931): 448–66.

Hilts, P. "Dispelling Myths about AIDS in Africa." *Africa Report* 33 (1988): 26–32.

Hoch-Smith, J. "Radical Yoruba Sexuality: The Witch and the Prostitute." In Hoch-Smith and A. Spring, eds., *Women in Ritual and Symbolic Roles,* 245–67. New York and London: Plenum, 1978.

Hodgson, D. "Embodying the Contradictions of Modernity: Gender and Spirit Possession Among Maasai in Tanzania." In M. Grosz-Ngaté and O. Kokole, eds., *Gendered Encounters: Challenging Cultural Boundaries and Social Hierarchies in Africa,* 111–29. London: Routledge, 1997.

Houlberg, M. "Sirens and Snakes: Water Spirits in the Arts of Haitian Vodou." *African Arts* (Spring 1996): 30–35.

Hurskainen, A. "The Epidemiological Aspect of Spirit Possession Among the Maasai of Tanzania." In A. Jacobson-Widding and D. Westerlund, eds., *Culture, Experience and Pluralism: Essays on African Ideas of Illness and Healing,* 139–51. Uppsala: Academia Upsaliensis, 1989.

Hutchinson, S. "The Cattle of Money and the Cattle of Girls Among the Nuer, 1930–83." *American Ethnologist* 19 (1992): 300–306.

Iroko, A. F. "Cauris et esclaves en Afrique occidentale entre le xvie et le xixe siecles." In S. Daget, ed., *Colloque international sur la traite des Noirs,* I, 193–204. Nantes: Centre de Recherche sur l'histoire du monde atlantique, 1985.

Isichei, E. "On Being Invisible: An Historical Perspective of the Anaguta and Their Neighbours." *International Journal of African Historical Studies* 24 (1991): 513–56.

Ittmann, J. "Der Kupe in Aberglauben der Kameruner." *Der Evangelische Heidenbote,* 77–80, 94–95, 111–13. Basel, 1930.

———. "Der kultische Geheimbund djengu an der Kameruner Küste." *Anthropos* 52 (1957): 135–76.

James, D. "'I Dress in this Fashion': Transformations in *Sotho* Dress and Women's Lives." In H. Hendrickson, ed., *Clothing and Difference,* 34–65. Durham, NC and London: Duke University Press, 1996.

Jell-Bahlsen, S. "*Eze mmiri di egwu,* The Water Monarch is Awesome: Reconsidering the Mammy Water Myths." *Annals of the New York Academy of Sciences* 810 (1997): 103–34.

Jewsiewicki, B. "Painting in Zaire: From the Invention of the West to the Representation of Social Self." In S. Vogel, ed., *Africa Explores 20th Century African Art,* 130–51. New York and Munich: Centre for African Arts/Prestel Verlas, 1991.

Jones, G. I. "Mbari Houses." *Nigerian Field* 6 (1937): 77–79.

Kasfir, S. L. Review of T. Wendl and D. Weise, "Mami Wata, Der Geist der Weissen Frau" (film, Göttingen, 1988). *African Arts* 27 (1994): 80–82.

Kaspin, D. "Chewa Visions and Revisions of Power." J and J. H. Comaroff, eds., *Modernity and its Malcontents: Ritual and Power in Postcolonial Africa,* 34–57. Chicago and London: University of Chicago Press, 1993.

Kohnert, D. "Magic and Witchcraft: Implications for Democratization and Poverty-Alleviating Aid in Africa." *World Development* 24 (1996): 1347–55.

Kopytoff, I. "The Cultural Biography of Things: Commoditization as Process." In A. Appadurai, ed., *The Social Life of Things: Commodities in Cultural Perspective,* 64–91. Cambridge: Cambridge University Press, 1986.

Lan, D. "Resistance to the Present by the Past: Mediums and Money in Zimbabwe." In J. Parry and M. Bloch, *Money and Mmorality of Exchange,* 191–208. Cambridge: Cambridge University Press, 1989.

Lawuyi, O. "The World of the Yoruba Taxi Driver: An Interpretive Approach to Vehicle Slogans." *Africa* 58 (1988): 1–13.

Leclerc-Madlala, S. "Infect One, Infect All: Zulu Youth Response to the AIDS Epidemic in South Africa." *Medical Anthropology* 17 (1997): 363–80.

Lemarchand, R. "African Peasantries: Reciprocity and the Market." *Cahiers d'Études Africaines* 113 (1989): 33–67.

Lienhardt, G. "Getting Your Own Back: Themes in Nilotic Myth." In J. Beattie and Lienhardt, eds., *Studies in Social Anthropology,* 213–37. Oxford: Clarendon, 1975.

Lonsdale, J. "The Moral Economy of Mau Mau: Wealth, Poverty and Civic Virtue in Kikuyu Political Thought." In B. Berman and J. Lonsdale, *Unhappy Valley,* 315–504. London and Nairobi: James Currey, 1992.

Ludwar-Ene, G. "Explanatory and Remedial Modalities for Personal Misfortune in a West African Society with Special Reference to Witchcraft." *Anthropos* 81 (1986): 555–65.

MacGaffey, W. "Kongo and the King of the Americans." *The Journal of Modern African Studies* 6 (1968): 171–81.

———. "The West in Congolese Experience." In P. D. Curtin, ed., *Africa and the West,* 49–74. Madison: University of Wisconsin Press, 1972.

Manning, P. "Coastal Society in the Republic of Bénin: Reproduction of a Regional System." *Cahiers d'Études africaines* 29 (1989): 239–58.

Marshall, R. "Power in the Name of Jesus." *Review of African Political Economy* 52 (1991): 21–37.

———. "'God is Not a Democrat': Pentecostalism and Democratisation." In P. Gifford, ed., *The Christian Churches and the Democratisation of Africa,* 239–60. Leiden: E. J. Brill, 1995.

Masquelier, A. "Encounter with a Road Siren: Machines, Bodies and Commodities in the Imagination of a Mawri Healer." *Visual Anthropology Review* 8 (1992): 56–69.

Matory, J. L. "Government by Seduction: History and the Tropes of 'Mounting' in Oyo-Yoruba Religion." In J. and J. Comaroff, *Modernity and its Malcontents,* 58–85. Chicago and London: University of Chicago Press, 1993.

Mbembe, A. "Provisional Notes on the Postcolony." *Africa* 62 (1992): 3–37.

McCaskie, T. "Anti-Witchcraft Cults in Asante: an Essay in the Social History of an African People." *History in Africa* 8 (1981): 125–53.

———. "Accumulation, Wealth and Belief in Asante History." *Africa* 53 (1983): 23–43.

Mesaki, S. "Witch-killing in Sukumaland." In R. Abrahams, ed., *Witchcraft in Contemporary Tanzania,* 42–60. Cambridge: African Studies Centre, 1994.

Meyer, Birgit. "'If You Are a Devil, You Are a Witch and if You Are a Witch, You Are a Devil': The Integration of "Pagan" Ideas into the Conceptual Universe of Ewe Christians in Southeastern Ghana." *Journal of Religion in Africa* 22 (1992): 98–131.

———, "'Delivered from the Powers of Darkness': Confessions of Satanic Riches in Christian Ghana." *Africa* 65 (1995): 236–55.

Morton-Williams, P. "An Outline of the Cosmology and Cult Organization of the Oyo Yoruba." *Africa* 34 (1964): 243–61.

Mugambi, H. N. "From Story to Song: Gender, Nationhood and the Migratory Text." M. Grosz-Ngaté and O. H. Kokole, *Gendered Encounters: Challenging Cultural Boundaries and Social Hierarchies in Africa,* 205–22. New York and London: Routledge, 1997.

Musambachime, M. "The Impact of Rumor: The Case of the Banyama (Vampire Men) Scare in Northern Rhodesia." *The International Journal of African Historical Studies* 21 (1988): 201–15.

Odhiambo, E. S. A. "The Movement of Ideas: A Case Study of Intellectual Responses to Colonialism Among the Liganua Peasants." In B. A. Ogot, ed., *History and Social Change,* 165–85. Hadith 6, Nairobi, 1976.

Onwu, N. "Igbo Religion: Its Present Situation." *Africana Marburgensia* 18 (1985): 15–22.

Opoku, K. O. and K. O. Wicker, "Abidjan Mami Water Festival 1994." *Religious Studies News* (Nov. 1994): 17–18.

Osborne, L. "Does Man Eat Man? Inside the Great Cannibalism Controversy." *Lingua Franca* (April/May, 1997): 28–38.

Paulme, D. "Une religion syncrétique en Côte d 'Ivoire: le culte deima." *Cahiers d'Études africaines* 3 (1963): 5–90.

Paulus, J. P. "Le kitawala au Congo belge." *Revue de l'Institut de Sociologie Solvay* (1956): 257–70.

Paxson, B. "Mammy Water: New World Origins?" *Baessler-Archiv* N. S. 31 (1983): 407–46.

Peel, J. D. Y. "*Olaju*: A Yoruba Concept of Development." *The Journal of Development Studies* 14 (1978): 139–65.

Pemberton, J. "Eshu-Elegba: The Yoruba Trickster God." *African Arts* 9 (1975): 20–27, 66–70.

Piault, Marc-Henri, "Captifs du pouvoir et pouvoir des captifs." In C. Meillassoux, ed., *L'esclavage precoloniale,* 321–50. Paris: F. Maspero, 1970.

Pittin, R. "Women, Work and Ideology in Nigeria." *Review of African Political Economy* 52 (1991): 38–52.

Prince, R. "Indigenous Yoruba Psychiatry." In Ari Kiev, ed., *Magic, Faith and Healing*, 84–120. New York: Free Press, Collier Macmillan, 1964.

Richards, Paul, "Natural Symbols and Natural History: Chimpanzees, Elephants and Experiments in Mende thought." In K. Milton, *Environmentalism: The View from Anthropology*, 144–59. London: Routledge, 1993.

Rosen, David, "Dangerous Women: 'Ideology', 'Knowledge' and Ritual Among the Kono of Eastern Sierra leone." *Dialectical Anthropology* 6 (1981): 151–64.

Rosenthal, J. "Foreign Tongues and Domestic Bodies: Gendered Cultural Regions and Regionalized Sacred Flows." In Grosz-Ngaté and O. H. Kokole, eds., *Gendered Encounters: Challenging Cultural Boundaries and Social Hierarchies in Africa*, 183–203. London and New York: Routledge, 1997.

Salmons, J. "Mammy Wata." *African Arts* 10 (1977): 8–15.

Sanderson, S. "The Folklore of the Motor-car." *Folklore* 80 (1969): 241–52.

Savishinsky, J. "The Baye Faal of Senegambia." *Africa* 64 (1994): 211–17.

Schatzberg, M. "Power, Legitimacy and 'Democratisation' in Africa." *Africa* 63 (1993): 445–61.

Schmoll, P. "Black Stomachs, Beautiful Stones" in J. and J. Comaroff, *Modernity and its Malcontents*, 193–220. Chicago and London: University of Chicago Press, 1993.

Schneider, H. "Male-Female Conflict and Lion Men in Singida." In Simon Ottenberg, ed., *African Religious Groups and Beliefs*. Berkeley, CA: Folklore Institute, 1982.

Shaw, R. "The Politician and the Diviner: Divination and the Consumption of Power in Sierra Leone." *Journal of Religion in Africa* 26 (1996): 30–55.

Shorter, A. "The Migawo: Peripheral Spirit Possession and Christian Prejudice." *Anthropos* 65 (1970): 100–26.

Soyinka, Wole. "Neo-Tarzanism: The Poetics of PseudoTtradition." *Transition* 48 (April/June, 1975): 38–48.

Stoller, P. "Embodying Colonial Memories." *American Anthropologist* 96 (1994): 634–48.

Szombati-Fabian, I. and J. Fabian. "Art History and Society: Popular Painting in Shaba, Zaire." *Studies in the Anthropology of Visual Communication*, 1976 (3) 1–21

Tanner, R. E. S. "The Sorcerer in Northern Sukumaland." *Southwestern Journal of Anthropology* 12 (1956):437–43.

Taussig, M. "The Genesis of Capitalism Amongst a South American Peasantry: Devil's Labour and the Baptism of Money." *Comparative Studies in Society and History* 19 (1977): 130–55.

Toulabor, C. "Jeu de mots, jeu de vilains, Lexique de la dérision politique au Togo." *Politique Africaine* (1981): 55–71.

Turner, V. "Colour Classification in Ndembu Ritual: A Problem in Primitive Classification." In M. Banton, ed., *Anthropological Approaches to the Study of Religion*, 47–84. ASA Monographs, 3. London: Tavistock, 1966.

Ubah, C. N. "The Supreme Being, Divinities and Ancestors in Igbo Traditional Religion: Evidence from Otanchara and Otanzu." *Africa* 52 (1982): 90–105.

Vecsey, C. "The Exception Who Proves the Rules: Ananse the Akan Trickster." *Journal of Religion in Africa* 12 (1981): 161–77.

Watts, M. "The Shock of Modernity: Petroleum, Protest and Fast Capitalism in Industrialising Society." In A. Pred and M. Watts, eds., *Reworking Modernity:*

Capitalisms and Symbolic Discontent, 21–64. New Brunswick, NJ: Rutgers University Press, 1992.

———. "Oil as Money: the Devil's Excrement and the Spectacle of Black Gold." In S. Corbridge, N. Thrift and R. Martin, *Money, Power and Space,* 406–45. Oxford: Blackwell, 1994.

Wescott, J. "The Sculpture and Myths of Eshu-Elegba, the Yoruba Trickster." *Africa* 32 (1962): 336–54.

White, L. "Bodily Fluids and Usufruct: Controlling Property in Nairobi, 1917–1939." *Canadian Journal of African Studies* 24 (1990): 418–38.

———. "Cars Out of Place: Vampires, Technology and Labour in East and Central Africa." *Representations* 43 (1993): 27–50.

———. "Vampire Priests of Central Africa: African Debates about Labor and Religion in Colonial Northern Zambia." *Comparative Studies in Society and History* 35 (1993): 746–72.

———. "Tsetse Visions: Narratives of Blood and Bugs in Colonial Northern Rhodesia, 1931–9." *Journal of African History* 36 (1995): 219–45.

Willis, R. "Kamcape: An Anti-Sorcery Movement in South-West Tanzania." *Africa* 38 (1968): 1–15.

———. "Kaswa: Oral Traditions of a Fipa Prophet." *Africa* 40 (1970): 248–55.

Wilson, M. "Witch Beliefs and Social Structure." *The American Journal of Sociology* 56 (1951): 307–14.

Wintrob, R. "Mammy Water: Folk Beliefs and Psychotic Elaborations in Liberia." *Canadian Psychiatric Association Journal* 15 (1970): 143–57.

Yamba, C. B. "Cosmologies in Turmoil: Witchfinding and AIDS in Chiawa, Zambia." *Africa* 67 (1997): 200–23.

Unpublished Sources

Anthony, D. H. "Culture and Society in a Town in Transition: A People's History of Dar es Salaam 1865–1939." Ph.D. dissertation, University of Wisconsin, 1983.

Bastian, M. "My Head Was Too Strong! Body Parts and Money Magic in Nigerian Popular Discourse."

Baum, R. "The Slave Trade in Diola (Senegal) Oral Tradition." Paper presented to a conference on the Slave Trade in African and African-American memory, University of Chicago, 1997.

Geschiere, P. "Witchcraft, Kinship and the Moral Economy of Ethnicity." Paper presented to the Conference on Ethnicity in Africa, Edinburgh, 1995.

Shaw, R. "Mami Wata and the Sierra Leone Diamonds," Paper presented to African Studies Association meeting, Orlando, Florida, 1995.

Videos and films

Jell-Bahlsen, S. "Mammy Water: In Search of the Water Spirits of Nigeria. Video, University of California Extension Center, 1989.

Rouch, J. *Les maîtres fous.* Video, 1956. Reissued, New York, Iterama Video, 1986.

Tobias W. and D. Weise. *Der Geist der Weissen Frau.* Video, *Institut für den wissenschaftlichen Film,* Göttingen, 1988.

INDEX